CHIPEWYAN

NASKAPI

HAIDA

SIOUX

IROQUOIS

PAIUTE

POMO

NAVAJO

MOUND-BUILDER

PIMA

HOPI

WEST-INDIAN

MEXICAN

MAYA

CHIRIQUI

DJUKA

QUIMBAYAN

MANABI

MARAJO

MARQUESAN

ANCON

AUETO

TUBUAI

TRUJILLO

TIAHUANACO

EASTER ISLAND

CALCHAQUI

PATAGONIAN

THE BOOK OF TIKI

Our protagonist, an alien in the world of plastic and chrome

THE BOOK OF TIKI

THE CULT OF POLYNESIAN POP
IN FIFTIES AMERICA

by Sven A. Kirsten

TASCHEN

KÖLN LONDON MADRID NEW YORK PARIS TOKYO

Zombie Village

6485 SAN PABLO AVENUE • OAKLAND, CALIFORNIA

CONTENTS

Left: Sophisticated savages
Links: Zivilisierte Wilde
A gauche: Barbares civilisés

This book is dedicated to Tiki, man and god, deity of the artists, who, as is handed down in Polynesian mythology, possessed a sturdy sense of humor and irreverence that would certainly have made him delight in witnessing the extent of his influence in the Western world.

A document this rich in material was only made possible through the combined contributions of a group of generous individuals, fellow hunters and collectors who all these years have believed in and supported this project:

First and foremost Leroy Schmaltz and Robert van Oosting, the keepers of the tradition, without whom I would not have thought of this book; my father Harald who has always been supportive in all of my endeavors; fellow urban archeologists Jeff "Beachbum" Berry, Doug Miller, Pete Moruzzi, Otto von Stroheim, John English, Chris Nichols, Dale Sizer, Kiara Geller, Brian Marsland, Martin McIntosh, Mark Cunningham, Bobby and Al of the Bigfoot, Bamboo Ben, Greg Escalante, John Turner, Ted Haigh, Byron Werner, Bruce Elliott, Janet Austin, Chester and Cheryl; artists Moritz R., Kevin Kidney, Jody Daily, Bosko Hrnjack, Florian Gabriel, Mark Ryden, Andy Cruz, Josh Agle, Coop, and Laura Kikauka, Gordon Monnahan, Gordon W. and Lisa Brown; Tiki veterans Hans Richter, Michael Tsao, Eldon Davis and Victor Newlove; writers De Soto Brown, Domenic Priore, Jim Heimann, Alan Hess, Luis Reyes, Sylvia Stoddard, Dewey Webb, Diana Wagman, Frank de Caro; and Charles Schneider. My special thanks go to Angelika and Benedikt Taschen for their instinctual acceptance of a project that year after year had met with indifference from American publishers

"AH, GOOD TASTE!
WHAT A DREADFUL THING!
TASTE IS THE ENEMY
OF CREATIVENESS."

PABLO PICASSO

A GUIDE FOR THE URBAN ARCHEOLOGIST

DISCOVERING A LOST CIVILIZATION IN YOUR OWN BACKYARD

"The wood-rot malady is spreading among the idols—the fruit upon their altars is becoming offensive—the temples need rethatching."
(Herman Melville *TYPEE. A Peep at Polynesian Life*, 1844)

These observations on the fate of the ancient Polynesian civilization from one of the classics of South Seas fiction seem strangely appropriate to describe the fate that has befallen the American Tiki style of the 50s and 60s. Its symbols, the Tikis, are decaying, the "Polynesian" cuisine of that period has become the antithesis of health food, and most of the surviving examples of Tiki architecture appear dilapidated.

But just as Paul Gauguin was fascinated with the melancholy atmosphere of decay in Papeete, Tahiti's capital, detecting "the blurred surface of some unfathomable enigma" in this already tainted paradise, so can today's Urban Arche-

TOP RIGHT: Toppled Tikis, left to rot. Just like the natives of Hawaii in the 1820s, by the 1980s American believers had also become disenchanted and, as if waking up from a horrendous hangover, looked back in embarrassment at what they had worshipped in their Mai-Tai-induced euphoria. RIGHT: Urban archeologists examining a fallen idol at the defunct amusement park The Tikis in Lake Elsinore, California. BOTTOM RIGHT: A thrilling discovery at the thrift store

OBEN RECHTS: Umgestürzte Tikis, die langsam verwittern. Ähnlich den hawaiischen Eingeborenen der 20er Jahre des 19. Jahrhunderts hatten auch die amerikanischen Tiki-Anhänger in den 80er Jahren unseres Jahrhunderts ihre Illusionen verloren und schauten verstört auf das zurück, was sie in ihrer rauschhaften Begeisterung für die polynesischen Rituale angehimmelt hatten. RECHTS: Stadtarchäologen untersuchen eine umgefallene Götzenstatue in dem verfallenen Vergnügungspark The Tikis in Lake Elsinore, Kalifornien.

ologist appreciate remnants of that Paradise Lost of the American *dolce vita* we call Tiki style.

Tiki temples, once gracing every major American city, have vanished or been refurbished, the "uncouth jolly-looking images" (Melville) cast out with missionary zeal to make room for new gods (or styles). Waterfalls have ceased to flow like the mana (or the money) that built them, the Tiki torches have gone out, and outrigger beams been sawn off.

Yet the Urban Archaeologist has developed a sensitivity to lost cultures and their forgotten forms. He fearlessly travels to their sites in such remote and exotic places as Columbus, Ohio, or Pomona, in the urban sea of Los Angeles. For him, bobbing down some obscure freeway toward uncharted sub-suburbia on a smoggy day is as thrilling as steering the Kon-Tiki through a hurricane in the Pacific. Like an urban beachcomber, he sifts through the debris of consumer culture in thrift stores, yard sales, and used-book stores— in search of the artifacts and ephemera that provide pieces to the puzzle of the lost culture that brought forth such concepts as that of the Urban Polynesian Paradise. With sense of wonder intact, the Urban Archeologist realizes that one does

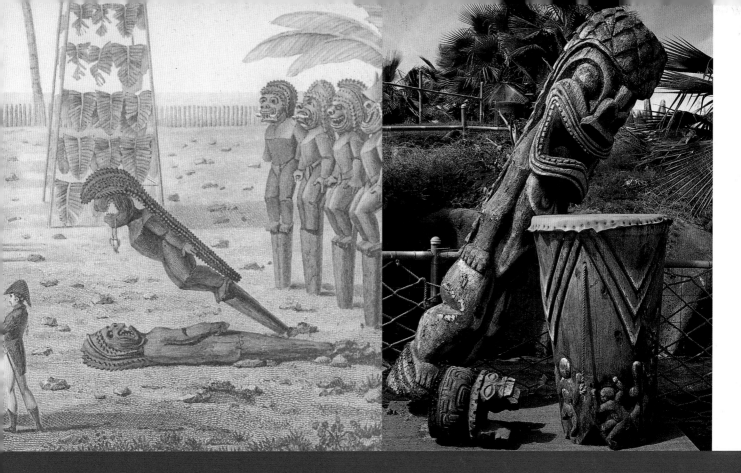

not always have to search far to explore the mysteries of forgotten ancient traditions, but that strange treasures can lie right in your own neighborhood, hidden under the layers of progress and development. It is our aim to nurture this ability to see the marvelous in the seemingly mundane through this book, your guide to Tiki culture in America.

Artifacts of the Tiki cult. LEFT: A drinking vessel from the Outrigger, Monterey, California. RIGHT: a. Ancient scriptures enlighten the researcher. b. Tiki temple regalia: swizzle sticks (cocktail stirrers) from the Chin Tiki, Detroit, Michigan, and the Hawaiian Village, Tampa, Florida. c. Matchbooks often reveal the exact site of vanished Polynesian palaces.

Artefakte des Tiki-Kults. LINKS: Ein Trinkgefäß aus dem Outrigger, Monterey, Kalifornien. RECHTS: a. Alte Schriftstücke geben dem Forscher wichtige Aufschlüsse. b. Tiki-Tempel-Souvenirs: Cocktailquirler aus dem Chin tiki, Detroit, Michigan, und aus dem Hawaiian Village, Tampa, Florida. c. Streichholzheftchen verraten häufig die genaue Adresse inzwischen verschwundener polynesischer Paläste.

Objets du culte tiki. A GAUCHE: Un récipient à bois-son provenant de l'Outrigger, Monterey, Californie A DROITE: a. Des anciennes inscriptions éclairent le chercheur. b. Joyaux d'un temple tiki : bâtonnets à cocktail du Chin Tiki, Detroit, Michigan, et du Hawaiian Village, Tampa, Floride. c. Les pochettes d'allumettes révèlent souvent l'emplacement exact de palais polynésiens disparus.

SP111 / 50c

"Sprightly...informative...ribald"
—New York Herald Tribune

WAIKIKI BEACHNIK

H. Allen Smith
author of
Low Man on a Totem Pole
Smith picks up where
Michener leaves off

The islander
Exotic Foods &
Drinks of the Islands
385 N. LA CIENEGA · LOS ANGELES

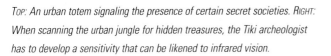

TOP: An urban totem signaling the presence of certain secret societies. RIGHT: When scanning the urban jungle for hidden treasures, the Tiki archeologist has to develop a sensitivity that can be likened to infrared vision.

OBEN: Ein städtisches Totem, das auf die Anwesenheit verschiedener Geheimgesellschaften hinweist. RECHTS: Wenn der Tiki-Archäologe den Stadtdschungel durchforstet, muss er – als sei er mit einem Infrarot-Blick ausgestattet – ein Gespür für verborgene Schätze entwickeln.

CI-DESSUS: Un totem urbain signalant la présence de certaines sociétés se-crètes. A DROITE: Lorsqu'il explore la jungle urbaine, l'archéologue du tiki doit développer une sensibilité aux trésors cachés proche de la vision à infrarouge.

First Palm in Calif. 1769   *2/17/20*

2

IN THE BEGINNING...

Ever since its fall from grace, humanity has yearned to find its way back to the paradise it was cast out of. When the first reports of the South Sea Isles reached the Old World, the tales seemingly described this lost haven. Polynesia became the metaphor for Eden on earth. But as the distant shores of the South Pacific were out of reach for most mortals, other mythical lands were sought out by the explorers.

One such place was "California," a mysterious island (it was believed to be a continent on its own) reputed to be endowed with Amazons and pearls. Even though once this *terra incognita* was settled and these flights of fancy proved to be an exaggeration, California has retained its status as a golden dream

RIGHT: Back to the primitive, but with air-conditioning, please. Naive cave painting in the basement of the Kahiki in Columbus, Ohio. MIDDLE: Modern Adam and Eve dreaming of an earthly Eden
BOTTOM: Shangri-La–California-Polynesia!

RECHTS: Zurück zum Ursprünglichen, aber bitte mit Klimaanlage. Naive „Höhlenmalerei" im Untergeschoss des Kahiki in Columbus, Ohio
MITTE: Heute träumen Adam und Eva von einem irdischen Paradies.
UNTEN: Shangri-La–California-Polynesia!

À DROITE: Retour au primitif, mais avec l'air conditionné, s'il vous plaît. Des peintures rupestres naïves dans le sous-sol du Kahiki à Columbus, Ohio.
AU CENTRE: Adam et Eve modernes rêvant d'un Eden terrestre.
CI DESSUS: Shangri-La – California–Polynesia!

PAGE 16: The doors to paradise and their guardian

SEITE 16: Das Tor zum Paradies und sein Wächter

PAGE 16: Les portes du paradis et leur gardien

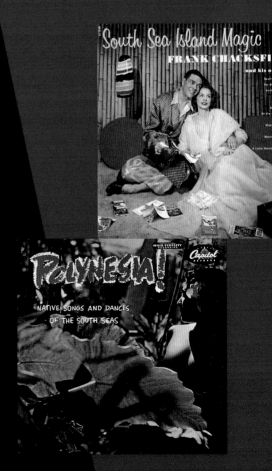

destination. Generation after generation arrived here, seeking to realize their own version of paradise. One such interpretation was the tropical garden of the South Sea Isles.

Thus the first palm tree was planted and tropical flora was propagated. And since not only the biosphere but also the psychosphere was present in California, a Polynesian Americana soon began to take shape. Tiki temples were erected, and for a while the people believed. They came to worship the cult of modern primitivism, naively engaging in such (now taboo) practices as alcoholism, racism, chauvinism, and pig-eating.

And as Californians emulated Polynesia, the rest of the nation looked to California for lifestyle guidance. Soon every major city in America was home to at least one Polynesian palace.

SKETCH ~ RAIN FOREST

XONA XAI RESTAURANT

HOT SHOPPES INC

ARMET + DAVIS AIA ARCHITECT
2440 W. THIRD ST. LOS ANGELES

3

TIKI—WHO WAS HE?

In the beginning was the word, and the word was: "TIK"!—at least according to renowned language archeologist and linguist Merrit Ruhlen of Palo Alto, California. He traced the origin of all human language back to this magic three letter word, surviving today as "toe," in the word *digit* (and obviously, *dick*). Endowed with such archetypal power, it is does not seem surprising that "Tiki" became the buzzword of a generation. But "Tiki" was not only close to the first word uttered by mankind: In Polynesian mythology; it is also the synonym for the first man. Looking the term up in A.W. Reed's *Concise Maori Dictionary*, one finds this expansion of the term:

1. TIKI: First man, or personification of man. Through ancestor worship this Maori Adam evolved into a half-god, and eventually "Tiki" was used as a term for all depictions of man, as we find in its next meaning:

LEFT: A Maori meeting house, rendered by George French Angas in 1846. MIDDLE: A Marquesan Tiki. Although neither the Hawaiian nor the Tahitian idiom contains the term "Tiki," in Polynesian pop all graven images, from Easter Island to Fiji, became members one happy family: The Tikis.

LINKS: Ein Maori-Versammlungshaus in einer Darstellung von G. F. Angas, 1846. MITTE: Ein Tiki von den Marquesa-Inseln. Obwohl weder die hawaiische noch die tahitische Sprache den Begriff „Tiki" kennt, wurden im polynesischen Pop alle Götzenbilder Mitglieder einer einzigen glücklichen Familie: den Tikis.

A GAUCHE: Un temple maori, dessiné par George French Angas en 1846. AU CENTRE: Un tiki des Marquises. Bien que ni la langue hawaïenne, ni la langue tahitienne ne possèdent le terme « tiki », dans le pop polynésien, toutes les images taillées devinrent membres d'une seule famille heureuse : les tikis.

2. TIKI:

grotesque carving of a man decorating a house. A concise description of the kind of Tiki we find in these pages. But as we read on, the word reveals an even deeper significance:

3. TIKI: A phallic symbol. Indeed, in Maori lore, "Tiki" was the name for the procreative power and sexual organ of the god Tane, creator of the first woman. In the Austral Islands south of Tahiti, "Tiki-roa" (the long ancestral figure) was the nickname for the penis, and "Tiki-poto" (the short ancestral figure) endearingly designated the clitoris. For a word that holds such creative powers, it does not surprise us to find yet another meaning on the Marquesas Islands:

4. TIKI: God of the artists. To demonstrate that Tiki was indeed the muse of many artists, known and unknown, is one of the humble aspirations of this book. This seems to be perfectly suited to be the long needed protector of the artists.

POLYNESIAN IDOL AND ITS DEVOTEES.

RIGHT: Not all, but definitely most suburbanites were unaware of the phallic nature of the lawn decorations they erected in their backyards.

RECHTS: Nicht alle, aber doch die Mehrheit der Vorstädter war sich des phallischen Charakters ihres Gartenschmucks nicht bewusst.

A DROITE: La très grande majorité des banlieusards ignoraient la nature phallique des décorations qu'ils édifiaient dans leurs jardins.

The name of the creator / Der Name des Schöpfers / Le nom du Créateur

PRIMITIVE ART IN CIVILIZED PLACES

"Anyone who has ever seen them is thereafter haunted as if by a feverish dream."
(Karl Woermann on Tikis in *Geschichte der Kunst aller Zeiten und Völker,* 1900–1911)

The concept of using so-called "primitive" art to contrast and augment the smooth lines of modern design has its origin in the inspiration the founding fathers of modern art found in the seemingly naive and savage aesthetic. When, in the early 20th century, more and more "artificial curiosities" (African and

Oceanic) made their way from the colonies to western European cities, a young generation of artists, including Picasso, Miro, Klee, and Ernst, used the inspiration they drew from primitivism to challenge the accepted concepts of what art was. As Gauguin put it, studying the established classical arts "disgusted and discouraged me, giving me a vague feeling of death without rebirth."

Pablo Picasso underwent his seminal experience ("suddenly I realized why I was a painter!") upon viewing the collection of primitiva at the Musée d'Ethnographie du Trocadero in Paris. In fact, as early as 1919 he was hailed as "an old adept of the Tiki." This was probably due to the fact that by around 1910 Picasso was the proud owner of a Marquesan Tiki that would

FRESNO, CALIFORNIA

PAGE 24: The in-crowd at the Imperial Luau cocktail hour in Pompano Beach, Florida
PAGE 26, TOP LEFT: Tiki and poet Guillaume Apollinaire in Picasso's studio, c. 1910; TOP RIGHT: Three gods of pop culture: Brigitte Bardot, Picasso and Tiki
TOP: The primitive and the modern meet at the Tropicana Lodge in Fresno, California, in 1961. The Los Angeles architectural firm of Armet & Davis was the leader in California Coffeeshop Modern, also known as Googie style. The architects erected several Tiki temples, including the Kona Kai in Philadelphia and the Kon-Tiki in Montreal.

SEITE 24: Die In-Clique im Imperial Luau zur Cocktail-Stunde in Pompano Beach, Florida
SEITE 26, OBEN LINKS: Tiki und der Dichter Guillaume Apollinaire in Picassos Atelier, ca. 1910; OBEN RECHTS: Drei Götter der Popkultur: Brigitte Bardot, Picasso und Tiki
OBEN: Begegnung des Primitiven und Modernen im Tropicana Lodge in Fresno, Kalifornien, 1961. Das Architekturbüro Armet & Davis in Los Angeles war führend in der Einrichtung moderner kalifornischer Coffeeshops, deren Stil auch als „Googi" bezeichnet wurde. Sie bauten mehrere Tiki-Tempel, zum Beispiel den Kona Kai in Philadelphia und den Kon-Tiki in Montreal.

PAGE 24 : La foule branchée à l'heure du cocktail à l'Imperial Luau, Pompano Beach, Floride
PAGE 26, EN HAUT À GAUCHE : Tiki et le poète Guillaume Apollinaire dans l'atelier de Picasso vers 1910 ; EN HAUT À DROITE : Trois dieux de la culture pop : Brigitte Bardot, Picasso et tiki
CI-DESSUS : Le primitif et le moderne se rencontrent au Tropicana Lodge de Fresno (Californie), en 1961. La société Armet & Davis de Los Angeles fut le premier architecte du Moderne Coffeshop californien, également connu sous le nom de Googie style (style gogo). Ils construisirent plusieurs temples tiki, tels que le Kona Kai à Philadelphie et le Kon-Tiki à Montréal.

later accompany him throughout the rest of his unparalleled career.

While primitive art was mainly appreciated by the avantgarde throughout the 20s and 30s, after the second World War it began, by virtue of this very association, to appeal to the affluent middle class: It was now associated with an artistic, bohemian lifestyle and a whimsical, playful attitude. By the late 1950s it was definitely de rigeur to have a striking tribal art piece to break the monotony of your contemporary living room decor. The time of the Tiki had come.

This strange watering hole rose out of the desert in Palm Springs in 1962 as the outgrowth of the imagination of Lyle Wheeler, art director of "South Pacific" (the movie). It has long since been reclaimed by the desert sands.

Das seltsame Wasserloch entstand mitten in der Wüste in Palm Springs im Jahr 1962, der Fantasie von Lyle Wheeler entsprungen, dem Artdirector des Films „South Pacific". Schon lange liegt es unter dem Wüstensand begraben.

Ce curieux bar, fruit de l'imagination de Lyle Wheeler (responsable des décors du film «South Pacific»), surgit dans le désert de Palm Springs en 1962. Cet endroit a depuis longtemps été recouvert par les sables du désert.

29

San Francisco

4½ DAYS

868 MILES 18 HOURS

2091 MILES

2228 MILES 4½ DAYS

Los Angeles

PRE-TIKI AND THE BIRTH OF POLYNESIAN POP

COURSE OF THE
MATSON LINERS
IN THE *South Pacific*

"Oh to be born on one of the South Sea Isles as a so-called savage, for once to enjoy human existence as pure and untainted by a fake after-taste." (Goethe, 1828)

The wish to forsake the benefits of civilization for a simpler, natural life-style is as old as "civilization" itself.

Escapist dreamers and serious philosophers found that the early travelogues from the South Sea voyages of Cook and Bougainville described the perfect alternative living conditions in contrast to the affected society of Old Europe. Melville extolled the naturalness of the native girls: "I should like to have seen a gallery of coronation beauties, at Westminster Abbey, confronted by this band of Island girls; their stiffness, formality and affectation, contrasted with the artless vivacity and unconcealed natural graces of these savage maidens."

PAGE 30/31: A flower garland of South Sea icons from the early 40s

ABOVE: An early rendition of a South Sea paradise

ABOVE RIGHT: "A bewildered Botanist", discovering an exotic specimen, from the "Cruise of the Kawa".

RIGHT: "The Author and his Island Bride"

SEITE 30/31: Die Attraktionen der Südsee als Blumengirlande, Anfang der 40er Jahre

OBEN: Frühe Darstellung eines Südseeparadieses

OBEN RECHTS: „Ein verblüffter Botaniker" entdeckt eine exotische Pflanze, aus „The Cruise of the Kawa"

RECHTS: „Der Autor und seine Insel-Braut"

PAGE 30/31: Les attraits des mers du Sud sous forme de guirlande fleurie, début des années 40

CI-DESSUS : Une ancienne représentation d'un paradis des mers du Sud. CI-DESSUS À DROITE : «Un botaniste perplexe» découvrant un spécimen exotique, d'après «La Croisière du Kawa». À DROITE : «L'Auteur et sa fiancée des îles »

The fair climate, natural beauty, passionate natives, and abundant resources of exotic foods seemed to promise an existence free of the restraints and stresses created by the cultured communities of the Western world. In fact, adventure stories in the escapist vein set in Polynesia became so popular that in 1921 G. P. Putnam's Sons published a parody on such South Seas expeditions entitled *The Cruise of the Kawa*. The need for such fare was so great that although the book was clearly a satire by virtue of the photos alone it was accepted far and wide as a genuine narrative and its author was invited to speak in front of the National Geographic Society. The *Kawa* proved that fiction was preferable to fact when it came to renditions of par-

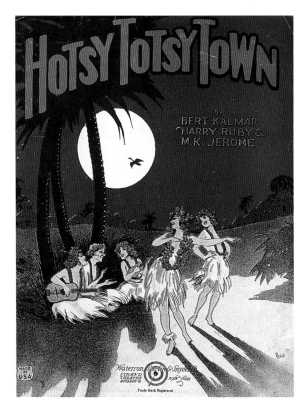

Aloha - Clifton's "Pacific Seas"
618 So. Olive St., Los Angeles

LEFT PAGE: *Hawaiian slide guitar and ukelele tunes like "I'd Like to See Some More of Samoa" were all the rage in America in the early twenties;* MIDDLE: *The Zombie was a predecessor to the Tiki as an agent of the ominous side of Paradise.*
ABOVE: *The elaborate exterior of Clifton's Pacific Seas was mirrored on the inside with fake palmtrees, neon lilies and a sherbet-gushing volcano. Built by the architectural firm of Welton Becket in the late 1930s, it made way for a parking lot in 1960.*

LINKE SEITE: *Hawaiische Gitarren- und Ukelele-Lieder wie „I'd Like to See Some More of Samoa" waren in den frühen 20er Jahren in Amerika äußerst beliebt;* MITTE: *Der Zombie war ein Vorläufer von Tiki – als ein Abgesandter der bedrohlichen Seite des Paradieses.* OBEN: *Die aufwendig gestaltete Außenansicht von Clifton's Pacific Seas hatte im Inneren ihre Entsprechung mit künstlichen Palmen, Neonlilien und einem Brausepulver-Vulkan. Das Lokal wurde in den 30er Jahren von dem Architekturbüro Welton Becket gebaut und mußte 1960 einem Parkplatz weichen.*

PAGE DE GAUCHE: *Des mélodies à la guitare hawaïenne ou à l'ukulele telles que «I'd Like to See Some More of Samoa» faisaient fureur en Amérique au début des années vingt;* AU CENTRE: *Le zombie précéda le tiki comme messager de cette face obscure du Paradis.* CI-DESSUS: *Au décor extérieur très élaboré du Clifton's Pacific Seas répondaient à l'intérieur des faux palmiers, des lis en néon et un volcan crachant de la limonade. Construit par le bureau d'architectes de Welton Becket à la fin des années 1930, l'établissement fut remplacé par un parking en 1960.*

LEFT: The Hula girl became the exotic siren for the entertainment seeking lounge clientele of the early 20th century, projecting her naked breasts on embossed matchbooks (right, and page 99) that gave the user the tactile sensation of actual nubile mounds under their fingertips.

RIGHT PAGE: This South Seas watering hole in the megalopolis of Chicago was completely decked out with bamboo, rattan and tropical foliage to help you forget the concrete canyons outside.

LINKS: Das Hula-Girl war die exotische Sirene einer Nachtclub-Klientel des frühen 20. Jahrhunderts, die sich gut unterhalten lassen wollte. Die barbusigen Mädchen waren auf geprägten Streichholzheftchen (rechts und Seite 99) zu bewundern, sodass der Gast das Gefühl hatte, mit den Fingerspitzen richtige kleine Hügel zu berühren.

RECHTE SEITE: Dieses Südsee-Lokal im Großstadtmoloch Chicago war vollständig mit Bambus, Rattan und tropischen Pflanzen ausgestattet, um den Gast die Betonwüsten draußen vergessen zu lassen.

A GAUCHE: La Houla girl devint la sirène exotique des clients de bars en mal de divertissement au début du vingtième siècle. Elle offrait ses seins nus en relief sur les pochettes d'allumettes (à droite, et page 99); l'usager avait vraiment l'impression de poser les doigts sur des rondeurs.

PAGE DE DROITE: Ce bar des mers du Sud à Chicago était entièrement tapissé de bambou, de rotin et de plantes tropicales qui faisaient oublier les blocs de béton à l'extérieur.

Hollywood entertainers like Al Jolson favored
tropical decor like the sitting room above.

Hollywood-Entertainer wie Al Jolson fühlten sich
in tropischen Einrichtungen besonders wohl.

Des artistes d'Hollywood tels qu'Al Jolson adoraient
les décors tropicaux.

adise on earth. And it established the spirit of whimsy that from then on was to permeate Polynesian pop. But originally a much more archetypal instinct was addressed by the reports from Polynesia. "On the isle of Ota-heite, where love is the principal occupation, the preferred luxury, or, more precisely, the unique luxury of the inhabitants, the bodies and souls of the women, are formed to perfection." (Joseph Banks, 1743–1820, naturalist on Captain Cook's *Endeavour*). Statements like this transformed the nude native girl, the *wahine*, into Eve in the Polynesian Garden of Eden. She became the first and foremost an icon of Polynesian pop, embodying the promise of unconditional love. Soon other images like the palm tree, the native hut, the outrigger canoe, and all sorts of exotic flora and fauna joined her in the gallery of popular symbols of Oceanic culture. So far the Tiki was just one of many characters in the storybook land of Polynesia Americana. The Hawaiian guitar made its appearance when the big Hawaiian music craze hit the mainland in the 1920s. Hawaiian entertainers became sought-after nightclub acts, and the clubs themselves began to emulate the tropical theme. Floor-to-ceiling bamboo and rattan, lush tropical plants, and murals of the Islands were the ingredients these early urban getaways used to create the illusion of having escaped to the South Seas. And soon the popular imagination focused on another image. Ever since the early European Zoos had begun to exhibit real live "wild men" as part of their displays and journalists were mocking the swooning reactions of the society ladies, the simultaneous attraction and repulsion felt towards the savage, the allure of the "exotic other", had entered the civilized consciousness of the Western world. In Polynesian Pop this fascination took the form of the heathen idol, the Tiki.

37

"The system of idolatry, which prevailed among a people separated from the majority of their species by trackless oceans, and possessing the means, not only of subsistence but of comfort, in an unusual degree, presents a most affecting exhibition of imbecility, absurdity, and degradation." (Rev. William Ellis, "Polynesian Researches," 1831)

TiKi: RECReATiONAL LiFE-STYLE OF A GENERATION

By the 1950s Americans were ready to reap the rewards of the hard work that had brought them economic independence and affluence. They had emerged from the Second World War as heroes and were flying high on a cloud of international success and appreciation. But the same Puritan work ethic that had gotten them thus far also brought with it a whole package of traditional social and moral restrictions that were limiting their freedom to enjoy their prosperity.

Polynesian parties provided the outlet that allowed the man in the grey flannel suit to regress to a rule-free primitive naivety: Donning colorful aloha shirts

Bengt
Danielsson
ANTHROPOLOGIST ON THE KON-TIKI VOYAGE

(which did not have to be tucked in!), getting intoxicated by sweet exotic concoctions with names that resembled a lilting infant idiom (Lapu Lapu, Mauna Loa Puki), eating luau pig with bare hands, and engaging in hula and limbo contests provided the opportunity to cut loose and have fun in an otherwise conservative society.

Another freedom that the "suburban savage" identity offered was that of beholding images of bare-breasted native women as long as it was in the context of anthropological interest — in other words, the practice of a sort of National Geographic eroticism. Thus the century-old myth of guilt-free sex was perpetuated, if not in action at least in the imagination. But as the wahine and all the other clichéd icons of South Sea story-book-land were recruited again, a new figurehead of Polynesian pop emerged: the carved native idol commonly referred to as Tiki. Notwithstanding the fact that the term did not exist in the Hawaiian or Tahitian languages, or that the stone sculptures of Easter Island were actually called *moai*, in Polynesian pop, all Oceanic carvings became members of one happy family: the Tikis. These primitive effigies were the counteragents in the modern world of plastic and chrome: priapic monuments to the primal urges that were otherwise

The Tiki and the three graces: At Tropics Motel (Blythe, California,1963) an upside-down palm tree created the palm root hairdo (page 38).

Der Tiki und die drei Grazien. Im Tropics Motel (Blythe, Kalifornien, 1963) wurde eine Palme auf den Kopf gestellt – fertig war die Palm-wurzelfrisur (Seite 38).

Le tiki et les trois Grâces, Tropics Motel, Blythe, Californie, 1963. On retourne le palmier et le tour est joué: la coupe de cheveux «racines de palmier» est née (page 38).

suppressed under the ordered cleanliness of 50s suburbia.

Although the form they took was inspired by their Polynesian predecessors, American Tikis were more often than not free-form interpretations of several island styles, mixed with a good dose of cartoon whimsy and a dash of modern art. Even those that could be called "authentic" were merely reproductions of the few originals that had survived the "utter abolishment" by zealous missionaries. This liberal attitude towards counterfeiting had actually begun in the Hawaiian Islands with the early Western contacts, seen in the following report from 1825:

"The officers of the HBM ship *Blonde*, when here, were anxious to procure some of the ancient idols, to carry home as curios. The demand soon exhausted the stock at hand: to supply the deficiency the Hawaiians

The Tiki easily found his place in the bohemian world of the playboy. RIGHT: Hugh Hefner at his pool, surrounded by his Playboy Bunnies and three masks from William Westenhaver's "Contemporary Idol" line BELOW: Tiki—God of the artists; a photograph by Bunny Yeager

Mühelos fand Tiki auch Eingang in die Bohemewelt des Playboy. RECHTS: Hugh Hefner an seinem Swimmingpool, umringt von seinen Playboy-Bunnies und drei Masken aus William Westenhavers Kollektion „zeitgenössischer Götzenbilder" UNTEN: Tiki, der Gott der Künstler; ein Foto von Bunny Yeager

Le tiki s'ntégra tout aussi facilement dans l'univers bohème de Playboy. A DROITE: Hugh Hefner au bord de sa piscine, entouré de ses Playboy Bunnies et par trois masques de la ligne «Idole Contemporaine» de William Westenhaver CI-DESSOUS: Tiki – le dieu des artistes, une photographie de Bunny Yeager

made idols, and smoked them, to impart to them an appearance of antiquity, and actually succeeded in the deception." (W.S.W. Ruschenberger, *Extracts from the Journal of an American Naval Officer*, 1841) And

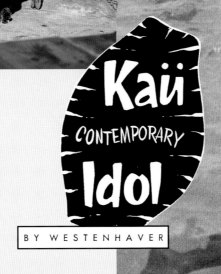

Kaü
CONTEMPORARY
Idol

BY WESTENHAVER

A NEW WORLD OF *Enchantment*

Island drums echo your footsteps as you enter this Polynesian posada yielding unforgettable revelry for pleasure seekers and adventurous appetites. Here you tread on enchanted grounds of an authentic Polynesian Village recreated with captivating mystery and beauty . . . the tempting thrills of the Tahitian Room . . . the haunting delights of the Hawaiian Room . . . the splendors of the Samoan Hut . . . and the carefree relaxation in the Cannibal Cocktail Lounge.

Aglow with the allure of the South Seas, your dining hours become heart-throbbing adventures accented with intriguing decor. Take your seat in a mighty throne chair and welcome the gracious gifts of this romantic restaurant.

Polynesian Village
Exotic Food and Drink

Cantonese and Mandarin
DISHES

Native chefs have prepared a potpourri of Polynesian delicacies for you . . . a medley of Mandarin fare . . . captivating Cantonese cuisine garnished with the flair of Oriental service. Enjoy such irresistible delights as Lobster Cantonese . . . Samoan Beef . . . Royal Shrimp Cashew . . . Hamsteaks Hong Kong . . . Mandarin Duck . . . to bewitch you with undeniable taste sensations.

The Tiki Calls . . .

. . . Aloha Luau's trademark is the Tiki . . .
. . . Watch for one of the largest hand-hewn palm gods of the South Seas at the gate entrance, where you will receive the welcome of Aloha Luau's host, Jaisohn Hyun . . .

. . . With a beautiful Hawaiian lei . . .

. . . With an orchid for the lady . . .

For Reservations

ONE CALL:
SPruce 3-1311
OR WRITE
ALOHA LUAU
7272 E. GAGE AVE.
COMMERCE, CALIF.

AUTHENTIC
Entertainment

. . . With each luau, there is always the finest South Sea island entertainment — hula, Samoan and Tahitian dancers, singers and musicians, fire and knife dancers . . .

DANCING — SOUTH SEAS
. . . Grass hut dancing — with rain on the roof . . .

Aloha Luau

over a century later, primitive art collector Pablo Picasso, who was a thrifty flea market shopper, proclaimed:

"You don't need the masterpiece to get the idea. The concept or component of a style is entirely accessible in second-rate examples and even fakes." And so American artists, imbued with the spirit of Tiki, did not hesitate to re-create the godheads in their own whimsical manner.

A perfect example of this style is the Tiki that Alec Yuill-Thornton designed for Tiki Bob's bar in San Francisco. Part George Jetson, part modern

The Evolution of Polynesian Pop

1930s

And The 'Beachcomber' Style

1940s

Trader Vic's
And The 'Trader' Style

W.W.II Soldiers Return
From South Pacific.
James Michener's Best Sellers

PRE-TIKI

- - - **1950s** - - -

TIKI

Don The Beachcomber and
Trader Vic's Proliferate

Stephen Crane's
LUAU
**Tikis Appear
In Greater Numbers**

Thor Heyerdahl's
KON-TIKI
And **Aku-Aku**
Bestsellers

Crane's
KON-TIKI
Chain

Tourist Culture
Jet Travel Opens Hawaii
Hawaii Gains Statehood

1960s

Danny Balsz's
The Tikis
The Heyday of Tiki

Backyard Polynesian Culture

Motels And Apartments
Go Tiki

1970s

DEVOLUTION BEGINS

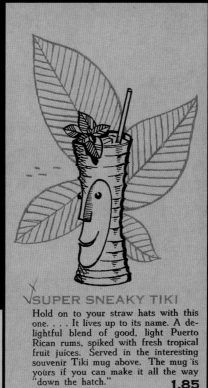

SUPER SNEAKY TIKI
Hold on to your straw hats with this one. . . . It lives up to its name. A delightful blend of good, light Puerto Rican rums, spiked with fresh tropical fruit juices. Served in the interesting souvenir Tiki mug above. The mug is yours if you can make it all the way "down the hatch." **1.85**

primitive, this sculpture has very little in common with any Oceanic artifacts. But, together with the signature Tiki of Stephen Crane's Luau, it actually marks the beginning of Tiki style. For the first time, a Tiki was employed as a logo, serving as an entrance guardian, appearing as an icon on the menu and matchbooks, and assuming the form of mugs and salt and pepper shakers. "Sneaky" Bob Bryant had worked as Trader Vic's bar manager, but when they had a falling out in 1955, Bob moved down a block from the Trader's Cosmo Place location and opened his own bar. An attempt to franchise his concept at the Capitol Inn in Sacramento was short lived. Bob also opened *Tiki Bob's Mainland* on Bush Street where he offered lingerie fashion shows to draw in the business crowd at lunchtime.

Thus Tiki became the star in the Polynesian pop theater, his name christening a multitude of establishments across America from Alabama to Alaska, and his many varied forms adorning just as many "watering holes of the civilization weary." The Tiki image reached the peak of its prominence when it was used as a logo for the Warner Brothers TV series *Hawaiian Eye,* which was beamed into American living rooms from 1959 to 1963, subliminally implanting its archetypal form into the minds of the hypnotized suburbanites.

But just as Tiki fever reached its peak, the big generational divide of the 60s put an end to it. The children of the Tiki revellers decided to create their own

LEFT PAGE: A simplified overview of the stylistic and historic influences that formed Tiki style. The "Big Three" (Don, Vic and Steve) are symbolic for all the individuals like Tiki Bob who gave the style it's variety and unique charm.

LINKE SEITE: Ein vereinfachter Überblick über die stilistischen und historischen Einflüsse, aus denen sich der Tiki-Stil entwickelt hat. Die „Großen Drei" (Don, Vic, Steve) stehen symbolisch für all diejenigen, die wie Tiki Bob dem Stil seine Vielfalt und seinen einzigartigen Charme verliehen haben.

PAGE DE GAUCHE: Une chronologie sommaire des influences historiques et stylistiques qui ont généré le style tiki. Les «Big Three» (Don, Vic et Steve) symbolisent tous ceux qui, tels Tiki Bob, donnèrent à ce style son charme bien à lui et sa diversité.

TIKI BOB'S

POST AND TAYLOR   SAN FRANCISCO

POLYNESIAN CHOW AND GROG

LEFT PAGE: The first Logo Tiki
LEFT: Alec Yuill-Thornton, designer of the Tiki Bob's Tiki, illustrated this Trader Vic tome in 1952. BELOW: "Tiki Bob" Bryant (right), raising the mug to Jerry Bundsen, aide to columnist Herb Caen.

LINKE SEITE: Der erste Logo-Tiki
LINKS: Alec Yuill-Thornton, der den Tiki für Tiki Bob's entworfen hat, illustrierte dieses Trader Vic-Buch von 1952. UNTEN: „Tiki Bob" Bryant (rechts) hebt den Becher auf Jerry Bundsen, Mitarbeiter von Kolumnist Herb Caen

PAGE DE GAUCHE: Le premier logo tiki
A GAUCHE: Alec Yuill-Thornton, créateur du tiki de Bob's Tiki, illustra ce volume de Trader Vic en 1952. CI-DESSOUS: « Tiki Bob » Bryant (à droite), portant un toast à Jerry Bundsen, l'assistant du billettiste Herb Caen.

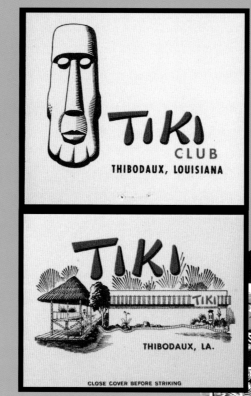

TiKi CLUB THIBODAUX, LOUISIANA

TiKi TiKi THIBODAUX, LA.

CLOSE COVER BEFORE STRIKING

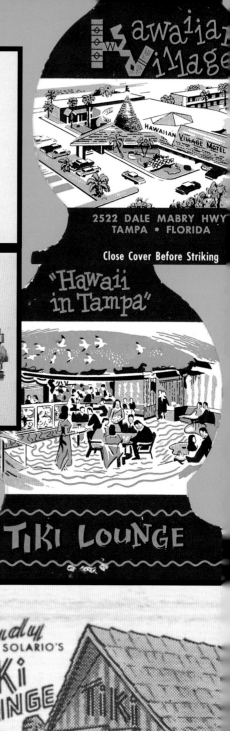

Hawaiian Village

2522 DALE MABRY HWY TAMPA • FLORIDA

Close Cover Before Striking

"Hawaii in Tampa"

TiKi LOUNGE

Nirvana, where Free Love and other-worldly happiness became an immediate reality. Alcohol was no longer the drug of choice as marihuana and psychedelics became recreational avocations and the sexual revolution seemingly did away with all Puritan notions of monogamy. Together with the tropical cocktails, the greasy sweet faux-Chinese cuisine termed "Polynesian" clashed with the growing health food consciousness.

The "British invasion" shifted the young generation's attention toward another strange foreign cult, the Beatles. The Kinks lamented a plastic Polynesia in "Holiday in Waikiki," whining "… and even all the grass skirts were PVC!" Just as two centuries earlier the Polynesian natives had realized that the white explorers were not gods when they drew Captain Cook's blood in the skirmish at Kealakekua Bay and were able to kill him, Americans suffered a traumatic

Dancing Every Night

TiKi SUPPER CLUB Next to Chick-N-Box Restaurant MOBILE, ALA.

ORCHESTRA DAILY • OPEN SUNDAYS

Rudolf SOLARIO'S TiKi LOUNGE TiKi

50

TIKI LODGE

509 No. Riverside
Medford, Ore. 97501

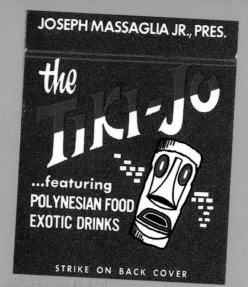

JOSEPH MASSAGLIA JR., PRES.

the TIKI-Jo

...featuring
POLYNESIAN FOOD
EXOTIC DRINKS

STRIKE ON BACK COVER

TIKI-KAI
371-7588

456-6320
549 - 2nd AVE.

MECCA BAR
Tiki Cove
Fairbanks
. . . ALASKA .

CLOSE COVER FOR SAFETY

EXOTIC
Atmosphere
TIKI
ISLAND

3743 SO. WESTERN AVE
LOS ANGELES

341-7766

Club Tiki

Please Close Cover Before Striking

Tiki Men's Salon
IN THE
TAHITIAN VILLAGE
13519 LAKEWOOD BLVD.
DOWNEY, CALIF.

★ ★ ★

HAIR STYLING

ENTERTAINMENT
Dancing
ROSCOE
at DESOTO
CANOGA PARK
Host - FLORIAN

PETE ARMENTA

FOR SAFETY

Tiki Hut
25 SEPULVEDA BLVD.
SEGUNDO, CALIF.

1718 WALNUT

pub Tiki

PARK
FREE

1815 Walnut

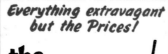

Everything extravagant
but the Prices!

the pub

51

Polynesian Floor Shows
South Pacific Room

THURSDAY 10:15 p.m.

SUNDAY 10:15

FRIDAY 10:00 p.m. and 12:00 p.m.

SATUR 10:00 and 12:00

SHELTER ISLAND'S **BALI HAI** RESTAURANT POINT LOMA, CALIF.

Down With Fake 'Kon-Tiki'!

A pestilent rash of "Polynesian" restaurants is spreading across the face of this land of ours. I confess that, initially, I smiled upon these eating-houses. But they degenerate in quality, and I yearn for food, not for pseudo-Pacific cuteness. Down with cuisine and decor a la Kon-Tiki!

The Kon-Tiki fad now extends to Podunk and Tuxedo Junction. Certain wholesalers thrive by selling nothing but grass matting, imitations of Easter Island figures, and the other paraphernalia of "South Seas" dining. Thor Heyerdahl, ethnologist and author of that delightful book "The Voyage of the Kon-Tiki," must be aghast at the architectural and gastronomic atrocities committed in the name of his balsa raft.

Primarily, the trouble with these sham-Pacific restaurants is that the cooks don't really know how to prepare Polynesian or Micronesian or Indonesian or Malayan dishes—how could they? — and that the proprietors think garish ersatz-Tahiti decor will atone for the dubious fare and the high prices. I confess that a few of these dining-rooms are pleasant, with their fantastic drinks and almond-eyed waitresses. But here I reproach the typical "atoll" masquerade just off the throughway, with its thin veneer of fakery and its insipid adaptation of American-Chinese menus.

Ignorance Is Indigestion

blow to their own godliness when President Kennedy was killed in 1963. It was the beginning of the end, marking the loss of youthful innocence in their own eyes and those of the world.

Exotica and the Tiki style were denounced as contrived rituals of the imperialist establishment at the same time that the Vietnam war developed into an ugly mistake, with native huts and palm trees burning on TV. Young protesters were marching on the Capitol in Washington while Richard Nixon was drinking Mai Tai's at his favorite hang out, the Washington *Trader Vic's*.

In the 70s, the thus segregated Polynesian style was watered down further through a certain "Jimmy Buffetization,"—the introduction of a

generic tropical island theme with no definite identity. Be it the Caribbean, Mexico, or Polynesia, everywhere was Margharita-ville. The popular TV show *Fantasy Island* typified this new "politically correct" detachment from cultural complicity, creating a world of white wicker colonial-style decor mixed with exotic plants.

The fern bar replaced the Tiki bar.

The 1980s was the decade of destruction—the abolishment of Tiki and his culture. Either completely razed or renovated beyond recognition, Polynesian palaces disappeared without ever having been acknowledged as a unique facet of American pop culture. Purely an expression of a popular fad, they had always been denounced and ignored by the culture critics in their own time; now they represented merely an embarrassing lapse of taste. Unnoticed and without mourning, a whole tradition vanished.

LEFT PAGE, TOP: In the eyes of their children, these wanna-be natives had lost all sense of shame; LEFT: An Los Angeles Times edict from 1965, representing the prevailing opinion of the "Taste-police" ABOVE, LEFT: Watering hole of the ruling class: Trader Vic's at the Capitol Hilton, Washington, D.C.; RIGHT: Tiki Bob's today

LINKE SEITE, OBEN: In den Augen ihrer Kinder hatten diese Möchtegern-Eingeborenen jedes Schamgefühl verloren; LINKS: Ein Verriß in der Los Angeles Times von 1965, der die damals vorherrschende Meinung der „Geschmackspolizei" wiedergibt. OBEN LINKS: Ein Bar-Restaurant der herrschenden Klasse: Trader Vic's im Capitol Hilton in Washington, D.C.; RECHTS: Das Tiki Bob's heute

PAGE DE GAUCHE, EN HAUT: Aux yeux de leurs enfants, ces pseudo-indigènes avaient perdu tout sens du ridicule; À GAUCHE: Un article au vitriol du Los Angeles Times de 1965, qui reflète l'opinion de la «Police du Goût». CI-DESSUS, À GAUCHE: Le bar de la classe dirigeante: Trader Vic's au Capitol Hilton, Washington, D.C.; À DROITE: Le Bob's Tiki aujourd'hui

ERECTING A TiKi TEMPLE

HALE TiKi

The construction of a "Hale Tiki" (House of Tiki) was an elaborate undertaking, not only because of the various exotic materials used, but owing to the unusual concepts that were employed to fill the attending Tiki devotees with amazement and delight as they filled themselves with tropical libations.

This chapter will enlighten the reader on the exterior and interior motifs that define the architecture of Tiki style, and in so doing help establish the thus-far unrecognized style as a part of American pop culture. Though there is a distinct tradition that has been followed since Don the Beachcomber, with certain devices being employed and elaborated on again and again, what characterizes Tiki style is how the individual entrepreneurs who were struck with Tiki fever re-created it in their own way. From fake interior jungles to drink presentation rituals, personal imaginations ran wild as American developers followed the call of Tiki and conjured up

NATIVE DWELLINGS
OF THE PACIFIC AREA

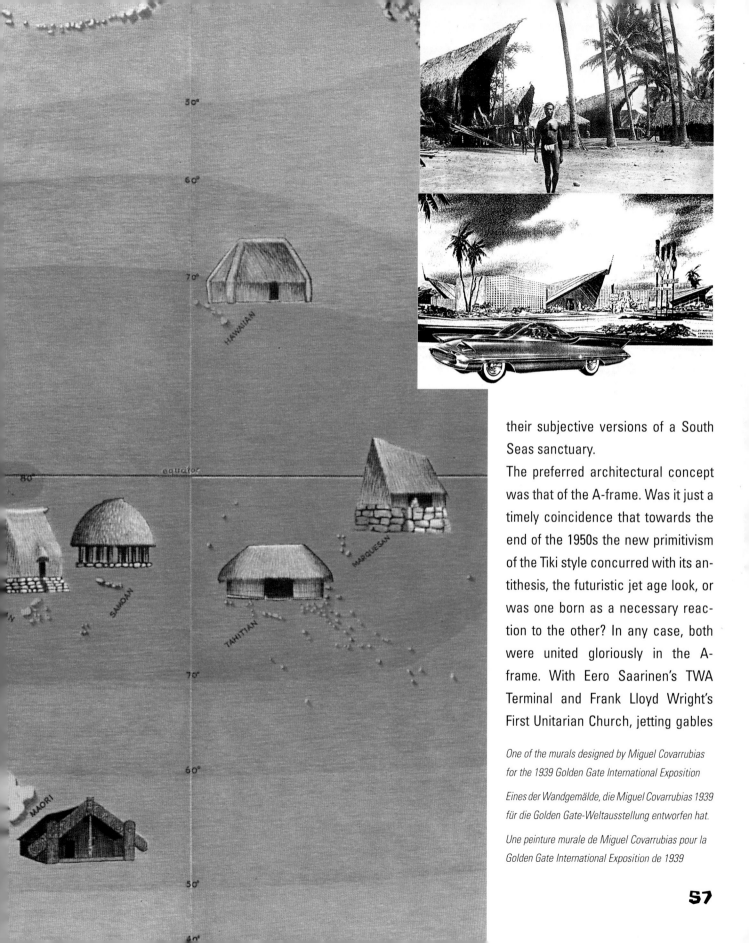

their subjective versions of a South Seas sanctuary.

The preferred architectural concept was that of the A-frame. Was it just a timely coincidence that towards the end of the 1950s the new primitivism of the Tiki style concurred with its antithesis, the futuristic jet age look, or was one born as a necessary reaction to the other? In any case, both were united gloriously in the A-frame. With Eero Saarinen's TWA Terminal and Frank Lloyd Wright's First Unitarian Church, jetting gables

One of the murals designed by Miguel Covarrubias for the 1939 Golden Gate International Exposition

Eines der Wandgemälde, die Miguel Covarrubias 1939 für die Golden Gate-Weltausstellung entworfen hat.

Une peinture murale de Miguel Covarrubias pour la Golden Gate International Exposition de 1939

ABOVE: A New Guinea "Haus Tambaran"
ABOVE RIGHT: A Hawaiian Tiki Temple in 1816
RIGHT: A men's club house on Palau Island
RIGHT PAGE, TOP: A Maori meeting house, early 1840s;
BOTTOM: An American Tiki temple, early 1960s

OBEN: Ein „Haus Tambaran" aus Neuguinea
OBEN RECHTS: Ein hawaiischer Tiki-Tempel von 1816
RECHTS: Versammlungshaus für Männer auf der Insel
Palau
RECHTE SEITE, OBEN: Ein Maori-Versammlungshaus um
1840; UNTEN: Ein amerikanischer Tiki-Tempel, frühe
60er Jahre

CI-DESSUS : Une « Haus Tambaran » de Nouvelle-Guinée.
CI-DESSUS À DROITE : Un temple tiki hawaïen en 1816. A
DROITE : Un club pour hommes sur l'île de Palau
PAGE DE DROITE, EN HAUT : Un temple maori, au début
des années 1840; EN BAS : Un temple tiki américain,
au début des années 1960

became a favorite plaything of modern architects, mirroring the space-age optimism also found in Cadillac tail fins.

By happenstance the majority of traditional Oceanic domiciles were palm huts, and as such A-shaped. But since the native structures of the Polynesians were—with the exception of the elaborately carved Maori meeting houses—rather plain, other South Sea culture groups were enlisted. The New Guinea cult house, or

reservations SU 2-9400

Judges'
"Beyond the Reef"

16590 W. NORTH AVE. (AT CALHOUN RD.)
BROOKFIELD, WISCONSIN

Aloha! from the Judges'
"Beyond the Reef"
CHARCOAL BROILED
OPEN HEARTH

STEAKS
SEAFOODS
CHICKEN
Enticing COCKTAILS
that "capture island enchantment"

Air Conditioned   (Closed Mondays)

ABOVE: A Wisconsin log cabin turned "Tiki"
RIGHT PAGE: Stephen Crane's first Kon-Tiki outpost,
1959, Montreal, designed by Armet & Davis, L.A.

OBEN: Eine Blockhütte in Wisconsin, im Tiki-Stil
umgewandelt. RECHTE SEITE: Stephen Cranes erstes
Kon-Tiki-Lokal, 1959, Montreal; entworfen von
Armet & Davis, Los Angeles

CI-DESSUS: Une cabane du Wisconsin transformée
en tiki. PAGE DE DROITE: Le premier poste avancé Kon
Tiki de Stephen Crane, 1959, Montréal; dessiné par
Armet & Davis, Los Angeles

Haus Tambaran, with its sweeping gable and mask-decorated front, and the ceremonial meeting house as found on Palau, Micronesia, (also known as the men's club house!) with its colorful story-board paintings, were the inspiration for many American Tiki temples. The Jetsons met the Flintstones as middle-class modern primitives parked their shuttle crafts in front of these spaceships from planet Tiki and willingly entered the dimension barrier to another world where for a while they could become members of the Tiki tribe.

A-frames were easy to build, and so traditional structures like Wisconsin log cabins or classic downtown business buildings were transformed into pagan palaces by the addition of a peaked entrance. Chinese restaurants "updated" their style with the hut look to benefit from the Polynesian craze. But what happened behind the big A?

To symbolize the threshold to another reality, the entrance often required traversing a bridge crossing a stream fed by a lava rock waterfall. The archetypal elements of fire and water were brought into play with gas-fed Tiki torches (sometimes installed as beacons on top of the gables) and exterior and interior waterfalls that provided a subtly gurgling background. Imposing Tikis flanked the entrance,

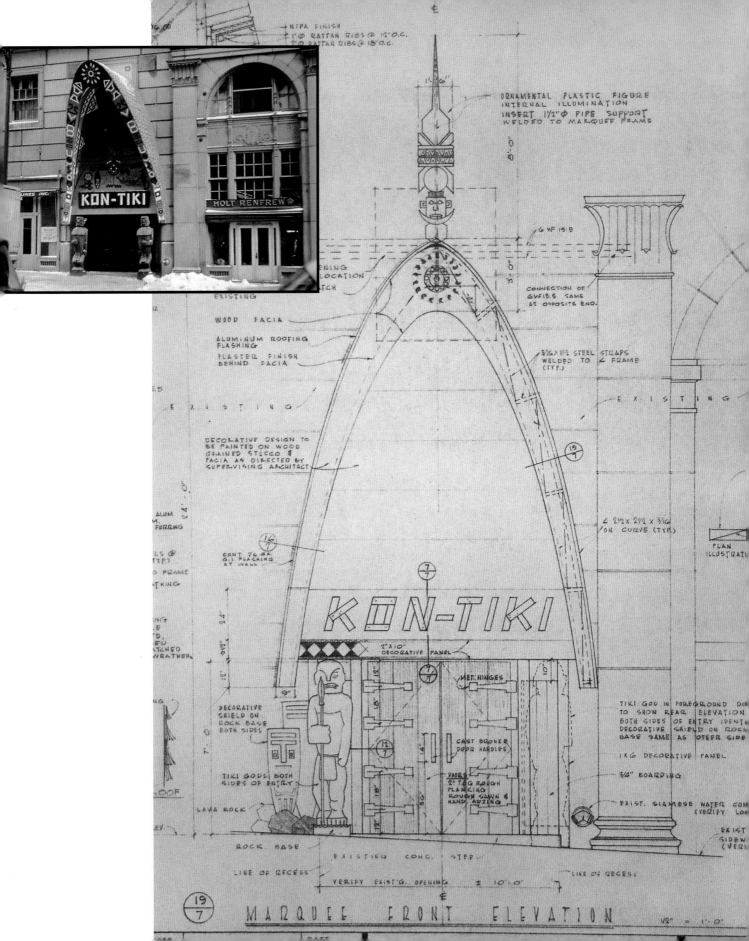

NIPA FINISH
1"Ø RATTAN RIBS @ 12" O.C.
?"Ø RATTAN RIBS @ 18" O.C.

ORNAMENTAL PLASTIC FIGURE
INTERNAL ILLUMINATION
INSERT 1½"Ø PIPE SUPPORT
WELDED TO MARQUEE FRAME

6 WF 15.5

CONNECTION OF
GWF15.5 SAME
AT OPPOSITE END.

...NING
...LOCATION
...TCH
EXISTING

WOOD FACIA

ALUMINUM ROOFING
FLASHING

PLASTER FINISH
BEHIND FACIA

3/16 x 1½ STEEL STRAPS
WELDED TO ∠ FRAME
(TYP.)

EXISTING   EXISTING

DECORATIVE DESIGN TO
BE PAINTED ON WOOD
GRAINED STUCCO &
FACIA AS DIRECTED BY
SUPERVISING ARCHITECT

15
7

∠ 2½ x 2½ x 3/16
ON CURVE (TYP.)

PLAN
ILLUSTRATI...

16
7

CONT. 26 GA.
G.I. FLACHING
AT WALL

7
7

KON-TIKI

2" X 10"
DECORATIVE PANEL

7
7

MET. HINGES

12"

10"

TIKI GOD IN FOREGROUND DO...
TO SHOW REAR ELEVATION
BOTH SIDES OF ENTRY IDENT...
DECORATIVE SHIELD ON ROCK
BASE SAME AS OTHER SIDE

1 X 6 DECORATIVE PANEL

3/4" BOARDING

DECORATIVE
SHIELD ON
ROCK BASE
BOTH SIDES

9"

18"

12
7

18"

CAST BRONZE
DOOR HANDLES

DOORS
2" T&G ROUGH
PLANKING
ROUGH SAWN &
HAND ADZING

TIKI GODS BOTH
SIDES OF ENTRY

EXIST. SIAMESE WATER CON...
VERIFY LOC...

LAVA ROCK

12"

EXIST
SIDEW...
(VERI...

ROCK BASE
LINE OF RECESS

EXISTING CONC. STEP.
VERIFY EXIST'G. OPENING   ± 10'-0"

LINE OF RECESS

19
7

M A R Q U E E   F R O N T   E L E V A T I O N   ½" = 1'-0"

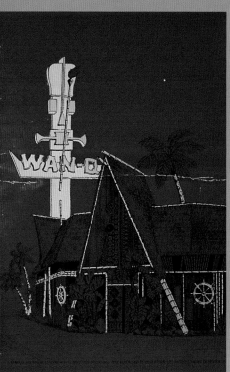

Left: Before and after: Seen from the same angle, a Chinese restaurant dresses up Polynesian to keep up with the trend. Below: Never realized, but dreamed of, were Tiki fast food franchises like the Tonga Pup.

Links: Vorher und nachher: Ein chinesisches Restaurant, aus demselben Blickwinkel gesehen; um im Trend zu liegen, wurde es im polynesischen Stil aufgepeppt. Unten: Nie verwirklicht, aber ewig erträumt: Tiki-Fastfood-Ketten wie der Tonga Pup

A gauche: Avant et après: vu sous le même angle, un restaurant chinois habillé à la mode polynésienne pour rester dans le coup. Ci-dessous: Jamais réalisés, mais rêvés, les fast-foods tiki franchisés comme le Tonga Pup.

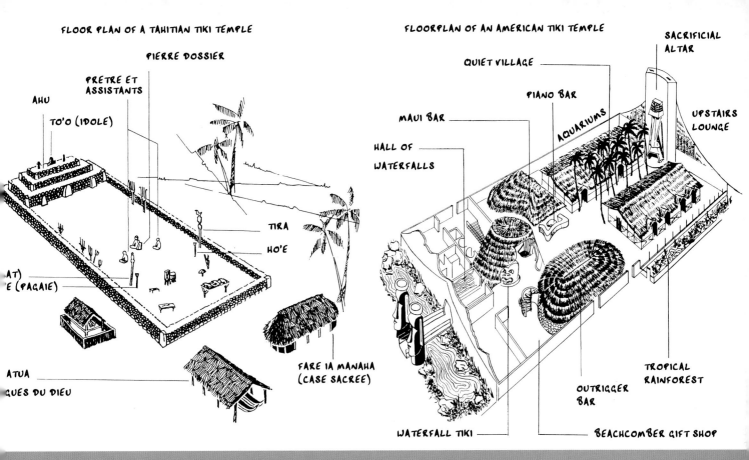

FLOOR PLAN OF A TAHITIAN TIKI TEMPLE

PIERRE DOSSIER

AHU

TO'O (IDOLE)

PRETRE ET ASSISTANTS

TIRA

HO'E

AT) E (PAGAIE)

ATUA

QUES DU DIEU

FARE IA MANAHA (CASE SACREE)

FLOORPLAN OF AN AMERICAN TIKI TEMPLE

SACRIFICIAL ALTAR

QUIET VILLAGE

PIANO BAR

MAUI BAR

AQUARIUMS

UPSTAIRS LOUNGE

HALL OF WATERFALLS

TROPICAL RAINFOREST

OUTRIGGER BAR

WATERFALL TIKI

BEACHCOMBER GIFT SHOP

popped out of the jungle foliage, and were used as support posts and other architectural details.

The interior was a multi-layered environment appealing to all the senses. The various rooms with evocative names like "Black Hole of Calcutta" or "Lounge of the Seven Pleasures" were constructed from floor-to-ceiling with exotic woods, bamboo, rattan, Tapa cloth, and other organic naturals. Primitive weapons and masks hung on the walls, while beachcomber lamps and assorted flotsam on the ceiling provided the next layer. Murals of island life and three-dimensional dioramas further

Below: Apartment architecture in Los Angeles

Unten: Apartment-Architektur in Los Angeles

Ci-dessous: Style d'architecture d'un appartement, Los Angeles

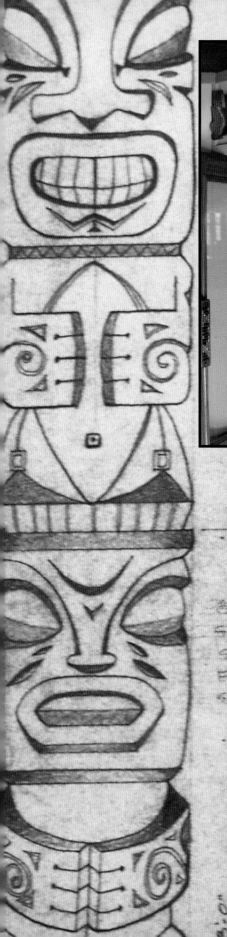

THE BALI HAI
IS MADE OF
WOODS FROM

Germany
Walnut

Tahitian
Ti

CALIFORNIA
REDWOOD

WEST INDIES
BLUE GUM

MEXICO

CHINESE
TEAK

AFRICA
BENIN

PHILIPPINE
MAHOGANY

England
Brown Oak

HAWAII
KOA

TROPICS
The Waikiki Room
The Polynesian Room
The Bamboo Lounge
The Outrigger Bar
The Surfboard Lounge
The Lanai Room
Reservations TAYLOR 6201-2
4:30 P.M. till 2:30 A.M.
Sundays 12 till 9:30 P.M.
1721 N. Main St.
Dayton's Finest
"Goodie" Sable
Maitre de & Mgr.

enhanced the illusion of being in a faraway place.

Another important texture was that of human skin. Many establishments prided themselves on their scantily clad exotic waitresses; live counterparts to the black velvet paintings that were also part of the regular decor of Tiki lounges. For the white-collar warriors of the 1950s, this exposure held a special allure that was further fueled by the Polynesian floorshows that had become standard entertainment in many South Seas supperclubs. That the Samoan Firedancers and Tahitian Hula Girls were often of South American or Asian heritage was not important. The costumes and the music, the exotic textures, the tropical decor, and the potent libations all worked together to dissolve any petty concerns about authenticity, thus allowing the Tiki reveller to become a believer in the hyper-reality of the urban Polynesian paradise.

KONA KAI F
MARRIOTT MOT
LOWER MER

While Exotica music provided the soundscape of the Tiki temple, this album had an actual piece of burlap glued on to it to provide the listener with the tactile experience of a primitive texture.

Während Exotica-Musik für den Klangteppich im Tiki-Tempel sorgte, war auf dieses Plattencover sogar ein echtes Stück Jute geklebt – so konnte der Hörer erfahren, wie sich ein solch ursprünglicher Stoff anfühlt.

Tandis que la musique « Exotica » fournissait l'ambiance sonore du temple tiki, cet album avait un véritable morceau de toile d'emballage collé sur sa couverture afin de procurer à l'acheteur l'expérience tactile d'une texture primitive.

A.I.A.

ARCHITECTS
2440 WEST THIRD STREET
LOS ANGELES, CALIFORNIA

LEFT: *The Tonga Room, Fairmont Hotel, San Francisco*
1940s: The hotel pool is turned into an ocean liner.
Early 60s: A Mondrian-style Chinese modern attempt
Late 60s: A Polynesian palace, complete with rain effects

LINKS: *Der Tonga Room, Fairmont Hotel, San Francisco*
40er Jahre: Der Hotel-Pool als Ozeandampfer
Frühe 60er Jahre: Ein an Piet Mondrian erinnernder
'modern-chinesischer' Versuch
Späte 60er Jahre: Ein polynesischer Palast, komplett mit
Regen-Effekt

A GAUCHE: *Le Tonga Room, Fairmont Hotel, San Francisco*
Années 40: La piscine de l'hôtel transformée en un
transatlantique
Début des années 60: une tentative sino-moderne inspi-
rée de Mondrian
Fin des années 60: un palace polynésien avec pluie arti-
ficielle

Left and below: Beachcomber lamps, the firmament of "Polynesia-Americana"
Below: The logo "Tiki" at the Tiki Jo in Santa Monica, carved by Ely Hedley

Links und unten: Beachcomber-Lampen, das Firmament von „Polynesia-Americana"
Unten: Der Logo-Tiki am Tiki Jo in Santa Monica, geschnitzt von Ely Hedley

A gauche et ci-dessous: Les lampes «Beachcomber», le firmament du «Polynesia-Americana»
Ci-dessous: Le logo tiki, sculpté par Ely Hedley, au Tiki Jo de Santa Monica

Murals that could be switched into a night mode with black light, dioramas with miniature South Sea island models, and entire fake jungle exteriors were among the concepts used to animate the dream.

Wandbilder, die mit schwarzem Licht in nächtliche Szenen verwandelt werden konnten, Dioramen mit Miniaturinseln der Südsee und komplette Dschungelinszenierungen gehörten zu den Entwürfen, mit denen der Traum wahr gemacht werden sollte.

Des peintures murales que l'on pouvait mettre en mode nocturne avec une lumière noire, des dioramas avec des reliefs d'îles des mers du Sud, et de faux décors de jungles tels étaient quelques-uns des dispositifs employés pour éveiller le rêve.

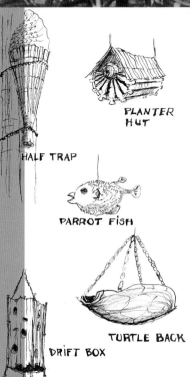

HALF TRAP

PLANTER HUT

PARROT FISH

DRIFT BOX

TURTLE BACK

KAUAI
OAHU
NIIHAU
Guam · 3337
Honolulu
MOLOKAI
MAUI
LANAI
KAHOOLAWE
HAWAII

Honolulu to Hollywood 2228 miles

Papeete to Hollywood 3490 miles

Hollywood
Catalina

Honolulu to Paqo Paqo 2276 miles

Honolulu to Papeete 2381 miles

Sydney 4420

Christmas Island

Suva
FIJI

Upolu
Apia
SAMOA
I. Paqo Paqo
Tutuila

I. BORA-BORA
I. TAHAA
I. RAIATEA

Papeete

I. MOOREA
I. TAHITI

I. Huahine

I. Nuku-Hiva
I. Hiva-Oa
I. Tahuata
MARQUISES
I. Fatu-Hiva
Puka-Puka

I. Mururoa
I. Taro Voi
GAMBIER
I. Mangareva

Papeete to Panama 4486 miles

PITCAIRN

I. Aitutaki
COOK ISLANDS
I. Rarotonga

DON THE BEACHCOMBE

— MEA HOOMANAO — "A thing to remember" —

DON THE BEACHCOMBER–
FOUNDING FATHER OF
POLYNESIAN POP

Hollywood, 1934: America's "noble experiment" with prohibition had just ended. Highproof alcohol was in demand, and an emigré restauranteur from New Orleans named Ernest Beaumont-Gantt decided to experiment with rum. Maybe inspired by his home town's pirate history or the fact that his father, who owned a hotel in New Orleans, had taken him on trips to Jamaica, Ernest opened a small bar on McCadden Place in Hollywood, propped up some fake palm trees, and named it *Don the Beachcomber*. Here he blended and mixed the liquid gold like an alchemist in search of the sorcerer's stone, creating potent concoctions that allowed his customers temporarily to escape to distant shores, while outside the big city life rushed by.

Ernest identified with the Beachcomber persona so strongly that he legally changed his name to Donn Beach. Soon his expert mixology attracted the alcohol- and atmosphere-hungry film crowd, and in 1937 he expanded his operation into a South Seas hideaway that was to become the blueprint for the many entrepeneurs who would follow in

his footsteps: Like an island in the urban sea, the Polynesian paradise that Donn designed was meant to be a refuge from the teaming metropolis that surrounded it.

Upon entering, all the senses were assailed: Exotic materials like bamboo, lahaula matts, and imported woods provided the basic texture. Tropical plants, fresh flower leis, and bunches of bananas and coconuts cultivated the jungle atmosphere, while native weapons and other Oceanic artifacts spoke of savage civilizations. Jetsam and flotsam from the four corners of the world hung from the ceiling, amplifying the illusion of having arrived at some distant port of pleasure. An intermittent man-made rain-on-the-roof effect gave the impression of having escaped from a tropical downpour, while continous soft background music further lulled the patrons into exotic reveries. All this was enhanced by the effect of Don's potent cocktail creations that were sometimes served in whole pineapples, or at least heavily decorated with intriguing garnishes.

But what Donn Beach possessed in showmanship and imagination, he lacked in business smarts. This aspect was taken care of by his wife Cora Irene "Sunny" Sund. She had proposed a business partnership that flowered into a marriage in 1937, only to end in divorce three years later. But she kept a firm grip

ZOMBIE
Created at Don the Beachcomber, Hollywood in 1934. Often imitated, but never duplicated.

PI
Crushed fresh H
and light Cuba
in a hollo
baby pir

DON THE BEACHCOMBER

BRAND

JAMAICA RUM

TAHITIAN RUM PUNCH

Exotic tropical fruits admirably blended with Mexican limes and old Cuban Rums.

Cantonese food and
original rum cocktails
presented in an authentic
Polynesian atmosphere.

Sunny Sund,
President

rsonalized Chop Stick Cases
onging to established guests

Rums from far-away places

Miss Beachcomber of Hollywood 1933
Chicago 1940 - Palm Springs 1953

The inside of this souvenir menu shows the modest exterior of the Hollywood Beachcomber. Behind the bar, the urban archeologist can make out Don's three pet Tikis, the "Tahitian cannibal carvings."

Auf der Innenseite dieser Getränkekarte sieht man das bescheidene Äußere des Beachcomber in Hollywood. Hinter der Bar kann der Stadtarchäologe Dons drei hauseigene Tikis erkennen, die „Tahitischen Kannibalen".

L'intérieur de ce menu souvenir montre le modeste extérieur du Beachcomber de Hollywood. Derrière le bar, l'archéologue urbain peut remarquer trois tiki domestiques de Don, les «sculptures cannibales tahitiennes».

on the shop—so firm that when Donn returned from his stint as an air force colonel at the end of WW II, he found himself ousted from his own bailiwick. Sunny, who had directed the opening of the first franchise in Chicago in 1940, was now firmly in charge of the operation and did not need Don anymore, except in name.

Always more of an originator than a manager, Donn struck a deal to remain in an advisory position at the mainland *Don the Beachcomber's* while turning his creative energies to his pet project: opening his own place in Hawaii.

But Donn had also created an image, a figure: that of the 20th century urban
beachcomber, an individual somewhere between well-travelled connoisseur,
beach beatnik, and marina swinger. In the history of Polynesian pop other
Beachnik characters appeared, most notable among them Ely Hedley, also
known as "the original Beachcomber." A luckless grocer from Oklahoma, he
had followed the call of the Pacific Ocean and moved his family to Whites
Point, a beach cove near San Pedro in Los Angeles. Here he, his wife, and four
daughters built their house out of actual driftwood and started a successful
business making lamps and furniture with the flotsam that washed onto their

DON'T HELP!

front yard. Ely became so well known for his "Beachcomber Moderne" style that he was hired to decorate Tiki temples like *Trader Dick's* and *Harvey's* in Nevada. When the Tiki fever hit, he started carving Tikis and opened his *Island Trade Store*, first in Huntington Beach, later in Adventureland in Disneyland. After making his definite mark on Tiki style, Ely Hedley retired to the Islander apartments in Santa Ana that he himself had decorated.

In the interim, *Don the Beachcomber* had become a commercial logo, the business changing hands twice and ending up under the ownership of the Getty Corporation. The figure had been modernized from Don's actual likeness into an anonymous suave swinger. The franchise had grown to 16 locations—some, like the Dallas and the Marina Del Rey facilities, looking like brown UFOs. Other Polynesiacs

BEACHCOMBER PARTIES ARE FUN... PLAN YOURS WITH... *Original* DON THE BEACHCOMBER

AUTHENTIC EXOTIC COCKTAIL MIXES
MAI TAI ❀ NAVY GROG ❀ SCORPION
❀ JUST ADD RUM

DON THE BEACHCOMBER®

ABOVE: Having lost his mustache and his baldness, a generic Beachcomber figure signaled the originator's loss of control of the image from the 1940s to the 60s. BELOW AND RIGHT: Numerous namesakes sprang up all over America.

OBEN: Die neu geschaffene Beachcomber-Figur ohne Schnauzbart und Glatze signalisierte den Machtverlust des Originals. UNTEN UND RECHTS: Die Namensvettern erschienen überall in Amerika.

CI-DESSUS : Ayant perdu sa moustache et sa calvitie, une figure générique de Beachcomber indiquait la perte de contrôle du créateur entre les années 1940 et les années 1960. CI-DESSOUS ET À DROITE : De nombreux homonymes surgirent dans toute l'Amérique.

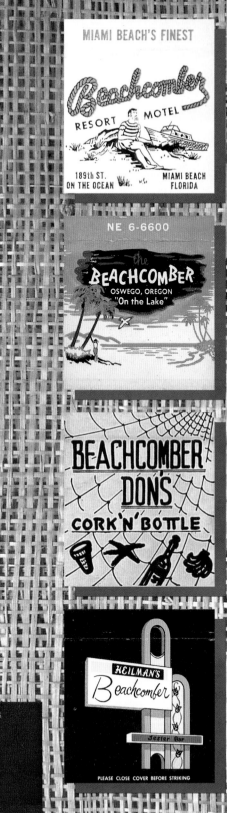

all over the States felt inspired by the Beachcomber concept, but none achieved Don's flair. He, meanwhile, had built himself a new kingdom at his International Market place in Waikiki. Here he continued to innovate and create "new ways of doing things" for Polynesia Americana. After Donn passed away in 1987, the remnants of the chain that bore his name closed within a few years, having in any case been devoid of his mana for a long time. But his formative influence on the phenomenon of Polynesian pop is unforgotten.

LEFT: Burt Hixson, proprietor of The Warehouse and Beachbum Burt's in Marina Del Rey. BELOW: Don Beach hosting one of his famous luaus in Hawaii in the 1950s. BELOW RIGHT: This sign is the last remnant of the original Hollywood Beachcomber restaurant.

LINKS: Burt Hixson, der Inhaber von The Warehouse und Beachbum Burt's in Marina Del Rey. UNTEN: Don Beach als Gastgeber bei einem seiner berühmten Luaus in Hawaii in den 50er Jahren. UNTEN RECHTS: Dieses Schild ist das letzte Überbleibsel des Original-Hollywood Beachcomber-Restaurants.

A GAUCHE: Burt Hixson, propriétaire de The Warehouse et de Beachbum Burt's à Marina Del Rey. CI-DESSOUS: Don Beach à l'un de ses célèbres Luaus à Hawaï dans les années 1950. CI-DESSOUS À DROITE: Ce signe est tout ce qui reste du restaurant Hollywood Beachcomber original.

TRADER VIC

The Americanization of Tiki as the god of recreation was a gradual process. One of his greatest emissaries was a man named Victor Bergeron, better known as Trader Vic. It was not so much that he openly glorified the godhead per se—he even utilized his own mythological figures, the *Menehune*, or "little people" of Polynesian legends—but beginning in the 50s, the Tiki was always by his side, and the Trader was a larger than life figure, an original, one of a dying breed of unique characters lacking in today's public arena.

A patriarch, a gentleman, and a chauvinist in one, Trader Vic was a successful restauranteur and an epicure who encouraged a generation of "sophisticated savages" to "go native" and create their own Polynesias in lounges, backyards, and bowling alleys. He elevated South Seas "chow and grog," as he liked to call it in his gruff manner, to an art. More than Don the Beachcomber, who supposedly found the name for his appetizer creation "Rumaki"

HINKY DINKS
The Home of The
FRANKENSTEIN

Where those merry souls who make drinking a pleasure—
Who achieve contentedness long before capacity,
And who, whenever they drink, prove able to carry it,
enjoy it, and remain gentlemen.

65th Street and San Pablo Avenue   Oakland, California

PRESS OF THE COURIER

ABOVE: Victor Bergeron's first tavern in Oakland,
before and after its conversion to a Polynesian pub
BELOW LEFT: Evidence of Vic's new persona
BELOW: The Oakland interior

OBEN: Victor Bergerons erstes Lokal in Oakland,
bevor es in einen polynesischen Pub umgewandelt
wurde
UNTEN LINKS: Beweis für Vics neue Rolle
UNTEN: Im Inneren des Oakland

CI-DESSUS: La première taverne de Victor Bergeron
à Oakland, avant et après sa conversion en pub
polynésien. CI-DESSOUS À GAUCHE: Une preuve mani-
feste de la nouvelle personnalité de Vic. CI-DESSOUS:
L'intérieur de l'établissement d'Oakland

by pointing his finger into the flipping pages of a Cook Islands dictionary, Trader Vic was a culinary innovator. After his success with "nouveau Polynesian" fare he was among the first to bring Mexican food to the American public (with his Señor Pico restaurants), and far ahead of his time he lauded sushi as a delicacy to be savored.

It all began at a joint called *Hinky Dinks* in Oakland, across the bay from San Francisco. This was the first establishment Vic built for himself in 1934, a wooden shack erected with his last five hundred bucks. In the history of Polynesian pop there have been certain "power places," like the *Beachcomber* in Hollywood, the *Luau* in Beverly Hills, the Lanai in San Mateo, or the *Bali Hai* in

San Diego, that emanated the mana of Tiki. *Hinky Dinks*, soon to become *Trader Vic's*, was one of them. The late Herb Caen, eminent San Francisco columnist, remembered it as "little more than a beer joint, and yet you knew right away it was someplace special. Good places, as opposed to stinkers, have a distinctive and mysterious atmosphere—an immediate feeling of quality, dedication, success and self-confidence." But Victor Bergeron was an ambitious man with a knack for fancy cocktails, and that was exactly what people had a hankering for after the repeal of Prohibition. He went on a research trip to Cuba and Louisiana and studied with the top mixologists on location. But it was his visit to Los Angeles that was most influential. In his biography he reveals:

"We went to a place called the *South Seas* that doesn't exist anymore and even visited *Don the Beachcomber* in Hollywood. In fact, I even bought some stuff from *Don the Beachcomber*. When I got back to Oakland and told my wife about what I had seen, we agreed to change the name of our restaurant and change the decor. We decided that *Hinky Dinks* was a junky name and that the place should be named after someone we could tell a story about. My wife suggested *Trader Vic's* because I was always making a trade with someone. Fine, I became Trader Vic." Consequently, the wooden leg that he had inherited from a bout with tuberculosis as a child (and had entertained his customers with by unexpectedly sticking an icepick into it) became the result of an encounter with a shark, one of the many tales that were in keeping with Vic's new persona.

The candid revelation about the birth of Trader Vic came from a man who had not only equalled but superceded the achievements of his peer and predecessor. Gentleman Vic never had to deny his sources, because he never lost control of his venture as Donn did, and when the Polynesian

CAFE LAUREY · TAHITI

RUM THE SPIRIT OF THE AGES

It is always with great pleasure that I look back and reminisce on the important part that Rum has played in the molding of empires.

In the days of the ancients rum was drunk straight, or as a hot drink in cold weather, in England and the northern parts of our own country. Not satisfied with the strength of ordinary rum, the hearties drank Demerara Rum from British Guiana, straight, at 150 proof—God bless 'em! However, in the last half century rum and its mixtures have become famous among drinking people throughout the world. Unlike most of the distilled spirits of our times, specialists in the art of mixing rum drinks have arisen in centers of population and have become famous for their delicious creations made from rum. It is my pleasure to have drunk, in their original home, some of these concoctions that are offered at my bar.

In reviewing some of the outstanding mixologists throughout the world, I recall to you Pimm's Bar of London whose punches and mixtures served to His Majesty's forces are known throughout the empire and today are sold in bottle form under the name of Pimm's Cups. Then there is a little bar called Prospect of Whitby which has some outstanding drinks and in its efforts to please has become outstanding on the European continent.

We doff our hats to Frank Meier, formerly of the Ritz bar in Paris, not alone as a bartender par excellence but also as a great gentleman.

On our own continents it is best to begin with the Queen's Park Hotel, Trinidad, whose Queen's Park Swizzle is the most delightful form of anaesthesia given out at the present time. Olaffson's punch of Haiti has made the Haitian rum famous. Kelly's Bar on the Sugar Wharf, Jamaica, is famous for its Planter's Punch and Planter's cocktail, both of which have helped to glorify this spirit.

The greatest master of rum-mixing in all the West Indies, I can truthfully say, is Constantine at La Florida Bar, Havana. To him we owe our present Daiquiri and Cuban Presidente. He is also the originator of the Pino Frio. Travelers to Havana who do not visit La Florida have not fully seen Havana.

In our own country there was one grand old man who, many, many people will agree with me, was outstanding in this world of ours. It always gives me great pleasure to mention the late Albert Martin of the Bon Ton Bar on Magazine Street, near the old stock exchange in New Orleans. His rum cocktails were the finest obtainable, and if one desired a true Ramos Fizz in New Orleans, Albert Martin was the only man I know who could make it properly.

There is one other person I would like to mention who has done much to bring back the fine art of eating and drinking in our country. He has studied the mixtures of various rums; he has also become a collector of rums and at his bar may be found every type and brand of rum that this world produces. Some of the old ancients, fifty and sixty years old, true treasures to any rum connoisseur, may be had there for the asking. I salute Don the Beachcomber of Hollywood, the originator of such outstanding drinks as the Zombie and Missionary's Downfall.

Many of our later rum bars and also manufacturers of rum claim origination of their drinks. However, most of their concoctions have been taken from Don the Beachcomber or Albert Martin or Constantine of La Florida. Again I salute Don the Beachcomber as the outstanding rum connoisseur of our country.

Much time and consideration have been spent to obtain and bring to you many original formulas and some of my own mixtures which I offer here for your pleasure.

Trader Vic

DON THE BEACHCOMBER

RON HAVANA CLUB "LA FLORIDA" Pida RON HAVANA CLUB

ALBERT MARTIN'S BON TON BAR NEW ORLEANS

ABOVE AND LEFT: The first outpost in Seattle, The Outrigger opened in 1949. BELOW: WW II place mat illustration in typical Trader Vic style

OBEN UND LINKS: Die erste Filiale in Seattle, The Outrigger, die 1949 eröffnet wurde. UNTEN: Tellerunterlage aus dem Zweiten Weltkrieg mit typischer Trader Vic-Illustration

CI-DESSUS ET À GAUCHE: Le premier poste avancé à Seattle, The Outrigger, ouvert en 1949. CI-DESSOUS: Illustration du WW II dans le plus pur style Trader Vic

Due to these three Lousy Dirty Stinkers you're eating off of paper instead of my grass mats.

trend took off in the 1950s, he was positioned to take full advantage of it. Opening his first outpost, which he called *The Outrigger*, in Seattle in 1949, he followed with a flow of satellite supper clubs throughout the next decades: in San Francisco proper in 1951, Denver in 1954, Beverly Hills in 1955, Chicago in 1957, New York and Havana in 1958, and Portland in 1959. They were

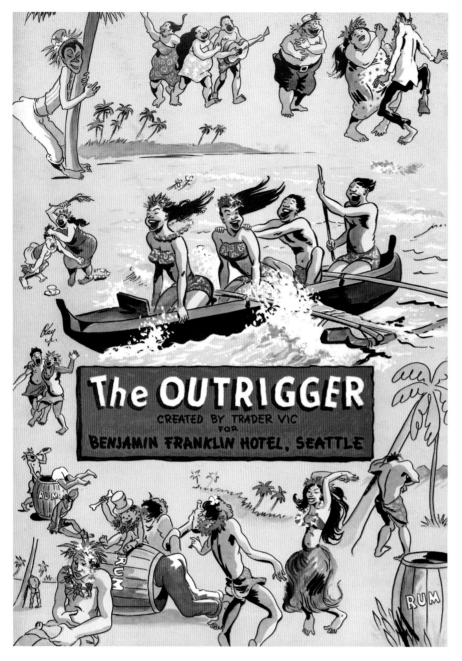

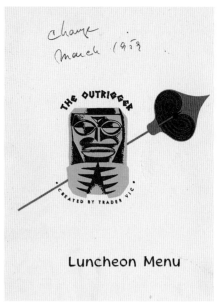

Luncheon Menu

The evolution of Trader Vic's menu covers is excellent proof of the emergence of the Tiki as the new emblem of Polynesian pop. While the illustrations in the 40s (previous pages and left) depicted the usual icons, in the early 1950s the Tiki took center stage (above, right page, pp. 90, 91).

Die Entwicklung der Umschläge der Trader Vic's-Speisekarten ist ein guter Beleg dafür, wie Tiki allmählich als neues Emblem für den polynesischen Pop aufkam. Während die Illustrationen aus den 40er Jahren (vorhergehende Seiten und links) die üblichen Titelzeichnungen zeigten, rückte Tiki in den frühen 50er Jahren in den Bildmittelpunkt (oben, rechte Seite und S. 90, 91).

L'évolution des couvertures de menus de Trader Vic's est une excellente preuve de l'émergence du tiki comme nouvel emblème du pop polynésien. Alors que les illustrations des années 1940 (à gauche et pages précédentes) employaient les symboles habituels, au début des années 1950 le tiki se mit à occuper le devant de la scène (en haut, page de droite et pages 90, 91).

followed by places in Boston, Houston, Dallas, Detroit, Atlanta, Kansas City, St. Louis, St. Petersburg, Washington, Vancouver, Scottsdale, London, Munich, and a host of other foreign locations.

Vic further expanded his influence with a string of cocktail and recipe books in which he preferably used merchandise from his new Trader Vic's Food Products company. In these publications he expounded his views upon social gatherings and middle-class eating habits in his characteristic Trader Vic lin-

TRADER VIC'S

the traders

go, which was quite different from the flowery prose he used in his menus:

"I've a lot of pet peeves to get off my chest concerning what cooks when you go over to somebody's house to chisel some food and drinks and I further contend that the average American hostess needs a swift kick in her culinary pants, so let's get about it. The tidbits usually served at cocktail parties simply slay me. After looking at hundreds of silver platters and their contents for many years, I've reached the conclusion that someone must have offered an annual Pulitzer prize for the most deadly hors d'oeuvre." The Trader was a salty son of a bitch, and people loved him that way.

When Hawaii became America's vacation destination of choice, Vic was approached to act as food consultant for United Airlines and the hotels of the Matson steamship line, which were the two main tourist transporters between the Islands and America. Earlier, around 1940, he had formed a partnership to open a place in Honolulu but pulled out as the result of a disagreement, leaving the other party the right to use the name in the Islands. The fact that a *Trader Vic's* was opened in Hawaii having originated in California—the

TRADER VIC'S®
Pomegranate Grenadine Syrup

MADE IN U.S.A.   COPR. 1946 BY TRADER VIC

INGREDIENTS: SUGAR, WATER, POMEGRANATE EXTRACTIVE REINFORCED WITH ARTIFICIAL FLAVORING, TARTARIC ACID AND ARTIFICIAL COLOR.

BOTTLED FOR **TRADER VIC'S FOOD PRODUCTS**
1545 Park Ave., Emeryville, California, U.S.A. 94608

NET CONTENTS 25.6 FL. OZ. (1 PT. 9.6 FL. OZ.)

same way *Don the Beachcomber,* Stephen Crane's *Kon-Tiki* and *Christian's Hut* proceeded—is curious and supports the claim that Polynesian pop is truly a facet of American pop culture which actually was imported to Hawaii to fulfill the expectations of the tourists.

This growth of the Trader's empire

(Z) MAI TAI DRINK SET
"Mai Tai" means the best, and here are four attractively packaged in a gift box. Mugs are 6" high and each holds a full pint. A real conversation piece. Use these mugs to serve Mai Tais and other unusual rum drinks this summer. Recipes and package of 8 green-twig swizzle sticks included.

$6.95 * Postpaid

TRADER VIC'S

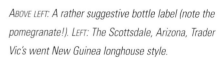

ABOVE LEFT: A rather suggestive bottle label (note the pomegranate!). LEFT: The Scottsdale, Arizona, Trader Vic's went New Guinea longhouse style.

OBEN LINKS: Ein recht verführerisches Flaschenetikett (beachten Sie den Granatapfel!). LINKS: Das Trader Vic's in Scottsdale, Arizona, war im Stil eines neuguineischen Langhauses gebaut.

CI-DESSUS À GAUCHE: Une étiquette de bouteille plutôt suggestive (notez la grenade!). A GAUCHE: Le Trader Vic's d'Arizona en Scottsdale adopta le style des habitations de Nouvelle-Guinée.

VOODOO GROG

Old
debbil Rum
conjures
throbbing drumbeats
and black magic

TIKI BOWL . . . .
A delightful punch served in earthen bowl supported by three Tikis-replicas of authentic Tahitian gods

The forerunner of the Tiki mug, the Tiki bowl, was based on actual Hawaiian objects (above right). Various Trader Vic's artifacts: an early skull mug, 1940s; Tiki cuff links; voodoo grog glass, late 1960s; salt and pepper shakers, still available today.

Der Vorläufer des Tiki-Krugs, die Tiki-Schale, war zeitgenössischen hawaiischen Objekten nachgebildet (oben rechts). Verschiedene Trader Vic's-Artefakte: ein früher Totenkopf-Krug, um 1940; Tiki-Manschettenknöpfe; ein Voodoo-Grogglas, späte 60er Jahre. Die Salz- und Pfefferstreuer kann man noch heute kaufen.

L'ancêtre de la chope tiki, la coupe tiki, fut inspiré par d'authentiques objets hawaïens (ci-dessus). Différents objets de chez Trader Vic's : une ancienne chope en forme de crâne des années 1940. Des boutons de manchette tiki de provenance indéterminée. Le verre à grog vaudou, à la fin des années 1960. Les salières et poivrières sont toujours disponibles aujourd'hui.

was made possible by the financial resources of major hotel chains like Western (now Westin) and Conny Hilton's. They could afford the elaborate construction a classy Tiki lounge required. And *Trader Vic's* was all class. Other South Sea joints, among them many that copied his monicker, served the foot soldier, whereas Vic's was the officer's club—not because Vic was a snob, but because he wanted to make a buck, and he succeeded in attracting the well-off. But ultimately, this selective clientele was also part of the reason for the chain's demise, because as the upper-class clique that frequented these ports of the palate died out, the younger generations sought out more affordable and less affected surroundings.

Sadly the outposts in Seattle, Washington, Vancouver, Portland, and even San Francisco have closed—some as recently as the 90s—and, in those that are left, misguided renovation efforts during the 1980s that caused the characteristic birdcage lamps and other traditional decor to be thrown out as "dust catchers," hotel hideways like the Chicago and Munich *Trader Vic's* remain (as of this writing) as rare examples of Tiki style.

ABOVE: The doors of the San Francisco Trader Vic's closed forever in 1994. FAR LEFT: Happy skiers clutching primitive lingams in Lake Tahoe, north of San Francisco. LEFT: The Holy Grail of the Tiki mug collector: a union of cocktail and Tiki culture

OBEN: Die Türen des Trader Vic's in San Francisco schlossen sich 1994 für immer. GANZ LINKS: Fröhliche Skiläufer in Lake Tahoe nördlich von San Francisco halten primitive Lingams in den Händen. LINKS: Der heilige Gral des Tiki-Krug-Sammlers, die Verbindung von Cocktail und Tiki-Kultur.

CI-DESSUS: Les portes du Trader Vic's de San Francisco se refermèrent définitivement en 1994. EXTRÊME GAUCHE: D'heureux skieurs exhibant des lingams primitifs au lac Tahoe, au nord de San Francisco. A GAUCHE: Le Graal du collectionneur de chopes tiki, l'union du cocktail et de la culture tiki

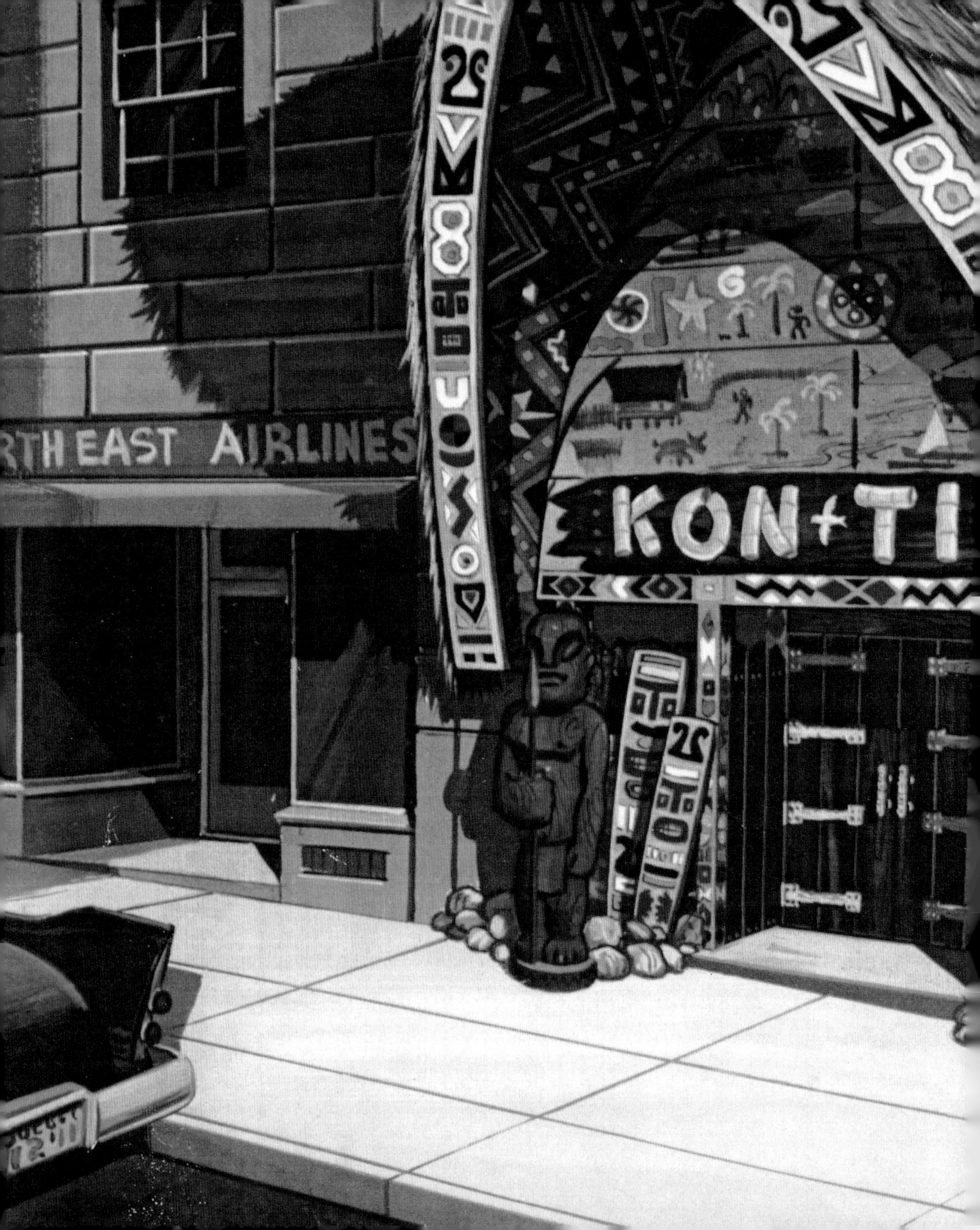

RTH EAST AIRLINES
KON TI

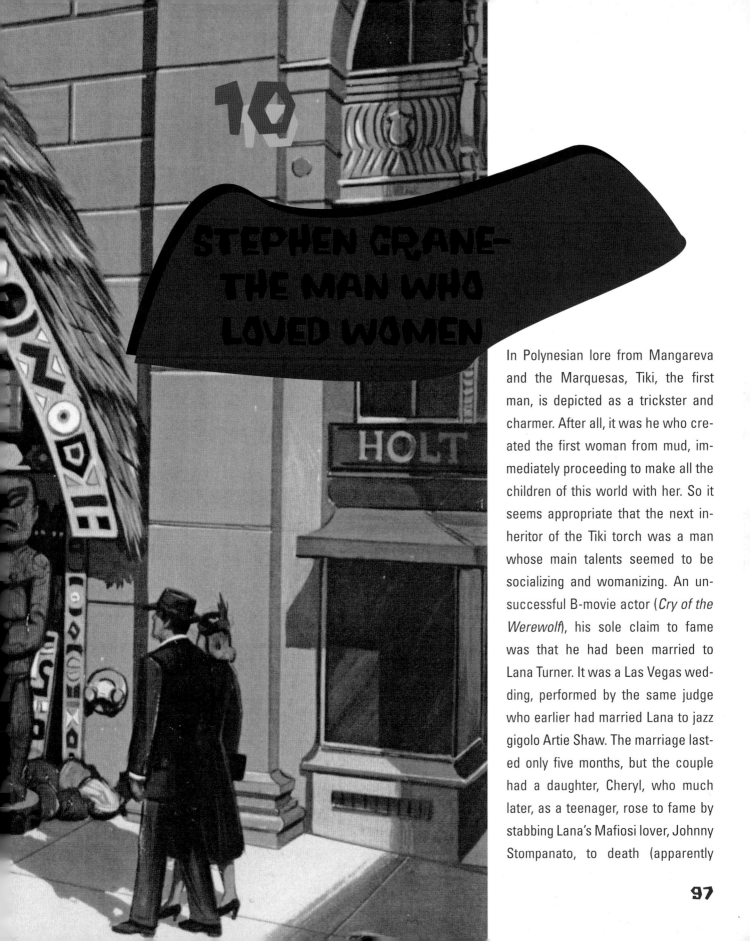

STEPHEN CRANE– THE MAN WHO LOVED WOMEN

In Polynesian lore from Mangareva and the Marquesas, Tiki, the first man, is depicted as a trickster and charmer. After all, it was he who created the first woman from mud, immediately proceeding to make all the children of this world with her. So it seems appropriate that the next inheritor of the Tiki torch was a man whose main talents seemed to be socializing and womanizing. An unsuccessful B-movie actor (*Cry of the Werewolf*), his sole claim to fame was that he had been married to Lana Turner. It was a Las Vegas wedding, performed by the same judge who earlier had married Lana to jazz gigolo Artie Shaw. The marriage lasted only five months, but the couple had a daughter, Cheryl, who much later, as a teenager, rose to fame by stabbing Lana's Mafiosi lover, Johnny Stompanato, to death (apparently

because she had earlier been molested by another of her mother's suitors, movie Tarzan Lex Barker). But Stephen remained on friendly terms with Lana while he went on seducing other film stars. The owner of Ciro's, Hollywood's main movie hangout in the forties, remarked after seeing Steve show up on three consecutive nights with Ava Gardner, Rita Hayworth, and Lana Turner: "This town's three top queens! I never saw anybody do that."

Luckily Stephen Crane's energies were soon directed towards his other talents: socializing and entertaining. In 1953 he opened his restaurant *The Luau* at 421 Rodeo Drive in Beverly Hills. The site had earlier housed the South Seas joint *The Tropics*, and Stephen elaborated on the theme, while aiming to retain the movie colony clientele. He did this in his own way, as his daughter Cheryl recalls in her biography *Detour- A Hollywood Story*: "He figured since men liked to hang out in spots that attracted women, he needed to bait the place like a honey trap ... At the core of Dad's honey trap was a little-known and never-voiced policy of allowing select and very expensive hookers to mingle discreetly at the bar. Often failed starlets, they were refined and beautifully dressed, their presence drawing men while not offending escorted women customers, who rarely recognized them for what they were." And to put the effect of the "Beauty and the Beast" archetype to full use, Crane profusely populated his paradise with Tikis, introducing them in his menu: "Of great interest are the TIKIS, the large and delightfully unlovely carvings about you. A TIKI is a pagan god, an idol. While today a majority of our

PAGE 96/97: The entrance to another world, Montreal, 1959

Left page: Stephen Crane with wife number four, the lovely Helen Demaree Crane, at the entrance to the Portland Kon-Tiki.

LEFT: A Tropics matchbook from the 40s, featuring "stand-out" breasts. The three monkeys were predecessors of the three Tahitian cannibal carvings used by the Luau, which took the place of the Tropics.

SEITE 96/97: Der Eingang zu einer anderen Welt, Montreal, 1959

LINKE SEITE: Stephen Crane mit seiner vierten Frau, der bezaubernden Helen Demaree Crane, am Eingang zum Kon-Tiki in Portland.

LINKS: Ein Streichholzheftchen aus dem Tropics mit „hervorstechenden" Merkmalen. Die drei Affen waren Vorgänger der drei tahitischen Kannibalen, Tikis, die das Luau verwendete, das Nachfolger des Tropics wurde.

PAGE 96/97: L'accès à un autre monde, Montréal, 1959

PAGE DE GAUCHE: Stephan Crane et sa quatrième épouse, la ravissante Helen Demaree Crane, devant l'entrée du Kon-Tiki à Portland.

A GAUCHE: Les pochettes d'allumettes des années 40 provenant du Tropics, avec sa caractéristique beauté des mers du Sud aux seins dénudés. Les trois singes étaient les prédécesseurs des trois Tahitiens cannibales, que le Luau, successeur du Tropics, a utilisés.

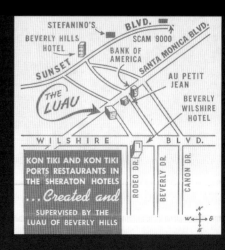

South Seas neighbors are of Christian faith, respect and deference is still extended to the gods of the elders, and we have with us here at THE LUAU such TIKIS as the god of rain, the god of sun, the god of war and others. The especially large-mouthed TIKI is the god of drink, The Loud-Mouthed One. The TIKI with the most ample tummy is our favorite, perhaps because he is the god of good food." This whimsical and naive attitude towards another people's extinct religion henceforth characterized Tiki style. For the first time, a Tiki resembling the two entrance-post carvings was used as an emblem on menus, matchbooks, postcards, and as the form for a ceramic lamp base, as well as salt and pepper shakers.

In the rest of the decor, Stephen was drawing strongly on the Beachcomber and Trader traditions—so strongly that art director Florian Gabriel recalls that as a requirement for his job as designer for Stephen Crane and Associates, he was asked to go to *Trader Vic's* at the Beverly Hilton (which once boasted

ABOVE: The Luau in the mid-50s. A-frames had not yet become fashionable. In the foreground: the classic ceramic Tiki condiment containers that were also used with the Kon-Tiki and Port o' Call inscriptions. RIGHT: The Luau logo Tiki as cocktail swizzle stick and on the menu cover

OBEN: Das Luau Mitte der fünfziger Jahre. Die A-Giebel waren noch nicht in Mode. Im Vordergrund: die klassischen Keramik-Tikis als Salz- und Pfefferstreuer, die ebenfalls mit den Inschriften „Kon-Tiki" und

„Ports of Call" in Gebrauch waren. RECHTS: Der Tiki vom Luau-Logo als Cocktail-Stäbchen und auf der Speisekarte

CI-DESSUS: Le Luau au milieu des années 1950. Les pignons en A n'étaient pas encore à la mode. Au premier plan, les tiki classiques en céramique servant de salière et de moulin à poivre et portant eux aussi les inscriptions «Kon Tiki» et «Port o'Call». A DROITE: Le tiki du logo Luau servant de bâtonnet mélangeur et ornant le menu.

THE LUAU

BEVERLY HILLS

LUAU
BEVERLY HILL.

ABOVE: Luau interior. BELOW: The first "Kon-Tiki"
RIGHT: An actual Tahitian beauty, Tarita, star from
"Mutiny on the Bounty" flanked by whitebread blon-
des Lana Turner and Debbie Reynolds, at the Luau.

OBEN: Das Innere des Luau. UNTEN: Das erste „Kon-
Tiki". RECHTS: Eine echte tahitische Schönheit, flankiert von den Platinblondinen Lana Turner und Debbie Reynolds: Tarita, Star aus „Meuterei auf der
Bounty", im Luau

CI-DESSUS: L'intérieur du Luau. CI-DESSOUS: Le premier
«Kon-Tiki». A DROITE: Une authentique beauté tahi-
tienne avec la blonde platinée Lana Turner et Debby
Reynolds. Il s'agit de Tarita, star de «Les Mutinés du
Bounty» en visite au Luau.

five fifteen-foot-high exterior Tikis)
and sketch a corner of the restaurant. He did so successfully, and then
and there formed a design team together with George Nakashima, who
had previously worked for Welton
Becket, architect of the Beverly
Hilton. They went on to help con-
struct the satellite islands that SCA
began to install in other American
cities at the end of the 50s.

The Sheraton Corporation, eager to

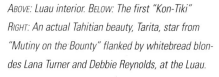

CREATED AND SUPERVISED BY
Kon-Tiki
Steve Crane
FOR THE
SHERATON-MT. ROYAL
1455 PEEL STREET, MONTREAL, CANADA

KON-TIKI

pull even with Hilton, had invited Crane to re-create his *Luau* in their hotel in Montreal, where it opened as the *Kon Tiki* in 1958, presenting to the astounded public "woodpanels handcarved by the Maoris with special designs to ward off evil spirits, New Guinea spears with bat-wing tips dipped in poison by headhunters, and a sacrificial altar." In the next years establishments in Portland (with three waterfalls!), Chicago, Dallas, Cleveland, and Honolulu fol-

MACAO

SAIGON

LEFT: These mugs, designed by Florian Gabriel for SCA, were used as cocktail vessels at the various Kon-Tiki Ports
BELOW: Pages from the Luau cocktail menu

LINKS: Diese von Florian Gabriel für SCA entworfenen Krüge wurden als Cocktailgefäße in den verschiedenen Kon-Tiki-Ports verwendet
UNTEN: Seiten aus der Luau-Cocktailkarte

A GAUCHE: Dans les divers Kon-Tiki, on servait les cocktails dans ces chopes dessinées par Florian Gabriel pour SCA. CI-DESSOUS: Page d'une carte des cocktails du Luau

lowed. The Chicago *Kon-Tiki Ports* and the Dallas *Ports o' Call* elaborated on the armchair traveller concept by giving every dining room a different theme: Papeete, Singapore, Macao, or Saigon. Their stories were pure Polynesian pop poetry: "PAPEETE-One of four exotic moorings at Ports o' Call Restaurant in the penthouse at Southland Center, Dallas, Texas. Nature has been tamed for this tropic hideaway. A waterfall babbles for your pleasure while local wildlife stands motionless to keep you at your ease. But spears and pelts remind the diner that simple life does have its excitements."

Yet the rift that reality was soon to create between the Tiki generation and its Vietnam-War-protesting children is probably best examplified by the description of the SAIGON room: "Oriental splendor and opulence mark this Port of Pleasure. Its fortunate inhabitants are surrounded by pure gold leaf, rare silks, fine crystal and once-forbidden temple carvings." What was poetic license in 1960 had turned painfully ironic by 1968. At the end of the seventies, an Iranian consortium offered Stephen Crane 4.1 million dollars for the *Luau*. In 1979 it was razed down right to the sub-basement, a signal for end of the Tiki era.

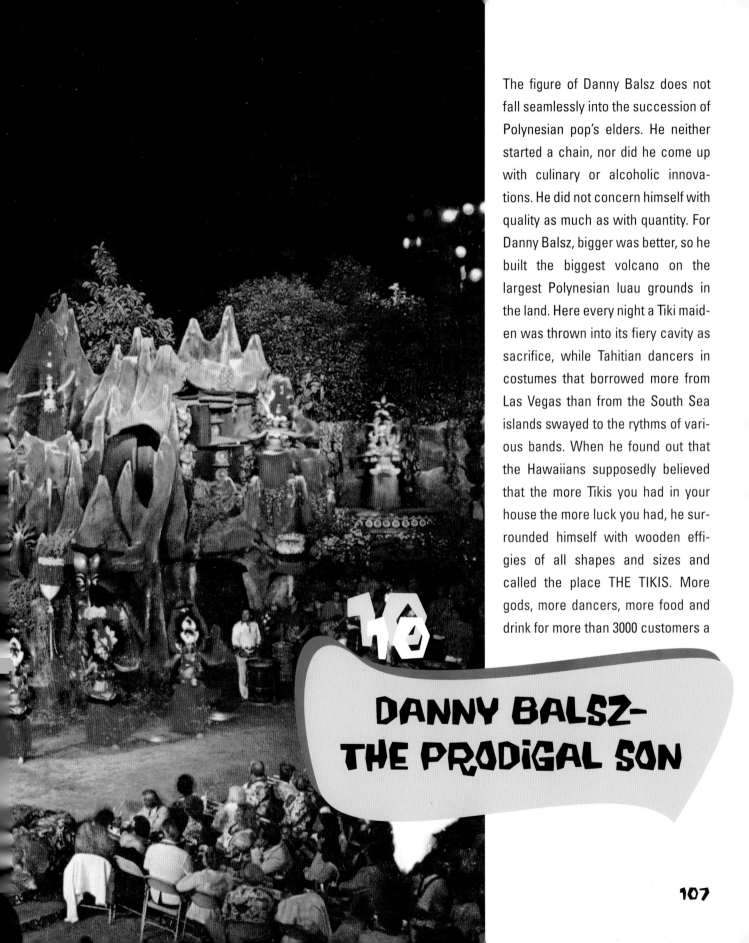

The figure of Danny Balsz does not fall seamlessly into the succession of Polynesian pop's elders. He neither started a chain, nor did he come up with culinary or alcoholic innovations. He did not concern himself with quality as much as with quantity. For Danny Balsz, bigger was better, so he built the biggest volcano on the largest Polynesian luau grounds in the land. Here every night a Tiki maiden was thrown into its fiery cavity as sacrifice, while Tahitian dancers in costumes that borrowed more from Las Vegas than from the South Sea islands swayed to the rythms of various bands. When he found out that the Hawaiians supposedly believed that the more Tikis you had in your house the more luck you had, he surrounded himself with wooden effigies of all shapes and sizes and called the place THE TIKIS. More gods, more dancers, more food and drink for more than 3000 customers a

10
DANNY BALSZ– THE PRODIGAL SON

107

night—it was Tiki for the masses, and Danny was Mr. Tiki!

THE TIKIS represents the culmination of the Tiki era, which peaked with unprecedented grandeur and decadence before crumbling into cultural oblivion. Stumbling upon the ruins of this forgotten Disneyland of the gods, I knew that its story had to be told one day. Before me lay the lost planet of the Tikis, the elephant graveyard of an extinct species. What had led to the demise of this once grand civilization?

The son of a nightclub owner in the bordertown of Mexicali, Danny Balsz moved to East L.A. with memories of forbidden glamor. He worked for ten years as a slaughter house butcher, until he decided to go into landscaping, specializing in waterfalls. In 1958 Danny was getting some supplies at a Japanese nursery in Monterey Park, a rural Los Angeles suburb wedged between four freeways. Stopping at a neighboring egg ranch,

PAGE 106/107: "The Tikis", Monterey Park, early 1970s
"They are cities of silence now, their builders lost. Where once walked youth and wisdom, now stand closely packed boles in deadly competition, struggling in vain against the strangle-hold of an army of parasites. The once pastel shaded facades of architectural masterpieces no longer gleam joyously in the bright sun. Yet there are relics which stand defiant, guarding another world of thought, a realm of unrevealed knowledge and a treasure house of intrinsic and esoteric wealth …" (from Atlantis. Mother of Empires, 1999, by Robert Stacy-Judd, archeologist and architect of the Mayan Revival Style)

Seite 106/107: „The Tikis", Monterey Park, Anfang der 70er Jahre
„Es sind jetzt Totenstädte, ihre Erbauer kennt keiner mehr. Wo einst Jugend und Weisheit einhergingen, stehen jetzt Baumstämme dicht bei dicht in tödlichem Wettkampf, die sich vergebens dagegen wehren, einer Armee von Parasiten ausgeliefert zu sein. Die einst in hellen Farben erstrahlenden Fassaden architektonischer Meisterwerke leuchten nicht mehr einladend im Sonnenschein. Und doch sind es Überreste, die trotzig dastehen als Wächter einer anderen Welt, eines anderen Denkens, eines Reichs von unentdecktem Wissen und einer Schatzkammer aus innerem und nur Eingeweihten zugänglichem Reichtum …" (Robert Stacy-Judd)

PAGE 106/107: «The Tikis», parc Monterey, début des années 1970
«Ce sont aujourd'hui des villes silencieuses dont le souvenir des fondateurs a disparu. Là où marchaient jadis jeunesse et sagesse, on trouve à présent des troncs d'arbres en rangs serrés, luttant en vain contre l'emprise d'une armée de parasites. Les façades, autrefois pastel, de chefs-d'œuvre architecturaux ont cessé de resplendir joyeusement au soleil. Il subsiste pourtant des reliques qui se tiennent debout, préservant un autre monde de pensée, un royaume de savoir caché et le trésor d'une richesse ésotérique…» (Robert Stacy-Judd)

he met the owner, Doris Samson. Four months later they were married. While helping Doris with her hens, Danny was developing his landscaping skills, slowly transforming the quarter-acre property into a tropical garden. In 1960 two college students asked Danny if they could hold a luau party on the lot. At this time, luau grounds for party rentals were springing up everywhere in the southland. Danny and Doris decided to slaughter all their chickens and go into the Polynesian party business. The timing was right, the place took off, and year for year Danny was pouring and sculpting more and more concrete into lava tunnels, stalagtite caves, and waterfalls, single handedly creating his own Xanadu.

By the late 60s, his predominantly blue-collar clientele was arriving by the busload from aircraft plants and trucking companies. The necessary supplies, such as 50,000 leis from the plastic-lei factory in Hughestown, Pennsylvania, and tons of pineap-

ples, were paid for in cash, and if there was money left, Danny bought more Tikis. "I had everything, man: Money, cars, rings!" reminisced Danny. But he wanted more. Danny's luck ran out when he committed the eternal sin: His fall from grace was was occasioned by his falling in love with Leilani, a Mormon Hawaiian dancer at *THE TIKIS*. The union of the *haole* and *wahine* was not sanctified by the gods, and even less so by Danny's wife and children, who had been the backbone of his family operation. And under pressure from fed-up neighbors, the city council revoked his entertainment license. The Polynesian three-ring circus was

LEFT: Danny Balsz posing with the biggest Tiki anywhere. This Hawaiian war god would spew fire.

LINKS: Danny Balsz posiert mit dem größten Tiki überhaupt. Dieser hawaiische Kriegsgott konnte Feuer speien.

A GAUCHE: Danny Balsz posant avec le plus grand des tiki. Le dieu de la guerre hawaiien pouvait cracher du feu.

Left: Decaying guardians of a bygone era

Above: One of the stranger artifacts of Tiki-dom, the Tikiccino machine

Right page: A brochure featuring the Tiki maidens; above: Pottery from The Tikis

Links: Zerfallende Wächter einer vergangenen Ära

Oben: Einer der seltsameren Gegenstände des Tiki-Kults, die Tikiccino-Maschine

Rechte Seite: Eine Broschüre mit Abbildungen von den Tiki-Kellnerinnen; oben: Keramikgefäße aus dem The Tikis

A gauche: Les gardiens décatis d'une époque oubliée

Ci-dessus: Un des objets les plus insolites du culte tiki, la machine Tikiccino

Page de droite: Une brochure montrant les serveuses du tiki; en haut: Des objets en porcelaine provenant du The Tikis.

over, it seemed. But Danny Balsz was a driven man. He packed up his Tikis and built them a new home at Lake Elsinore, further south of L.A. There he labored for years, re-erecting a complete new lava-land. Patiently his Tikis stood guard over it, awaiting the grand re-opening. But the times had changed, and the great day never came.

"The light that burns twice as bright burns half as long, and you have burned so very, very brightly. You're the prodigal son!
But I've done questionable things ...
Also extraordinary things, revealed in your time ..."
(from Ridley Scott's *Bladerunner*)

DINNER — "ALL YOU CAN EAT"

THERE IS NO PLACE LIKE THE TIKIS

KON-TIKI, AKU AKU, AND THOR

"The unsolved mysteries of the South Seas had fascinated me. There must be a rational solution to them, and I had made my objective the identification of the legendary hero TIKI."

Thus spoke a young Norwegian zoologist named Thor Heyerdahl in 1937, while struggling to survive on his island hideway of Fatu Hiva in the Marquesas, where he and his wife were sharing a pre-hippy existence. Thor and Liv had decided to forsake civilization and go "back to nature," living like primitives while researching the local fauna for his Oslo university. But when Thor heard old Tei Tetua, the last native who had tasted "Long Pig" (man), recite an old folk tale by the evening fire, everything changed. "Tiki, he was both god and chief. It was Tiki who brought my ancestors to these islands on which we live. Before that we lived in a great land far beyond the sea."

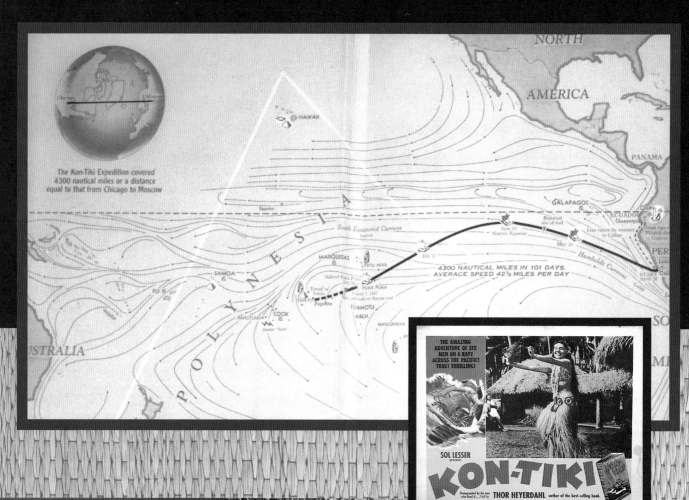

The Kon-Tiki Expedition covered 4300 nautical miles or a distance equal to that from Chicago to Moscow

4300 NAUTICAL MILES IN 101 DAYS.
AVERAGE SPEED 42½ MILES PER DAY

THE AMAZING ADVENTURE OF SIX MEN ON A RAFT ACROSS THE PACIFIC
TRUE! THRILLING!

SOL LESSER presents

KON-TIKI

Photographed by the men who lived it...Told by THOR HEYERDAHL author of the best-selling book.

KON-TIKI and I

A SKETCH BOOK of the famous KON-TIKI Expedition by the navigator of the voyage

ILLUSTRATIONS AND TEXT BY ERIK HESSELBERG

HOW 'KON-TIKI' GOT ITS NAME

Tiki was the name of the first great chief on Tahiti. He was regarded by the inhabitants as their divine ancestor, and stone statues like this were erected to his honor on many Polynesian islands.

The Voyage of the Kon-Tiki and Kon-Tiki film still and book cover
RIGHT PAGE: Not only motels and lounges took on the name, but even movie theaters like this one in Dayton, Ohio.

Die Reise der Kon-Tiki und Kon-Tiki-Standfoto und Buchumschlag
RECHTE SEITE: Nicht nur Motels und Bars legten sich den Namen zu, sondern auch Kinos wie dieses in Dayton, Ohio.

Le voyage du Kon-Tiki et une image du film « Kon-Tiki » et la couverture du livre
PAGE DE DROITE: Les motels et les bars ne furent pas les seuls à s'emparer du nom, des salles de cinéma l'empruntèrent aussi, comme celle-ci à Dayton, Ohio.

Kon Tiki RESTAURANT & MOTOR INN
RIVERSIDE · CALIFORNIA
ARMET & DAVIS A.I.A. ARCHITECTS

Thor was inspired to shift his object of study from snails and giant poisonous centipedes to the origin of the Polynesian race. He had noticed the likeness of the Marquesan stone tikis and petroglyphs to Incan idols in Peru, and for the next ten years he worked on his theory that the Pre-Incan high priest and sun-king Kon-Tici Viracocha, who had been forced to flee Peru by a waring chieftain, was identical with the Polynesian ancestor god, Tiki. Encountering nothing but scournful resistance from archeologists, ethnologists, linguists, and

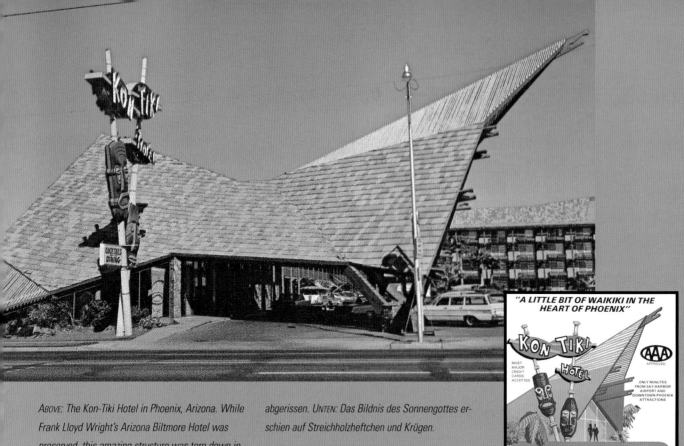

ABOVE: The Kon-Tiki Hotel in Phoenix, Arizona. While Frank Lloyd Wright's Arizona Biltmore Hotel was preserved, this amazing structure was torn down in 1997. BELOW: The likeness of the sun god appeared on matchbooks and mugs.

OBEN: Das Kon-Tiki-Hotel in Phoenix, Arizona. Während Frank Loyd Wrights Arizona Biltmore Hotel erhalten geblieben ist, wurde dieses Gebäude 1997

abgerissen. UNTEN: Das Bildnis des Sonnengottes erschien auf Streichholzheftchen und Krügen.

CI-DESSUS: Le Kon-Tiki Hotel à Phoenix, Arizona. Si l'Arizona Biltmore Hotel de Frank Lloyd Wright a été préservé, cette étonnante structure a quant à elle été détruite en 1997. CI-DESSOUS: L'effigie du dieu du soleil ornait les pochettes d'allumettes et les chopes.

Kona Kai Club
450 YACHT HARBOR DRIVE
SAN DIEGO, CALIFORNIA

CHARCOAL BROIL STEAKS OUR SPECIALTY

KON TIK

Stateline Village, I
Phone 773-931

sociologists, Thor set out to prove his theory in practice. He built a pre-Columbian balsa log raft, without using a single spike, nail, or wire rope, named it "Kon-Tiki," and proceeded to let himself and his five Scandinavian crewmen drift on the Humboldt Current from Peru to Polynesia.

After only three months on the open sea, the Kon-Tiki succeeded in reaching the Polynesian shores. The book about the voyage entitled *The Kon-Tiki Expedition* was first published in Norway in 1948, where it received unfavorable reviews, the whole endeavor being likened to "going over the Niagara Falls in a barrel." But this criticism did not deter the public's interest in the intrepid undertaking.

Shortly after publication in England and America in 1950, it became evident that the publishers had a best-seller on their hands. Eventually *Kon-Tiki* was translated into sixty differ-ent languages—the only book other than the Bible to reach this wide distribution. The film shot on the voyage met a similar fate, first being rejected by American distributors because of its technical flaws. Nevertheless it received the 1951 Academy Award for best documentary and was seen by millions of people. The world had just come out of the trauma of the Second World War and was longing for pacifist adventure.

The unprecedented worldwide Kon-Tiki fever further fueled America's fascination with Polynesian culture. Though "Tiki style" as a term was not in use during the 50s and 60s, the ver-nacular "Kon-Tiki style" was a popu-lar way to refer to Polynesian archi-tecture. Thor and Tiki, the Norse god of thunder and the Polynesian god of the sun, had united to become popu-lar heroes.

Heyerdahl's 1955 book about his Easter Island expeditition, *Aku Aku*, proved equally influential on Polyne-sian pop. The book's cover became such a popular icon that the giant stone statues, correctly termed *moai*, became known as Aku Aku heads, or even Aku-Tikis, making them into a widespread theme in American Tikidom.

TOP: Kon Tiki temple at Tiki Gardens in Florida
BOTTOM: Kon Tiki inspired men from all walks of life.

OBEN: KON-TIKI-Tempel in Tiki Gardens in Florida
UNTEN: Kon-Tiki inspirierte Menschen aus allen Lebensbereichen.

CI-DESSUS: Temple Kon Tiki à Tiki Gardens en Floride
EN BAS: Le Kon Tiki inspira des hommes aux modes de vie très divers.

TOP LEFT: Thor with stone giant. This image lodged itself in the public mind. LEFT: Mug, slot machine coin, paper fan, and menu cover from the Aku Aku at the Stardust Casino in Las Vegas

RIGHT PAGE: Motels and apartments invoked the protective spirits of Easter Island; BELOW: Interior of the Aku Aku, Las Vegas and an American export to Mexico.

OBEN LINKS: Thor mit Steinriesen. Dieses Bild prägte sich ins Bewusstsein der Öffentlichkeit ein. LINKS: Krug, Münze für den Spielautomaten, Papierfächer und Speisekarte aus dem Aku Aku im Stardust-Kasino in Las Vegas

RECHTE SEITE: Motels und Apartmenthäuser riefen die Schutzgeister der Osterinseln an; UNTEN: Blick ins Innere des Aku Aku, Las Vegas, und ein amerikanischer Exportartikel in Mexiko

CI-DESSUS À GAUCHE: Thor avec un géant de pierre. Cette image marqua profondément les esprits. A GAUCHE: Une chope, une pièce pour une machine à sous, un éventail en papier et la couverture d'un menu du Aku Aku au Stardust Casino de Las Vegas PAGE DE DROITE: Les motels et les résidences invoquaient les esprits protecteurs de l'île de Pâques; EN BAS: L'intérieur du Aku Aku, Las Vegas et un sous-bock américain exporté au Mexique

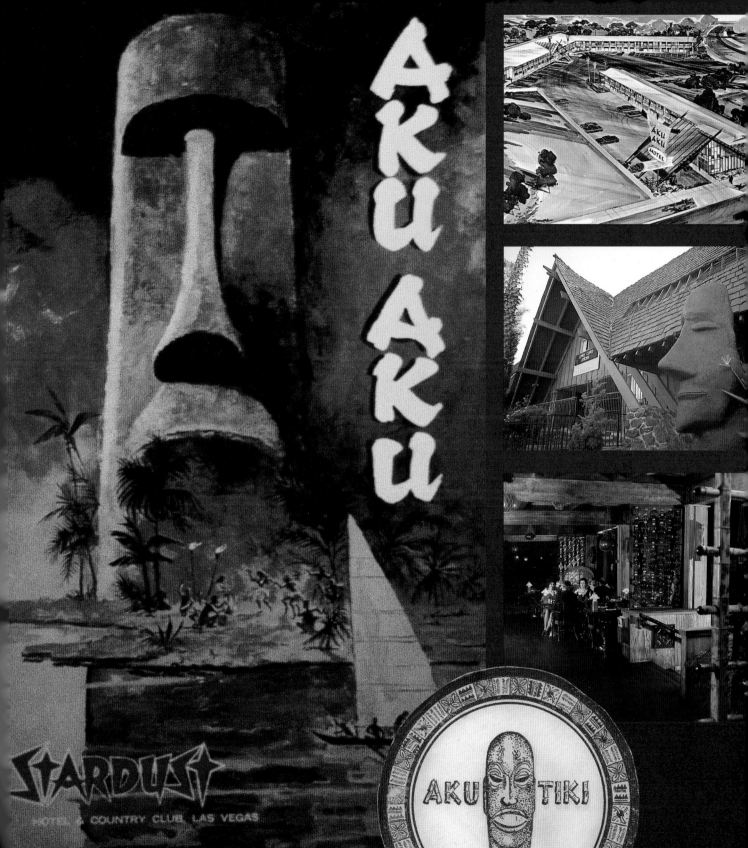

AKU AKU

STARDUST
HOTEL & COUNTRY CLUB LAS VEGAS

AKU TIKI
Acapulco, México

121

AN ORIGINAL SOUNDTRACK RECORDING
RCA Victor presents
RODGERS & HAMMERSTEIN'S
SOUTH PACI

A CAMERA

TODD-AO

COSTUMES
AND DANCERS

13
JAMES MICHENER, AND BALI HAI

"Bali Hai may call you, any night, any day.
In your heart you hear it call you, come away, come away.
Bali Hai will whisper, on the wind, on the sea,
here am I, your special island, come to me, come to me.
Your own special hopes, your own special dreams,
loom on the hillside and shine in the stream.
If you try, you will find me, where the sky meets the sea,
here am I, your special island, come to me, come to me."
(Rodgers & Hammerstein's *South Pacific*)

Thor was not the only bestselling author to make his mark on Polynesian pop.
During the Second World War a whole generation of American servicemen
had come into direct contact with Pacific island culture. James Michener had
been among them, and his fictional account of their plight, *Tales of the South*

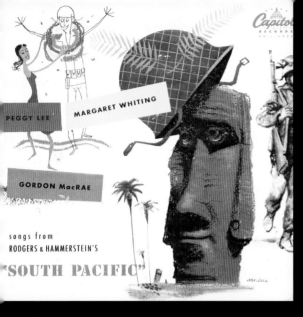

songs from
RODGERS & HAMMERSTEIN'S
'SOUTH PACIFIC'

Pacific, won him the 1948 Pulitzer Prize and tremendous popular success. A Broadway musical and a Cinemascope movie romanticized the actual hardships of war so successfully that a new idiom for the "exotic paradise" was created: the fictional "Bali Ha'i," the isle of the women. It became the new Shangri-La, everyman's dream island.

It was here that the novel's hero, Lt. Cable, experienced the age-old male fantasy of unconstrained love with a young exotic beauty. The story's protagonist is allowed the privilege of visiting the island, "a jewel of the vast ocean," on which "the French, with Gallic foresight and knowledge in these things, had housed all young women from the islands. Every girl, no matter how ugly or what her color, who

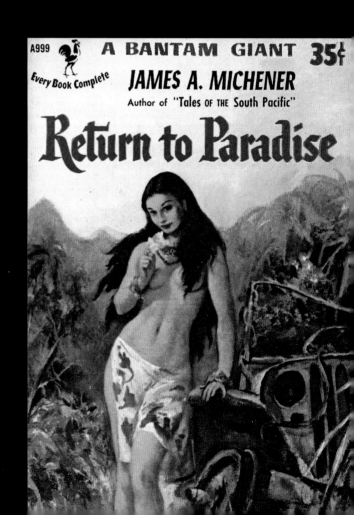

James A. Michener
TALES OF THE SOUTH PACIFIC

1948
PULITZER
PRIZE WINNER

THIS ABRIDGED
EDITION CONTAINS
14 OF THE ORIGINAL 19
STORIES

TOUGH, AMUSING, ROMANTIC
—ONE OF THE BEST NOVELS
TO COME OUT OF THE WAR!

A999   A BANTAM GIANT 35¢
Every Book Complete
JAMES A. MICHENER
Author of "Tales OF THE South Pacific"
Return to Paradise

LEFT PAGE: The soldier and the Wahine: The stuff dreams (male) are made of!

RIGHT AND BELOW: The origin of "Exotic Dancing?"

LINKE SEITE: Der Soldat und die Wahine: Der Stoff, aus dem die Träume (männlich) sind!

RECHTS UND UNTEN: Der Ursprung der Bezeichnung "Exotic Dancing"?

PAGE DE GAUCHE: Le soldat et la vahiné: l'étoffe dont sont faits les rêves (masculins)!

A DROITE ET CI-DESSOUS: L'origine de l'expression «Exotic Dancing»?

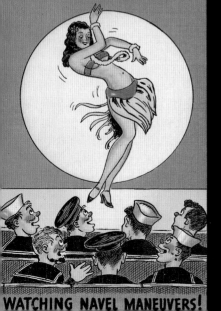

WATCHING NAVEL MANEUVERS!

might normally be raped by Americans was hidden on Bali Ha'i."(Michener) As lieutnant Cable's boat anchors, he is envied by every 1950s male reader: "For the first time in his life he had seen so many women, in fact any women, walking about with no clothes on above their hips …[L]ike the jungle, like the fruits of the jungle, adolescent girls seemed to abound in unbelievable profusion." (Michener)

Cable is swiftly rescued from the swarming maidens by the native matron Bloody Mary who wastes no time in setting him up with her beautiful virgin daughter, Liat. In the film our hero enters a romantic palm hut where Liat, a stunning beauty, awaits him, ready for love. No words are spoken—longing eyes, trembling lips: love is immediate and deep. The South Sea archetypes must be true, after all.

The fact that Americans from all walks of life had suddenly been exposed first

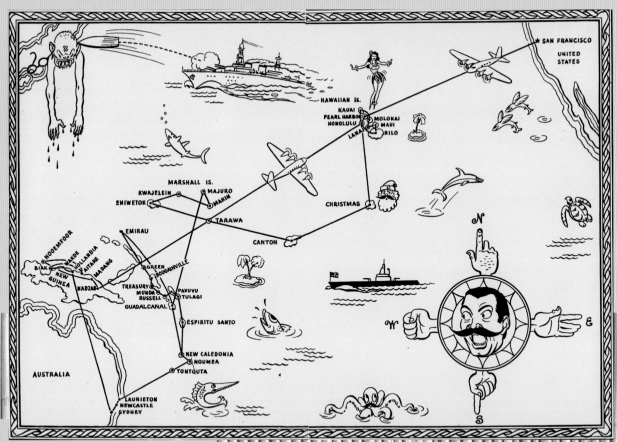

Above: Bob Hope's U.S.O tour map shows the extent of G.I. bases in the Pacific
Below: Little islands in urban America

Oben: Bob Hopes Tourneekarte zeigt die große Anzahl der G.I.-Basen im Pazifik.
Unten: Kleine Inseln im urbanen Amerika

Ci-dessus : Le plan de tournée de Bob Hope montre l'importance des bases militaires américaines dans le Pacifique.
Ci-dessous : Des îlots dans les villes américaines

hand to a completely strange culture left an indelible impression on America itself: "What am I doing here? How did I, Joe Cable of Philadelphia, wind up out here? This is Bali Ha'i, and a year ago I never heard of it. What am I doing here?" (Michener) The attitude was one of boyish wonder, and because the soldiers had been received warmly as saviors from the despised Japanese, the memories that remained of the South Pacific service were mostly of an exciting or pleasant nature. Consequently all over the U.S.A., little Bali Hai's popped up, serving those who had been there as well as those who had not.

James Michener followed the success of *South Pacific* with *Return to Paradise* in 1951. His further works included *Rascals in Paradise* (1957, with an account of Edgar Leeteg's life) and *Hawaii* (1959), establishing him firmly as the most-read author on Polynesia in the 50s.

The actual *Bali Ha'i* had been visited by Michener on the islet of Mono, near Guadalcanal. He remembered it as "a filthy, unpleasant village," but made a note of its name because he liked "its musical quality." This did not keep the Polynesian pop myth of Bali Ha'i from eventually getting re-imported to French Polynesia. In 1961, obviously infected by Tiki fever, a lawyer, a stockbroker, and a sporting goods salesman decided to abandon their civilized lives in the Los Angeles suburb of Newport Beach and made the move to Tahiti. Here they opened a hotel—and named it *Bali Hai*, of course. Fiction had conquered fact, as so often in Polynesian pop.

OTHER CELEBRATED TIKI TEMPLES

As mentioned earlier, the Tiki cult, like any other, had its "power places"—certain energy spots, where pure Tiki mana emanated freely and undiluted. Unfortunately we cannot portray or even mention all of these places in this book, which, although comprehensive, is far from a complete encyclopedia of the Tiki style. This chapter describes some of the still extant Tiki temples, most notably the *Mai* Kai and the *Kahiki*, which are possibly the two finest surviving examples of this vanished culture in America today. In an unprecedented and unusually enlightened move, the National Register of Historic Places has recently listed the *Kahiki*, a rare honor for a building dating from 1961 and one which hints at the re-emerging appreciation of Tiki style. We regret that we can do no more than to mention others, now mostly vanished, such as the *Lanai* in San Mateo, south of San Francisco; the *Tropics* in Dayton, Ohio; the *Hawaii Kai* in New York; and various obscure establishments in even more obscure places, such as the *Tur Mai Kai in* Kalamazoo, Michigan. They await discovery in later texts. The greeter to this chapter (left page) is a Mystery Girl who welcomes us at the entrance to the Tiki fountain of the *Kahiki* in Columbus, Ohio. The tradition of the Mystery Drink ritual was probably transmitted from the *Mai Kai*, where it seems to have originated in the tendency towards exotic waitress worship.

The first place of power we shall visit was once a whole island of Tiki temples. Appropiately enough, it was a man-made island created by the Navy from the sand they dredged out of San Diego bay to facilitate easier passage for their warships. What better place for artificial Polynesia than an artificial isle?

THE **BALI HAI,** SHELTER ISLAND, SAN DIEGO, CALIFORNIA

The first Tiki temple to be erected on Shelter Island was the Bali Hai, which had started out as *The Hut*, a subsidiary of *Christian's Hut* in Newport Beach. Only two years after its opening, the Hut's manager, Tom Hamm, took over the ailing business and transformed it into the most happening place in town. The *Bali Hai* had commanding views of San Diego Harbor, its own Yacht dock, and a Polynesian floor show that made it famous. It was popular not only with southern Californians, but with expatriate Polynesians

as well: they, unlike the academics who sneered at Tiki, were simply happy to have a place to reminisce about their heritage.

The "Mr. Bali Hai" logo Tiki was featured at the entrance and also in the shape of a mug, which to this day remains as a singular example of head-hunter whimsy. In a display case designed in the tradition of the Covarrubias Tiki map and filled with actual artifacts representing the Tiki styles of the various Polynesian Islands, the Bali Hai mug appropriately marks the location of its origin. But where did the strange head on top of the Bali Hai hail from? In a pertinent example of urban archeology, matchbook research can help to establish the source of this strange sculpture:

"MR. BALI HAI".
made Exclusively for the
BALI HAI
Restaurant
SanDiego, Calif.

ABOVE: The Tiki map display case at the Bali Hai. LEFT: The Mr. Bali Hai cocktail mug

OBEN: Schaukasten mit Tiki-Landkarte aus dem Bali Hai
LINKS: Der Mr. Bali Hai-Cocktailkrug

CI-DESSUS: La carte tiki du Bali Hai dans une vitrine
A GAUCHE: Le Mr. Bali Hai orne une chope à cocktail.

Just like in the islands: Hula dancing during the Polynesian floorshow at the Bali Hai

Wie auf den Inseln: Hula-Tanz bei einer polynesischen Nachtvorstellung im Bali Hai

Tout à fait comme dans les îles : danse polynésienne au Bali Hai

RIGHT: *Christian's Hut briefly opened in Hawaii in the late fifties, but "the Goof" had lost his mana.*

RECHTS: CHRISTIAN'S HUT *wurde in den späten fünfziger Jahren auf Hawaii eröffnet, aber der „Goof" verlor schon bald sein Mana.*

A DROITE : *Le Christian's Hut fut inauguré à Hawaii à la fin des années 1950, mais le charme était rompu.*

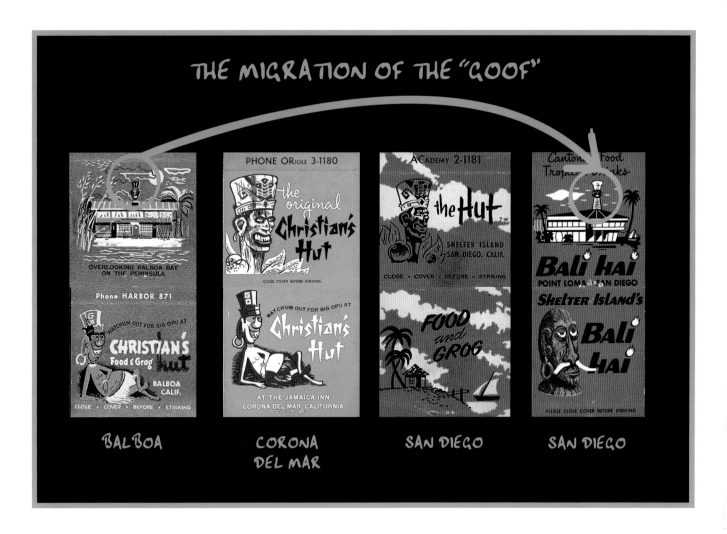

THE MIGRATION OF THE "GOOF"

BALBOA

CORONA DEL MAR

SAN DIEGO

SAN DIEGO

Marlon Brando as Fletcher Christian, 1961

Christian's Hut took its name from Fletcher Christian, famous mutineer of Her Majesty's ship *The Bounty*. In 1935 the story was filmed by MGM with Clark Gable playing the courageous officer. Catalina Island, off the coast of California, was chosen as location and turned into Tahiti. An entire Tahitian village was built, and at some point, 600 cast and crew members inhabited the isle. The bar that was located below Clark Gable's sleeping quarters became *Christ-ian's Hut*. When shooting finished, the Hut moved to Newport Beach, where it became a true power spot, with players like John Wayne and Howard Hughes among the regulars. The place spawned other franchises, but none ever achieved the fame of the original, which burned down in 1963. The actual meaning of the head, known as "the Goof," remains a mystery.

TAHITI restaurant
HALF MOON INN .... Shelter Island
San Diego, California.

FROM HWY. 101

BYRON ST. ROSECRANS ST.
HARBOR DRIVE
FROM SAN DIEGO

• Bali Hai

SHELTER ISLAND

San Diego Bay

NO.
ISL

2303 SHELTER ISLAND DRIVE
SAN DIEGO
(POINT LOMA)

The mana of the *Bali Hai* drew more Tiki temples to the Island. The strangest A-frame rose up across the way from the *Bali Hai* under the name of the *Half Moon Inn*, a project that Stephen Crane was initially involved in. Its restaurant once was to be named the Tahiti, but became instead

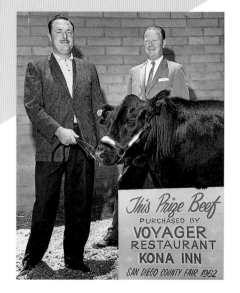

the *L'Escale*. The *Shelter Isle Inn*, the *Kona Kai Club*, and the *Kona Inn* all followed the Polynesian motif.

Today the Tiki touch has dissipated, has been mostly renovated away or, as in the case of the *Kona Kai Club*, has been completely obliterated, metamorphosed into Mediterranean style.

This Prize Beef
PURCHASED BY
VOYAGER
RESTAURANT
KONA INN
SAN DIEGO COUNTY FAIR 1962

These two gentlemen are proud to serve the cannibals at the Kona Inn.

Diese beiden Herren sind stolz darauf, die Kannibalen im Kona Inn bedienen zu dürfen.

Ces deux messieurs sont fiers de servir les cannibales qui fréquentent le Kona Inn.

THE **MAI KAI,**
FORT LAUDERDALE, FL

In the early 1950s two brothers from Chicago, Bob and Jack Thornton, decided to flee the icy winters of the Windy City in favor of tropical Florida. Here, inspired by the *Don the Beachcomber* outpost in their hometown, they began to create their own Polynesian haven, the *Mai Kai*. Since 1956 the *Mai Kai* has grown from a moderate four-room hut to a sprawling village with eight dining rooms, lush tropical gardens with waterfalls, and an abundance of Tikis. Bob Thornton always chose professional Polynesian pop artists to expand upon his realm, hiring George Nakashima and Florian Gabriel of Stephen Crane and Associates as art directors and using decor by

LEFT PAGE: A black velvet rendering of the Mai Kai
LEFT: The three Tahitian Cannibal Tikis as a coaster.
BELOW: The Mystery Girl, presenting the Mystery Drink at the sound of the gong

LINKE SEITE: Eine Darstellung auf schwarzem Samt im Mai Kai
LINKS: Die drei tahitischen Kannibalen-Tikis als Untersatz. UNTEN: wenn der Gong erklingt, serviert das Mystery Girl den Mystery Drink.

PAGE DE GAUCHE : Une représentation sur fonds de velours noir du Mai Kai
A GAUCHE : Dessous de verre à l'image des trois tikis cannibales tahitiens. CI-DESSOUS : Quand le gong retentit, la Fille Mystérieuse sert le Breuvage Mystérieux.

MAI-KAI
8mm
COLOR MOVIE

*Saronged
serving girls*

·

*Mystery Drink
Ritual*

Film and viewer
complete **9.95**
Film only **5.95**

MAIL-A-MOVIE, INC.
405 Professional Bldg.
Sunrise Center
Ft. Lauderdale, Fla.

Oceanic Arts in Whittier to give the *Mai Kai* that much claimed "authentic" touch.

The *Mai Kai* never had a specific logo Tiki, but made extensive graphic use of the Tahitian cannibal carvings that first appeared on the *Don the Beachcomber* menu. Another favorite fetish was a Cook Islands fisherman's god that became a rum bottle. The most notable artifact is perhaps the *Mai Kai* mystery bowl. The three Hawaiian war gods supporting it open their mouths to let the straws in. But apart from its extensive collection of carvings, the *Mai Kai* took pride in worshipping the beauty of the female form by providing the customer with a bevy of Bikini-clad beauties as waitresses. These poster girls were introduced as starlets and models in the Mai Kai periodical called "Happy Talk" (from a song in *South Pacific*), featured on yearly calendars, and in films depicting the Mystery Drink ritual.

The *Mai Kai* is now successfully run by such an Exotica girl, Mireille Thornton, the late Bob Thornton's wife, who came to the Mai Kai from Tahiti as a dancer. She is also the choreographer of the Mai Kai Polynesian revue, the longest running show of its kind. The mana of the *Mai Kai* undoubtedly inspired the spread of the Tiki cult in Florida, where to this day the Tiki archeologist can find bars and motels that emulate the image.

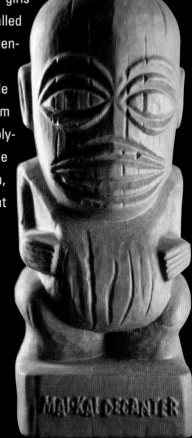

MAI KAI DECANTER

CATHY

MAY

JUNE 1972

JULY

OCTOBER

NOVEMBER 1972

DECEMBER

NOVEMBER

DECEMBER 1972

JANUARY

L. CARROLL

THE **KONA KAI,**
PHILADELPHIA, PENNSYLANVIA

The *Kona Kai* chain was Marriot's answer to Hilton's *Trader Vics* and Shera-ton's Kon-Tikis. In the sixties, the Kona coast was being pushed as the next Waikiki, and numerous mainland Tiki settlements, from restaurants to motels and apartment buildings, took on the name of this Hawaiian Promised Land. The Philadelphia *Kona Kai,* designed by Armet & Davis, was the flagship of the chain, with other islands opening in Chicago and Kansas City. It was a true Temple of Tiki, incorporating all the necessary paraphernalia including interi-or waterfalls and bridges as well as painted-glass dioramas. The origin of the classic Kona Kai logo Tiki can be traced back to an early rendition of the Armet & Davis designer Irving Weisenberg, and can be found in this book on the opening page of chapter seven. At this early stage still called "Hale Tiki," the figure bears only fleeting resemblance to the final result below, but the draw-ing of the entrance Tiki certainly gave birth to the Kona Kai's emblem.

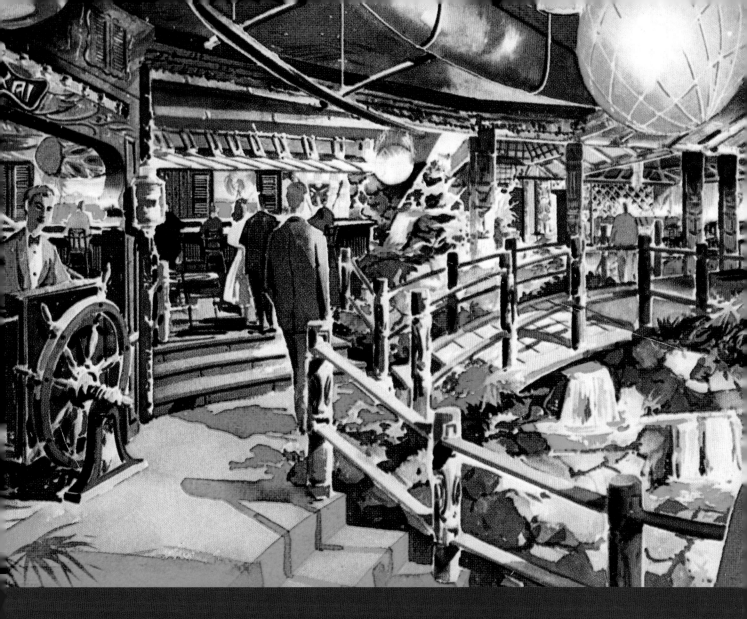

ABOVE: A detail of the Hale Tiki rendition reveals the source of the Kona Kai logo Tiki. The swizzle stick, which became a popular model for many other establishments, originated here.

LEFT PAGE: A fine modern Tiki, carved by Leroy Schmaltz of Oceanic Arts, against a modern concrete brick pattern designed by Armet & Davis, at the Chicago Kona Kai

OBEN: Ein Detail aus dem Hale Tiki macht deutlich, woher das Tiki-Logo des Kona Kai kam. Der Cocktailstab wurde in dieser Form auch in anderen Lokalen sehr populär, stammte aber von hier.

LINKE SEITE: Ein moderner Tiki, geschnitzt von Leroy Schmaltz (Oceanic Arts), vor einer modernen, gemusterten Betonwand, die von Armet & Davis für das Kona Kai in Chicago entworfen wurde.

CI-DESSUS: Ce détail du «Hale Tiki» révèle la source du logo tiki du Kona Kai. Le bâtonnet mélangeur qui devint si populaire dans de nombreux établissements vient d'ici.

PAGE DE GAUCHE: Un beau tiki moderne sculpté par Leroy Schmaltz d'Oceanic Arts devant un mur en béton à motifs modernes dessiné par Armet & Davis pour le Kona Kai de Chicago.

143

THE **KAHIKI,** COLUMBUS, OHIO

The urban Tiki Island concept took hold not only in the recreational states like Florida and California, where the climate facilitated the growth of palm trees and jungle foliage, but in colder zones as well. The effect of entering a tropical environment was amplified by the harsh conditions outside. The *Kahiki*, as can be seen by its floorplan on page 61, is a perfectly preserved example of such a Tiki sanctuary. The "main street" between the dining huts of the "Quiet Village" is lined by 40-foot-high fake palm trees, and some of the dining booths look out onto a rain forest jungle inhabited by live birds. Here a tropical storm erupts at regular intervals, while outside icicles form on the outrigger beams. A giant

LEFT PAGE: Coburn Morgan's original rendition of the Kahiki, 1961, and the Kahiki as it stands today
ABOVE: The "Quiet Village" and its god. RIGHT: Kahiki table setting with view onto the rain forest

LINKE SEITE: Coburn Morgans ursprünglicher Entwurf für das Kahiki, 1961, und das Kahiki heute
OBEN: Das „Stille Dorf" mit seinem Gott. RECHTS: Kahiki-Tischgarnierung mit Blick auf den Regenwald

PAGE DE GAUCHE: Le dessin original de Coburn Morgan pour le Kahiki, 1961, et le Kahiki aujourd'hui.
CI-DESSUS: Le «Paisible village» et son dieu
A DROITE: Une table du Kahiki avec vue sur la forêt tropicale

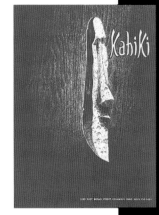

Easter Island fireplace idol looms over the whole scene.

Designed and built (surprisingly similar to the rendition) by Coburn Morgan for Lee Henry and Bill Sapp in 1961, the Kahiki is a treasure trove of Tiki art. "… above the door, authentic replicas of primitive art murals greet the visitor. With these designs, no evil spirits may enter." The black velvet paintings are signed "La Visse," apparently one of the many "students" of Edgar Leeteg. The Tiki tiles around the Mayan Revival-style entrance doors are identified as "Tectum Pan-L-Art." Unfortunately, this sanctuary has recently been threatened by an offer of a major drug-store chain. Go and see it while you can!

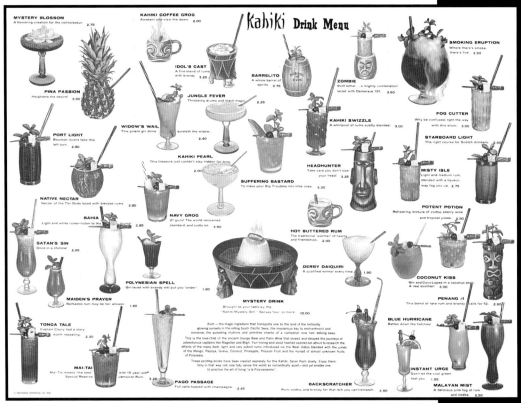

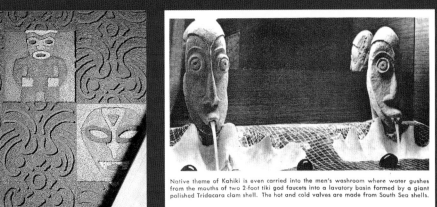

Native theme of Kahiki is even carried into the men's washroom where water gushes from the mouths of two 2-foot tiki god faucets into a lavatory basin formed by a giant polished Tridacara clam shell. The hot and cold valves are made from South Sea shells.

PAGE 146, LEFT: Famous people visited this Polynesian power place.
ABOVE: The front of Lee Henry's desk and Tectum Pa-L-Art Tiki tiles. RIGHT: Designer Coburn Morgan posing with war bride waitresses

SEITE 146, LINKS: Viele Berühmtheiten besuchten dieses polynesische In-Lokal.
OBEN: Die Vorderseite von Lee Henrys Schreibtisch und Tectum Pa-L-Art-Tiki-Kacheln. RECHTS: Designer Coburn Morgan posiert mit Kellnerinnen.

PAGE 146, À GAUCHE : De nombreuses célébrités ont fréquenté cet établissement polynésien en vue.
CI-DESSUS : La face antérieure du bureau de Lee Henry et des carrelages tiki du Tectum Pa-L-Art.
A DROITE : Le designer Coburn Morgan posant avec des serveuses, des épouses de guerre ayant suivi leur mari.

MENUS - L' ART TIKI

Menu covers are the oil paintings of Tiki style—portraits of Tikis and their temples that have long since vanished, like *Dorian's* in Whittier, California. This home of many graven images had a "Happy Talk" cocktail lounge, which took its name from a song from the musical *South Pacific*. "Happy talk" was used by Liat, Lt. Cable's island maiden as the naive native idiom for flirting. Apparently the menu rendition depicts two male Tikis involving a female Tiki in such "happy talk." Unfortunately no photographic record of this ensemble exists.

Menus also perpetuated the mythology of Polynesian pop by paying hommage to its forefathers like Don the Beachcomber, telling tales of the owners' adventures, or relating legends of Tiki, the god of recreation. Trader Vic established the tradition on the back of his 1947 menu (see page 83) by stating, "I salute Don the Beachcomber of Hollywood, the originator of such outstanding drinks as the Zombie and the Missionary's

The Tonga Lei in Malibu was a favorite hangout of the local beachcomber and surfer crowd until its motel began to attract drugs and prostitution. By the 1980s, Tiki had left the building.

Das Tonga Lei in Malibu gehörte zu den Lieblingslokalen der einheimischen „Beachcomber" und Surfer, bis sich im Motel Drogen und Prostitution breit machten. In den 80er Jahren hatte Tiki das Gebäude verlassen.

Le Tonga Lei à Malibu était le lieu de prédilection des «beachcombers» et surfers locaux jusqu'à ce que le motel commence à attirer la drogue et la prostitution. Dans les années 80, Tiki avait déserté l'endroit.

Downfall." The *Tahitian*, whose menu featured 68 tropical drinks, humbly continued the tribute:

"The Tahitian doffs its hat to Don the Beachcomber as the pioneer rum expert of the world. Don was the creator of many of our finest rum drinks, being most famous for the Zombie. He merits the applause of all lovers of fine foods and fine drink for his contributions towards the creation of a completely new type of restaurant. The Tahitian also salutes Trader Vic, who has made many contributions of delectable drinks and Polynesian-style foods. While we do not profess to excel these old masters, we sincerely believe The Tahitian to be one

The TahiTian

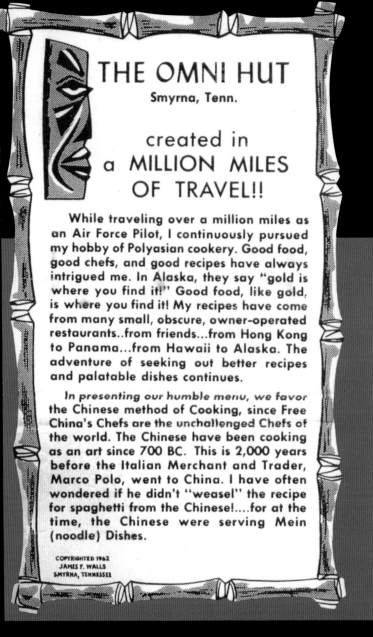

THE OMNI HUT
Smyrna, Tenn.

created in
a MILLION MILES
OF TRAVEL!!

While traveling over a million miles as an Air Force Pilot, I continuously pursued my hobby of Polyasian cookery. Good food, good chefs, and good recipes have always intrigued me. In Alaska, they say "gold is where you find it!" Good food, like gold, is where you find it! My recipes have come from many small, obscure, owner-operated restaurants..from friends...from Hong Kong to Panama...from Hawaii to Alaska. The adventure of seeking out better recipes and palatable dishes continues.

In presenting our humble menu, we favor the Chinese method of Cooking, since Free China's Chefs are the unchallenged Chefs of the world. The Chinese have been cooking as an art since 700 BC. This is 2,000 years before the Italian Merchant and Trader, Marco Polo, went to China. I have often wondered if he didn't "weasel" the recipe for spaghetti from the Chinese!....for at the time, the Chinese were serving Mein (noodle) Dishes.

COPYRIGHTED 1962
JAMES F. WALLS
SMYRNA, TENNESSEE

'famous'. How could they? Trader Dick's is brand new. I've connived, schemed, borrowed and begged for all the ideas and recipes we have here ... They are the very best I could steal from all the top Cantonese and Polynesian Restaurants from Honululu to New York. And I

of the top restaurants of its kind in the world."

This kind of gushy chivalry inspired Dick Graves, proprietor of *Trader Dick's* (see page 249), to cut the poetry and write in his menu: "Folks, I've never been to the South Seas ... none of these recipes are mine ... none of these have made the place

ought to know … I've snooped in all of them … I've swiped menus, bribed and talked to bartenders and cooks and copied every good thing I could find." With this uncharacteristic honesty Dick Graves actually described much more truthfully the competitive spirit that prevailed in Polynesian pop. The *Kona Kai* in Philadelpia expounded the following piece of menu mythology, making the customer believe he had arrived: "THE MYSTERY OF KONA KAI. Legend has it that Tiki, South Seas god of abundance and joyous comfort, once sought the most perfect setting for a timeless paradise full of laughter and happiness. He spent great effort and much time in sharpening his

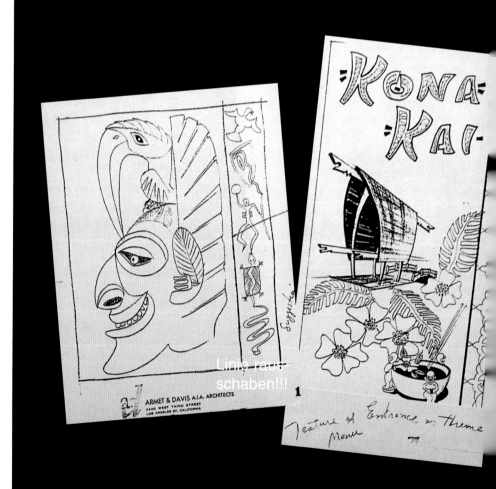

the ISLANDS

4839 N. Seventh Street
Just South of Camelback Rd.
Phoenix, Arizona

EAST ORANGETHORPE / FULLERTON

the palms

1010

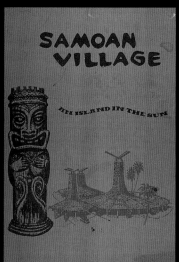

ABOVE: The Palms menu swiped its Tiki from the album cover for Les Baxter's "Ritual of the Savage" (bottom right). RIGHT: Menu covers from the Tur Mai Kai, Kalamazoo, Michigan, and the Samoan Village, Phoenix, Arizona

OBEN: The Palms klaute für seine Speisekarte den Tiki von der Plattenhülle von Les Baxters „Ritual of the Savage" (unten rechts). RECHTS: Speisekarten aus dem Tur Mai Kai in Kalamazoo, Michigan, und dem Samoan Village in Phoenix und dem Surfrider, Arizona

EN HAUT: Le menu de The Palms avait emprunté son tiki à la couverture du livre de Les Baxter «Ritual of the Savage» (à gauche en bas). A DROITE: Couvertures de menus du Tur Mai Kai, Kalamazoo, Michigan et du Samoan Village, Phoenix, Arizona.

the
HAWAIIAN

HOME OF THE
Yum
Yum ROOM

EXOTIC FOODS
by Johnny Quong

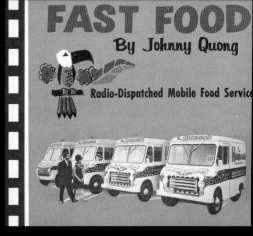

LEFT: Johnny Quong brought Tiki to Salt Lake City, Utah. His fast food delivery trucks had Tiki faces painted around their front grilles (above).

LINKS: Johnny Quong brachte Tiki nach Salt Lake City in Utah. Seine Lieferwagen für Fastfood hatten Tiki-Gesichter, die vorne um den Kühlergrill gemalt waren (oben).

A GAUCHE : Johnny Quong amena Tiki à Salat Lake City, Utah. Ses camions de livraison de fast-food avaient des visages de tiki peints autour de leurs calandres (en haut).

senses, so that he would know of a certainty when he had discovered his 'Garden of Eden,' he travelled throughout his land…. At last his sojourn led him to the sea … to a perfect lagoon called 'Kona Kai'. There he found the utter perfection he sought. This incredible bay was swept with soft trade winds, bathed in gentle sunlight, sheltered from storms and midday heat. Brilliant flowers grew in profusion and music ran soothingly from peaceful waterfalls. Tiki stays still at Kona Kai … basking in its utter perfection and blessing all his followers with abundant joy and happiness."

The Tiki gospel was orated in a much simpler fashion in the menu of the *Luau 400*, a New York Tiki temple: "TIKI is the traditional god of everything good…. Good health, good fortune, good times, and, oh yes, good food, are all part of the blessings bestowed by TIKI, the Polynesian god."

KAI KAI

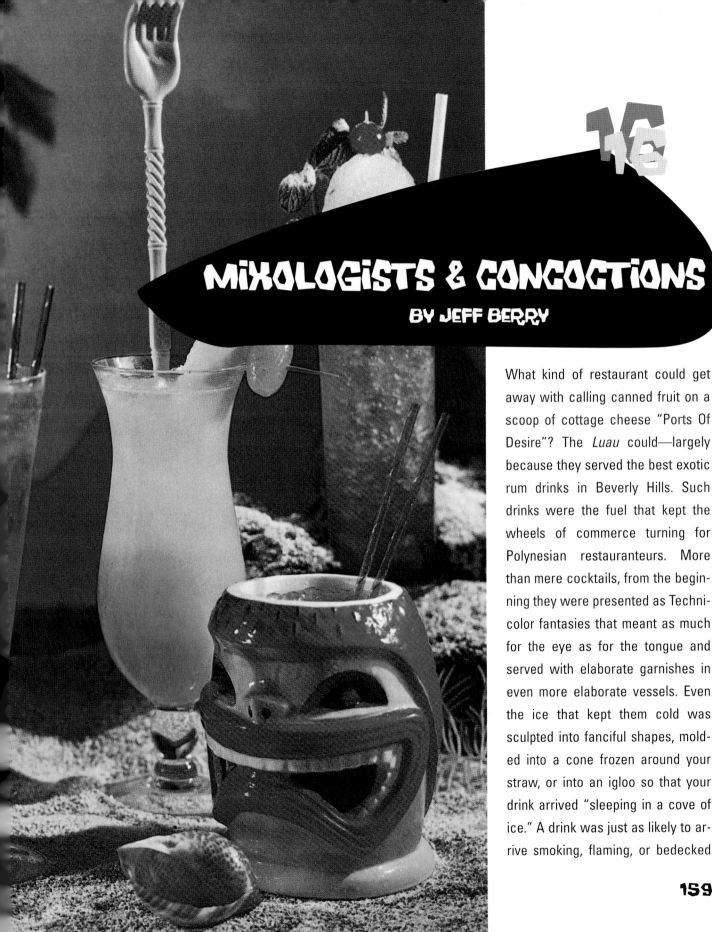

16

MIXOLOGISTS & CONCOCTIONS

BY JEFF BERRY

What kind of restaurant could get away with calling canned fruit on a scoop of cottage cheese "Ports Of Desire"? The *Luau* could—largely because they served the best exotic rum drinks in Beverly Hills. Such drinks were the fuel that kept the wheels of commerce turning for Polynesian restauranteurs. More than mere cocktails, from the beginning they were presented as Technicolor fantasies that meant as much for the eye as for the tongue and served with elaborate garnishes in even more elaborate vessels. Even the ice that kept them cold was sculpted into fanciful shapes, molded into a cone frozen around your straw, or into an igloo so that your drink arrived "sleeping in a cove of ice." A drink was just as likely to arrive smoking, flaming, or bedecked

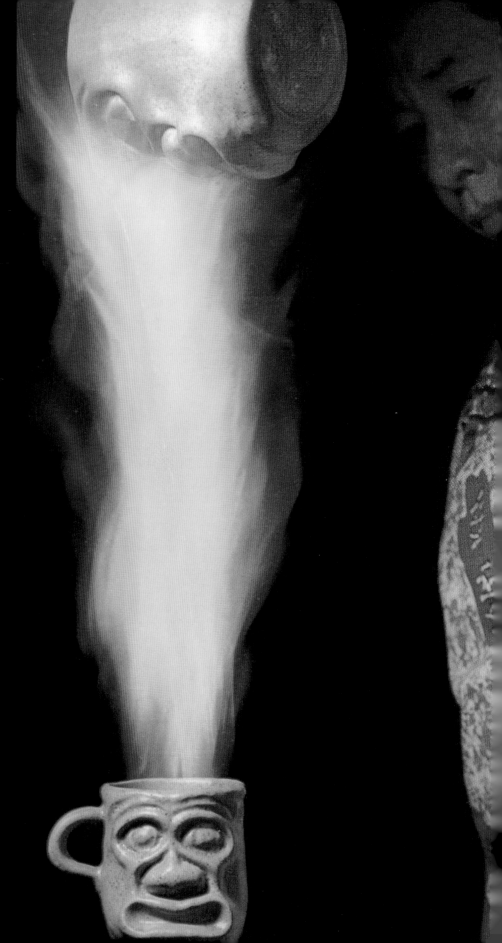

with a floating gardenia in which a hidden pearl awaited your discovery. This was the cocktail as Conversation Piece. When you left a Polynesian restaurant, you didn't talk about the food—you talked about the "Mystery Drink," or the "Penang Afrididi," or "Pele's Bucket Of Fire." And the management itself usually started the conversation going on the menu, where flowery, poetic descriptions accompanied fetishistically rendered color illustrations of a drink. Said *The Islander* of its Mount Kilauea, "An eruption of the finest in imported rums fired with the sacred nectars of the Tiki Gods."

As you might expect, these concoctions didn't always taste as good as they looked. But the best tropical drinks could be complex, layered, at once subtle and voluptuous, with a delicate balance between sweet and sour, strong and light, fruity and dry. And the best tropical drinks originated at *Don The Beachcomber's*.

When Don opened his first bar in 1934, rum was déclassé. Alcoholics were "rummies." Only sailors and stewbums drank demon rum; the smart set drank whiskey and gin. So why didn't Don invent whiskey and gin drinks? Because rum was cheaper. When Prohibition ended, cases of the stuff could be had for as little as 70 cents a quart. In Don's

case, frugality was the mother of invention. But Don didn't create his "Rum Rhapsodies" out of thin air. Nash Aranas, former supervisor and "director of authenticity" for the Beachcomber restaurant chain, acknowledged in 1989 that Don had "spent time in the West Indies where he got the rum idea." Don presumably encountered the Jamaican Planter's Punch and the Cuban Daiquiri; both of these drinks are simple combinations of lime, sugar, and rum—three ingredients that became the building blocks for most of Don's creations. To the lime he added pineapple, papaya, and passion fruit; to sugar he added anise, vanilla, and almond extract; to rum he added liqueurs, flavored brandies … and more rum.

Much more rum. Because Don had discovered that mixing dark rums with light rums created entirely new, more complex base flavors for his juices and syrups to accent. "Don would sit there all day with his cronies mixing drinks," remembers Aranas. "He would test, test, test, test, like a mad scientist." The combina-

Lapu Lapu

Exotic tropical fruit nectars harmoniously blended with the finest of imported rums.

Gold Cup

A frosty medley of fine Jamaican Rums, tree-ripened limes and golden nectar of the tropical sun.

Scorpion

A South Seas concoction of rums, fruit juices and brandy with a whisper of almond bedecked with gardenias and served with long straws.

Islander

Navy Grog

A truly great blending of exotic rums and tropical fruit juices with an accent of Pimiento Dram.

Islander's Pearl

A delicate Ambrosia of West Indies Rum and the fragrant nectar of the Gods blended with the smoothness of the virgin pearl.

Cobras Fang

Demerara Rum, Limes, and Currant Syrup coiled with aromatic bitters.

Mount Kilauea

Specialty of the Islander. An eruption of the finest in imported rums fired with the sacred nectars of the Tiki Gods.

Coffee Grog

Fine rums and Kona Coffee blended with wild honey and delicate spices of the Far East.

Tahitian

lending of sacred island h Passion Fruit nectar nest in tropical Golden

Vicious Virgin

Virgin Island Rums, fragrant fresh green limes, and Rock Candy Syrup in a passionate lagoon with floating lush Hawaiian flora.

Pi-Yi

Light rums blended together with romantic tropical juices of the islands and Polynesian spices served in a fresh Pineapple.

ABOVE: A treasure map of the rum producing island states adorned the back of Don the Beachcomber's menu.
RIGHT PAGE: Don himself, the archetypal mixologist, at work in his lab

OBEN: Eine Karte für Schatzsucher von den Rum-produzierenden Inselstaaten zierte die Rückseite der Getränkekarte im Don the Beachcomber.
RECHTE SEITE: Don persönlich, der Barmann schlechthin, bei der Arbeit in seinem Labor

CI-DESSUS: Une carte des îles productrices de rhum ornait le dos du menu de Don the Beachcomber.
PAGE DE DROITE: Don en personne, l'archétype du faiseur de mélanges, au travail dans son laboratoire

tions were endless and endlessly varied, resulting in such popular early inventions as the Vicious Virgin, the Shark's Tooth, the Cobra's Fang, the Dr. Funk, and the Missionary's Downfall.

Legend has it that Don's most famous drink, the Zombie, was improvised on the spot to help a hungover customer get through an important business meeting. When asked later how the cure worked, the customer said, "I felt like the living dead—it made a Zombie out of me." But the copy from a 1941 *Beachcomber* menu offers a different origin myth: "The Zombie didn't just happen. It is the result of a long and expensive process of evolution. In the experiments leading up to the Zombie, three-and-a-half cases of assorted rums were used and found their way down the drain so that you may now enjoy this potent 'mender of broken dreams'."

In a conversation shortly before his death, veteran mixologist Ray Buhen, one of the original *Beachcomber* employees in '34, told yet another story. "Don was a nice guy," recalled Buhen, who went on to open his own bar, the *Tiki Ti,* 27 years later. "But he'd say anything. He said he invented the Zombie, but he didn't. Or hardly any of his drinks." Buhen maintained that most of this work was done by "The Four Boys," a quartet of Filipino assistants Don had working behind the bar—a heretical notion, to be sure, but Ray's credentials as a source are impeccable: 62 years as a mixologist in the most famous Polynesian palaces, from the *Seven Seas* and the *Luau* to the *China Trader* and his own bar, serving the likes of Clark Gable, Charlie Chaplin, Buster Keaton, the Marx Brothers, and Marlon Brando.

Whatever their origins, Don's drinks became so popular so quickly that "four boys" soon were not enough. Don eventually had to hire seven full-time bartenders, each specializing in different drinks. Behind them were still more Filipino assistants, coring pineapples with piano wire, shaving big blocks of ice until their arms ached, and squeezing limes until the citric acid ate into their fingernails. To add insult to injury, strict security was enforced to make sure none of these assistants could memorize Don's secret recipes. Instead of labels, the bottles were identified only

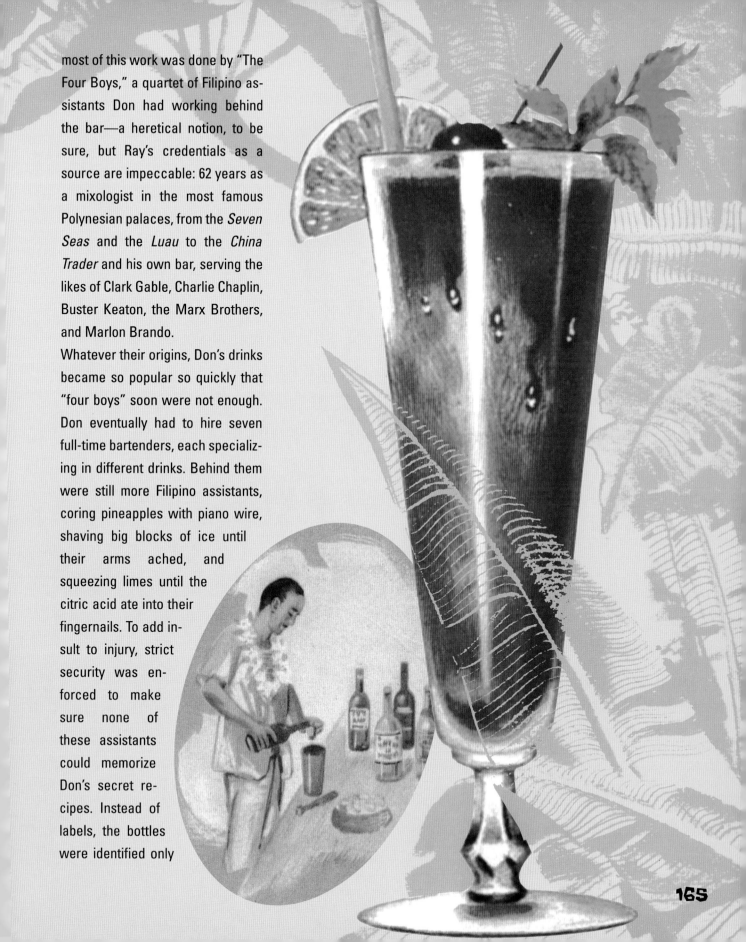

In his illustrious career Ray Buhen worked at almost every major Tiki bar in Los Angeles, opening his own "Tiki Ti" in 1960 (page 173), where today his son Mike is continuing the tradition.

In seiner beeindruckenden Karriere arbeitete Ray Buhen in fast allen größeren Tiki-Bars in Los Angeles und eröffnete 1960 sein eigenes Lokal, Tiki Ti (Seite 173), in dem heute sein Sohn Mike die Tradition weiterführt.

Au cours de son illustre carrière, Ray Buhen travailla dans quasiment tous les bars tiki importants de Los Angeles, ouvrant son propre Tiki Ti en 1960 (page 173) où aujourd'hui, son fils Mike perpétue la tradition.

by numbers and letters. According to a 1948 Saturday Evening Post article, "The recipes are in code and the mixers follow a pattern of code symbols indicating premixed ingredients, rather than actual names of fruit concentrates and rum brands. In this way, even if a rival restauranteur makes a raid on the Beachcomber help ... the renegade cannot take Don's recipes with him."

If Don was the Great White Father of the tropical drink, he had many Prodigal Sons. Rip-offs occured almost as soon as Don opened. At Harry Sugerman's *Tropics* nightclub in Beverly Hills, the Zombie became the Zulu: "One drink, you're important! Two drinks, you're impatient! Three drinks, you're impotent!" But while others were content to imitate Don, Trader Vic was more ambitious. "I didn't know a damn thing about that kind of booze," he wrote in his autobiography, "and I thought I'd like to learn." He traveled far and wide, observing internationally renowned mixologists such as Havana's Constantine Ribailagua (who created the *Papa Dobles*

"I call it a European Zombie — cognac, vodka, steinhager and beer....."

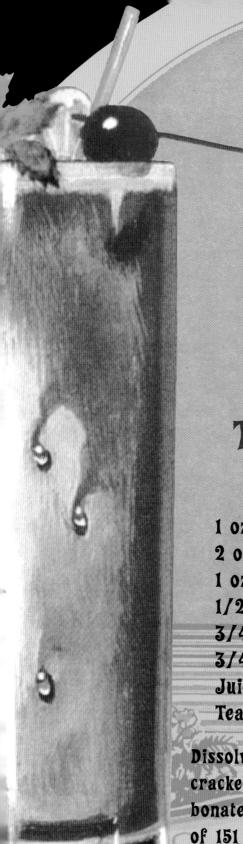

grapefruit daiquiri for Ernest Hemingway) and New Orleans' Albert Martin (of Ramos Fizz fame). By the time he returned to his Oakland saloon, Trader Vic was no longer an imitator. He was an innovator.

When Vic gave birth to the Scorpion, the Samoan Fog Cutter, and the Mai Tai, all of a sudden *he* became the one everybody was ripping off. "This aggravates my ulcer completely," he fumed when bars from Tahiti to Tulsa began taking credit for the Mai Tai. "Anyone who says I didn't create this drink," maintained Vic, "is a dirty stinker." He set the record straight with this characteristically modest tale: "I was behind my bar one day in 1944 talking with my bartender, and I told him that I was going to make the finest rum drink in

THE ZOMBIE

1 oz. dark Jamaican rum
2 oz. gold Barbados rum
1 oz. white Puerto Rican rum
1/2 ounce apricot brandy
3/4 oz. papaya nectar
3/4 oz. unsweetened pineapple juice
Juice of one large lime
Teaspoon finely granulated sugar

Dissolve sugar in lime juice, then shake everything well with cracked ice and pour into 14 oz. frosted lass. Add 1 oz. carbonated water and enough ice to fill glass, then float a dash of 151 proof Demerara rum. Garnish with mint sprig, pineapple cube skewered between one red and one green cocktail cherry, and powdered sugar sprinkled over all.

try a ...

MAI TAI

DON the BEACHCOMBER MIXES

the world. Just then Ham and Carrie Guild, some old friends from Tahiti, came in. Carrie tasted it, raised her glass, and said, 'Mai Tai—Roa Ae,' which in Tahitian means 'Out of this world—the best!' That's the name of the drink, I said, and we named it Mai Tai."

The controversy over who invented the Mai Tai didn't end until Trader Vic took the matter to court, filing a lawsuit against the Sun-Vac Corporation in 1970. By that time, Sun-Vac was licensing a *Don the Beachcomber* line of pre-mixed bottled drink syrups; ironically, Sun-Vac was claiming that it was Don

himself—the man Vic freely admitted copying more than thirty years before—who had invented the Mai Tai. The suit was eventually settled out of court in favor of Vic.

As exotic rum drinks became big business and the Polynesian palaces that served them proliferated, competition became even more fierce. Unlike Don and Vic, the new upstarts had no claim to fame, so they sought bragging rights for their restaurants by creating their own celebrity bartenders–often by entering staff members in cocktail competitions sponsored by rum companies. The restaurant could then advertise its own prize-winning cocktail created by its own legendary bartender, and the rum company could advertise that the winning recipe featured their rum. In 1953, an anonymous waiter at the *Luau* named Popo Galcini was entered in one such contest sponsored by Ron Rico; he won and achieved instant stardom, despite

VICTOR J. BERGERON (Trader Vic) and MRS. CARRIE GUILD WRIGHT
at Trader Vic's original Bar in Oakland, California

"I've sworn at this bar a few times since I built it 35 years ago, so to settle the argument over the origin of the 'Mai Tai' I will swear just once again to get the record straight.

At this bar in 1944 I designed and originated the 'Mai Tai' drink as it is still known and made today ... I served it to my good friends from Tahiti, Ham and Carrie Guild, and asked them to name it."

Oakland — 1970

"I, too, hereby solemnly swear that on a summer night in 1944 Trader Vic served us a delightfully-flavored drink in an oversized glass filled with fine ice and asked us to suggest an appropriate Tahitian name.

One sip, and my natural reaction was to say 'Mai Tai-Roa Aé', which in Tahitian means 'Out of this world — the best' ... Well, that was that! Vic named the drink 'Mai Tai'."

Carrie Wright

Oakland — 1970

MAI TAI
1 oz. aged Jamaican rum
1 oz. St. James Martinique rum
1/2 ounce Curaçao
Juice of one lime
1/4 oz. orgeat syrup*
1/4 oz. sugar syrup
Hand shake with crushed ice. Sink lime shell into drink and garnish with mint sprig. (*Orgeat is a commercially available almond-flavored syrup.)

rumors that the contest, like most of its kind, was rigged. Nevertheless, Galcini was soon poached from the *Luau* by the popular West L.A. groggery Kelbo's, where he began the first of a series of lucrative bartending gigs culminating at *The Outrigger* in Laguna Beach. *The Outrigger's* drink menu proudly boasted of "Prize Award Winning Cocktails by POPO," including the "Pikake," which took first place at another of those dubious cocktail competitions in 1958.

No longer scorned as déclassé, by the mid-50s rum had come full circle, largely due to the proselytizing of Vic and Don, who began blending and selling their own labels. The smart set abandoned their whiskey and gin for demon rum, now romanticized as the drink of "adventurers of the sea" and "the most talked about and fabulous potion of all ages" (at least, according to the Hawaiian Room in Omaha, Nebraska). Some places boasted not just a massive selection of rums, but a massive selection of rum drinks. "There is a choice of 36 tropical drinks," reported a contemporary restaurant review of the China Trader in Burbank, "and a professor from Cal Tech set a record by working his way through sixteen before succumbing to a rum torpor." We can

Kelbo's, once the beachcomber hideaway in Los Angeles, is now a strip club.

Kelbo's, ehemals der Zufluchtsort für Beachcomber in Los Angeles, ist heute eine Strip-Lokal.

Le Kelbo's, jadis le refuge des beachcombers de Los Angeles, est aujourd'hui une boîte de strip-tease.

OUTRIGGER APPETIZERS

FRIED SHRIMP 1.50 RUMAKI....1.35	GEE BOW GAI ....each .50	FRIED SUI GOW 1.50
CRAB MEAT EGG ROLL 1.50	CHINESE BARBECUED PORK 1.50	TERIYAKI STEAK 1.75

From the far corners of the wide world, the Outrigger has assembled the recipes for these exotic drinks. Some are world famous, all are delightful adventures into the mysterious art of Rum drinks.

THE OUTRIGGER COCKTAIL 1.00

The Wedding of Light Puerto Rican Rum, — Apricot Liqueur Makes this Cocktail Delightfully Refreshing with a Distinct "Boo-Kay" (Prize Award Winning Cocktail at the U. K. B. G. West Coast Cocktail Competition, 1958— by POPO)

GOLD CUP 1.00

A Frosty Presentation of Fine Jamaica Rums, Tree Ripened Limes, Syrup, a Few Scant Drops of the "Devil's Own Brew" Very Tongue Loosening . . . Fine Whet to the Negligent Stomach

LIN TIK 1.00

A Delicate Blend of Jamaica and Puerto Rican Rums, Our Own Sweetening Formula, Luscious Tropical Limes, Angostura Bitters Our "Barmeister" Lost his Jiggers Over this Potion

PIKAKE 1.00

Light Puerto Rican Rums, Acapulco Limes, Splash of Van Der Hum Liqueur . . . Spiced Elixir From South Africa. (First Award Winning Cocktail at the U. K. B. G. West Coast Cocktail Competition—1958 by POPO.)

FOG CUTTER 1.60

A Medley of Rum and Brandy, a Whiff of Juniper, a Whisper of Almond. This Drink Either Cuts the Fog or Vice Versa. May We Remind You, the Vicer the Versa.

DR. JEKYLL 1.20

Light Puerto Rican Rum, Persian Limes, Pomegranate Syrup, Impregnated with Pernod (Illegitimate Descendant of "The Green Devil", Which Has Been Outlawed in Most Parts of the World.) Confucious Say: "One Man's Mede is Another Man's Persian."

THE SCORPION 1.60

Fresh Floating Gardenia Lends Enchantment to this Polynesian Favorite. Light Rums Delicately Blended with Tropical Fruit Juices. It's Wickedly, Juicedly Good.

KINI POPO 1.50

Light Puerto Rican Rums, Acapulco Limes Popo's Own Sweetening Formula. Sip with Straws From a Hula Skirt and Watch the Backfield in Motion.

PLANTER'S PUNCH 1.25

Heavy-Bodied Jamaica Rums, Cane Syrup, Luscious Green Limes, Aromatic Bitters . . . a Noble Concoction by Heritage the Classic Long Drink of Jamaica.

TAHITIAN RUM PUNCH 1.00

A Frosty Presentation of Golden Rums and Passion Fruit Nectar. This One Cools Everything Except the Skin. Rum and Not Water is Drunk in the Tropics For Reducing Temperature.

IKA IKA 1.75

Fine West Indies Rums Subtly Blended with Pomelo Juice. Less Sweet and More Potent . . . Kicks Like Bottled Jet Fuel!

PUKKA PUKKA 2.00

French Martinique Rum, Key West Limes— Flavoring Liqueurs. This is Another One to Watch Cautiously Lest Your Pedal Extremities Fold up at Some Inappropriate Moment, A Drink Strictly for Pukkah Sahibs.

PENANG PUNCH 1.75

The Ingenious Union of West Indies Rums, Tropical Fruit Juices—a Few Scant Drops of "Green Muse." This is Strictly a Thinking Man's Tipple.

SUFFERING BASTARD 1.65

Name Conceived by Joe Scialom, "Barmeister," Formerly with the Shepherd's Hotel in Cairo. Rhum St. James, Persian Limes—Flavoring Liqueurs. Over-Consumption of this otherwise Friendly Stimulant and Equalizer May Hex You.

SINGAPORE GIN SLING .1.50

A Delightful Combination of Gin, Lime, Cherry Liqueur—Ginger Beer. The Original Sandakan Sling, Named After the Borneo Port Where it was Invented, now Known as Singapore Sling, Made Famous at the Raffles Bar in Singapore. Decidedly Delicious . . . Slow Acting, But Insidious. "Jaga-Baik-Baik-Tuan" or "Take Carem Master."

only hope he never made it across town to the *Luau*, which boasted no less than 74 exotic drinks—including the Martiki, their "Polynesian answer to a dry Martini."

By the 1960s, even the most sophisticated postwar intellectuals were flocking to Tiki bars. Film directors Bob Fosse and Stanley Kubrick were both regulars at the New York *Trader Vic's*—where, in 1964, Kubrick first voiced the idea that four years later would become *2001: A Space Odyssey*. (We don't know what he was drinking, but he must have given that Cal-Tech professor a run for his money.) In his autobiography, Gore Vidal recalled taking eminent historian Arthur Schlesinger and Nobel-prize winning economist John Kenneth Galbraith to the *Luau*, where, "awash in rum," they broke several spokes off the entrance's huge ship's wheel, shouting "This is the ship of state!" Frank Sinatra was a big fan of the Navy Grog served at the Palm Springs *Don the Beachcomber's*. He was a generous tipper, recalls bartender Tony Ramos, "but he'd scream and shout if he wasn't served fast enough."

As the 1970s dawned, popular tastes began to change. Eventually the Missionary's Downfall gave way to the Screaming Orgasm, and the master mixologists of the golden age scattered to the four winds—taking their expertise, experience, and "secret ingredients" with them. Ask today's bartenders to make you a tropical drink, and the sickly sweet results will sadly confirm Tony Ramos's assertion that exotic cocktail mixology is "a lost art."

However, as of this writing there are still a small handful of places that offer the real thing. The *Mai Kai* in Fort Lauderdale, Florida, and the *Kahiki* in Columbus, Ohio, still serve communal Mystery Drinks in smoking bowls, presented by scantily clad native girls to the sound of ceremonial gongs. And the late Ray Buhen's

SCORPION BOWL

- ounces orange juice
- ounces fresh lemon juice
- 1/2 ounces orgeat syrup
- ounces light Puerto Rican rum
- ounce brandy

Blend with two cups crushed ice and pour into tiki bowl. Add ice cubes to fill. Garnish with a gardenia and serve with long straws. Serves four.

Tiki Ti, now run by his son Mike, is still serving 72 impeccably mixed exotic drinks to the citizens of Los Angeles.

What better way to close this chapter on American alcoholic history than with the words of Ray himself: "It's escapism. It's not real. It's ballyhoo," he said of the faux Polynesian cocktail. And then: "Oh, that was the best time."

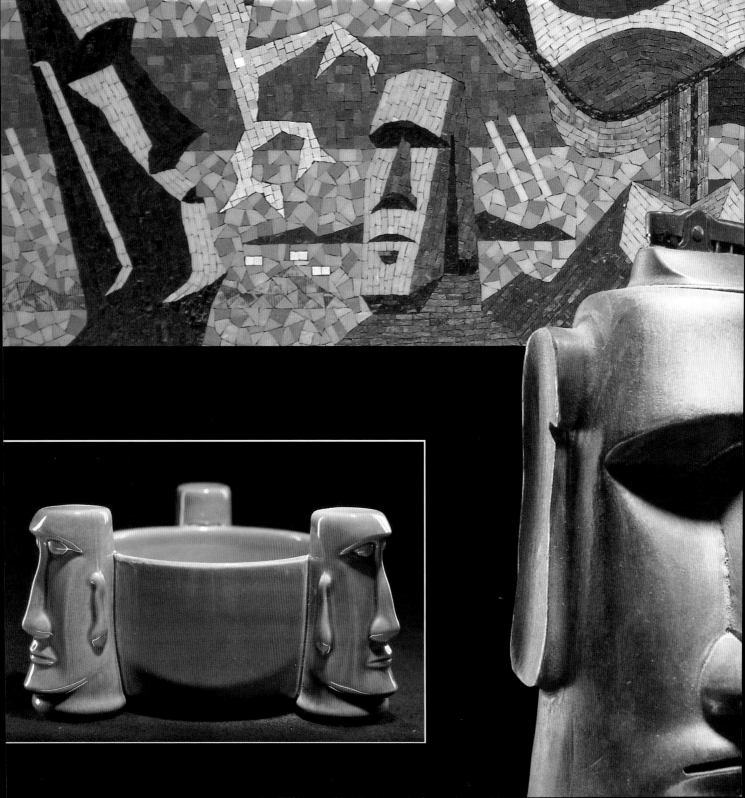

17
HUNTERS AND COLLECTORS

"At first, illustrating a humble story, the objects unfold by degrees a wider meaning, until at last the heart is touched." (Henry Mercer, Collector, 1898)

Like an ancient shard of pottery containing the macrocosm of a whole culture, the Tiki mug is the embodiment of Tiki style. Many an urban archeologist has been excited by the find of such a strange vessel, often representing the first clue to a forgotten Tiki temple. Daring expeditions to remote sites have been occasioned by the cryptic inscriptions found on these ceramics—inscriptions sometimes yielding clues to further artifacts. Thus splendid Polynesian paradises have taken shape again in the memory of the beholder and their histories have been wrested from oblivion.
The infinite variety and whimsical style of the Tiki mug speaks of the creative spirit that pervaded the follow-

ers of Tiki. Its use as a container during the ritual of imbibing so-called Polynesian potions in order to reach an altered state of consciousness underlines the affiliation of Tiki with Cocktail Culture.

A multitude of Tiki bars created specific logo mugs that were unique to their temples and often purchased by rum-happy customers as souvenirs of their brief vacation on these urban islands. But once at home, as time passed, many Tiki mugs ended up in the attic, regarded as temporary lapses of good taste committed in a mood of bohemian daring—aesthetic one-night stands regretted the morning after sobering up. Although the origin of the first true Tiki mug (we estimate around the late 1950s somewhere in California) is shrouded in mystery, the concept of using a human effigy as a receptacle is quite old and connects modern mug collectors to a darker tradition: Andreas Lommel, di-

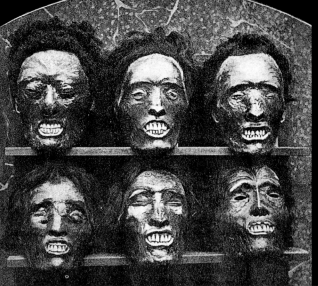

Top Left: Tiki at Kelbo's, L.A.; middle: Maori Mokomai; right: Kelbo's mug; bottom left: Headhunter cocktail container from Ren Clark's Polynesian Village, Fort Worth (p. 44).

Oben links: Tiki im Kelbo's, L.A.; mitte: Maori Makomai; rechts: Kelbo's-Krug; unten links: Kopfjäger-Cocktailgefäß von Ren Clarks Polynesian Village, Fort Worth (S. 44)

En haut, à gauche: Tiki au Kelbo's, Los Angeles; au centre: Mokomai maori; à droite: chope du Kelbo's; en bas à gauche: Récipient à cocktail de chasseur de têtes du Ren Clark's Polynesian Village, Fort Worth (page 44).

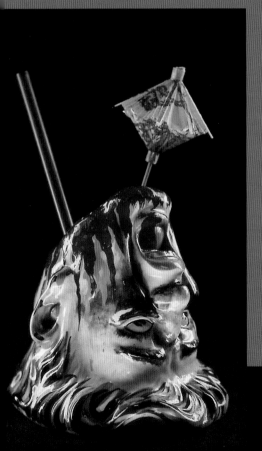

rector of the Munich Museum of Anthropology, describes in *Prehistoric and Primitive Man* how the belief that the human head contained the largest share of *mana* (or life-power) led to head worship and ultimately to the custom of headhunting, with the purpose of accumulating as much mana as possible. According to Lommel, "In widely separated areas of the Pacific, vessels shaped like human heads were clearly substitutes for captured trophies."

Thus contemporary Tiki mug collectors can be likened to 20th-century headhunters, lining up their prizes like tribal relics on the skull rack in the ceremonial *Haus Tambaran*. The collecting of heads as souvenirs is not entirely without precedence. Although recently Tiki mug collecting has become an obsession for some, it will hardly reach the extremes described by Major-General Robley in

RIGHT: The Mainlander mug, which took its design from a Witco fountain (far right).
BOTTOM: Witco Tiki fountain manufacture

RECHTS: „Mainlander"-Krug, der seine Form von einem Witco-Springbrunnen hat (ganz rechts).
UNTEN: Witco-Tiki-Springbrunnenmanufaktur

A DROITE: Chope du «Mainlander» qui tire son design d'une fontaine de Witco (extrême droite).
EN BAS À DROITE: La manufacture de fontaines Tiki de Witco

The Mainlander
SAINT LOUIS

LEFT: Self-portrait mug (1889) and mug sketche by Paul Gauguin

LINKS: Selbstbildnis als Krug (1889) und Krugzeichnungen von Paul Gauguin

AU CENTRE À GAUCHE: Chope autoportrait (1889) et dessins de chopes par Paul Gauguin

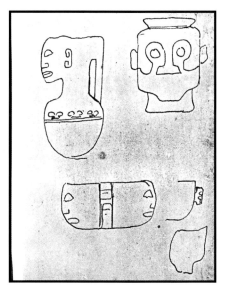

New Zealand, in his *Traffic in Heads* in 1896: "Until Europeans began to visit New Zealand and to settle here, the Maoris' *Moko-mai* (dried and tatooed heads) were of sentimental interest only [Robley's take on ancestor worship? – author] and had no commercial value. But the desire on the part of museums and collectors to possess them as curiosities caused a large demand to spring up. The Maori for his part was eager to obtain fire-arms, ammunition and iron implements. His reluctance to part with the heads was overcome, and such brisk a traffic sprang up that the demand exceeded the supply. It considerably reduced the population of New Zealand; but stocked the museums of Europe with barbaric

ABOVE: The "Sneaky Tiki" mug and utensils from the Polynesian Room on the top floor of Harvey's Wagon Wheel Hotel and Casino in snowy Lake Tahoe, California. RIGHT: The Pub Tiki's cryptic mug design becomes clearer after viewing the plate imprint.

OBEN: Der „Sneaky Tiki"-Krug und Utensilien aus dem „Polynesian Room" im Obergeschoss von Harveys Wagon Wheel Hotel and Casino im verschneiten Lake Tahoe, Kalifornien. RECHTS: Die geheimnisvolle Form des Pub-Tiki-Kruges wird verständlicher, betrachtet man das Logo auf dem Teller.

EN HAUT: La chope du «Sneaky Tiki» et des ustensiles du «Polynesian Room» au niveau supérieur du Harvey's Wagon Wheel Hôtel et Casino au Lake Tahoe enneigé, en Californie. A DROITE: Le dessin crypté de la chope du Pub Tiki devient plus clair lorsque l'on regarde le motif sur l'assiette.

Left: The Beauty and the Beast motif is ingeniously realized in this unique Hawaii Kai Tiki mug from New York.
Below: Another variation on the theme from the same site

Links: Das „Die Schöne und das Biest"-Muster ist bei diesem einzigartigen „Hawaii Kai"-Tiki-Krug aus New York großartig umgesetzt.
Unten: Eine Variation zu dem Thema von demselben Ort

A gauche: Le thème de la Belle et la Bête est ingénieusement réalisé dans cette chope Tiki unique du «Hawaii Kai» de New York.
En bas: Une autre variation du même site sur le thème

The modern Marquesan design of these Tiki mugs by Paul Marshall Products (P.M.P.) was a big hit. They were not only adopted by restaurants and suburban partyers alike, but they also spawned a whole family of articles, ranging from party lights to soap-on-a-rope.

Das moderne Marquesa-Design dieser Tiki-Krüge von Paul Marshall Products (P.M.P.) war ein Riesenerfolg. Sie wurden nicht nur von Restaurants und auf Vorstadt-Partys benutzt, sondern brachten eine ganze Familie von Artikeln hervor, von Party-leuchten bis zu „Soap on a rope".

Le design Marquises moderne de ces chopes Tiki par Paul Marshall Products (P.M.P.) fut un grand succès. Elles ne furent pas seulement utilisées par les restaurants et les noceurs suburbains, mais donnèrent naissance à toute une gamme d'articles, des lampes de fête au « savon à cordelette. »

face culture; furthermore, as commercial enterprise, the traffic was not without profit. Freshly done and inferior heads took the place of the genuine: when well preserved, it was felt that a newly tatooed head looked just as good as an aged one. The chiefs were not slow in taking advantage of the discovery and set

Above: Westwood Tiki mugs came in a variety of designs that all shared a graphic, rather stiff style. Pictured here is an almost complete dish set, including oil and vinegar bottles.
Below: What Toby Tiki products lacked in style, they made up for by inventive suggestions (right).

Oben: „Westwood"-Tiki-Krüge gab es in verschiedensten Ausführungen, die graphisch, aber eher steif wirkten. Hier sieht man einen fast vollständigen Geschirrsatz, einschließlich Essig und Öl-Flaschen.
Unten: Was „Toby"-Tiki-Produkten an Stil fehlte, machten sie durch ihren Erfindungsreichtum wett (rechts).

En haut: Les chopes Tiki «Westwood» connurent une variété de designs qui avaient en commun un style graphique plutôt rigide. On voit ici un ensemble de table presque complet comprenant même les flacons d'huile et de vinaigre.
En bas: Le manque de style des produits Tiki du «Toby» était compensé par des suggestions inventives (à droite).

to work to kill the least valuable of their slaves, tatooing their heads first as though they had belonged to men of high rank, then drying and selling them. J. S. Wood claims, "In the first place no man who was well tatooed was safe for an hour unless he was a great chief, for he might be at any-time watched until he was off his guard and then knocked down and killed, his head sold to the traders. Old grudges were raked up and small local wars undertaken to keep up the supply. The traffic continued to increase, and as the quality deteriorated, the dealers became dissatisfied, and some of them, who went personally to select living slaves whose heads they were willing to buy, were overtaken by a fate that deserves little pity."

Modern Tiki mugs were mostly manufactured in Japan, the cheapest source for promotional gift items. The leading producer was O.M.C., or

TD-325 MAR-HITI SET
This Tiki mixing tumbler is an exact ceramic reproduction of a Tahitian Tiki woodcarving. From this we derived the name MAR-HITI SET. The "Mar" for that ever popular cocktail - the martini "Hiti" from Tahiti.
The mixing tumbler has other uses too, such as mixing other cocktails, as a vase and due to its large (20 oz. approx.) capacity makes an ideal beer Tiki.
The Tiki Head drinking cups also double as dispensers for cigarettes, mustard, relishes and other condiments.

TOBY DESIGNS

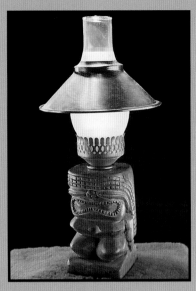

Otagiri Merchandising. Restaurants would send in their designs for O.M.C. to mold 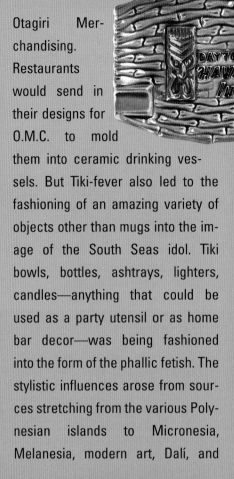 them into ceramic drinking vessels. But Tiki-fever also led to the fashioning of an amazing variety of objects other than mugs into the image of the South Seas idol. Tiki bowls, bottles, ashtrays, lighters, candles—anything that could be used as a party utensil or as home bar decor—was being fashioned into the form of the phallic fetish. The stylistic influences arose from sources stretching from the various Polynesian islands to Micronesia, Melanesia, modern art, Dalí, and

TIKI HIBACHI

REGISTERED

CANAPE
SNACKS
COFFEE
WARMER

E WITH : A PACKAGE OF SKEWERS
LIFTER ASBESTOS TABLE PAD

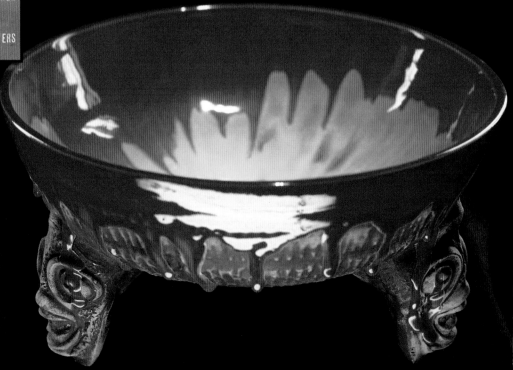

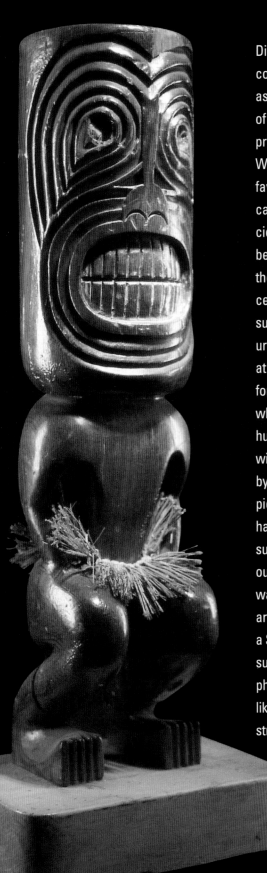

Disney. Authenticity and cultural correctness were secondary as long as the artifacts embodied the spirit of Tiki, a combination of savagery, primitivism, and whimsy.

When the urban Tiki cult fell out of favor, these god-heads were discarded or hidden, just as their ancient Polynesian counterparts had been after the missionary efforts on the islands had done away with ancestor worship and idolatry. Today such relics are being unearthed by urban archeologists in thrift stores, at flea markets, and yard sales. Unfortunately the internet has somewhat taken the challenge out of Tiki hunting, allowing armchair explorers with the necessary time and money by means of a few mouseclicks to pick up rarities that otherwise would have necessitated daring efforts such as investigative expeditions to outlying suburbs. Obsessive price wars on auction web sites like e-bay are the result, jacking up the rate of a St. Louis Mainlander mug to an absurd $103. This kind of greedy trophy-hunting is rather unsportsmanlike. On the other hand we must strongly discourage field collecting, which means ripping off artifacts from the few still extant Tiki sites whose already feeble mana will be further deplenished by such looting.

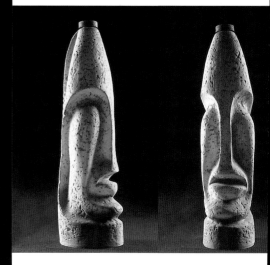

ABOVE: *A modern, a Dalí-esque, and a cartoon specimen.* RIGHT AND BOTTOM RIGHT: *Two wall hangings, by Hip and Coco Joe's, two Hawaii-based souvenir manufacturers.* BOTTOM: *This Tahitian love mask bears no trace of true Tahitian art.*

OBEN: *Ein modernes, ein an Dalí erinnerndes und ein Comicstrip-Exemplar.* RECHTS UND UNTEN RECHTS: *Zwei Wandbehänge, von „Hip" und „Coco Joe's", zwei Souvenirherstellern aus Hawaii.* UNTEN: *Diese „tahitische Liebesmaske" trägt keinerlei Spuren von echter tahitischer Kunst.*

EN HAUT: *Un spécimen moderne, un daliesque et un cartoonesque;* À DROITE ET EN BAS À DROITE: *Deux décorations murales censées être réalisées avec un composé de lave/plastique par «Hip» et «Coco Joe's», deux fabricants de souvenirs basés à Hawaii.* EN BAS: *Ce «Masque d'amour tahitien» ne porte aucune marque d'authentique art tahitien.*

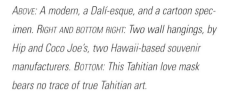

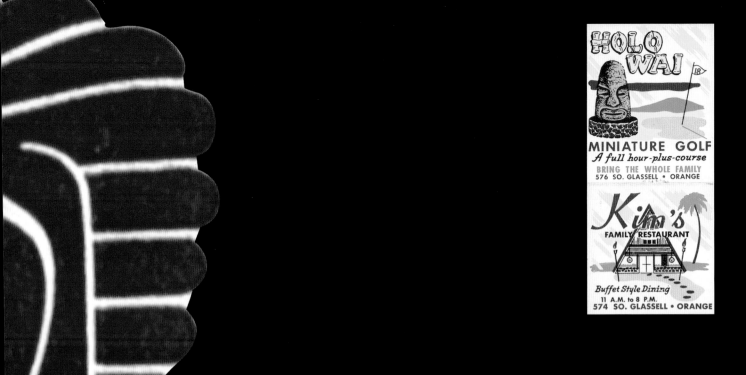

AND THE GODS WERE AMUSED

18

Hawaii, 1820, party time. Observing the natives at a hula marathon as they are offering leis (flower garlands) to a god-head, missionary Hiram Bingham tries to understand: "What purpose does your god serve, what is he good for?" Their simple answer puzzles him: "For play!" Incomprehensible to the early 19th-century Puritan, just over a century later this answer was something Americans were ready to understand. Their righteousness and modesty had brought them through the Depression and helped them win the Second World War. Economic security seemed within everyone's grasp and now the time had come to play. But the steadfast morals of the forefathers that constrained

SEE TIKI GARDENS

"South Sea Island Paradise in Florida"

TROPICAL PARADISE
by day

POLYNESIAN FANTASY
at night

Visit a strange and exciting world;
the enchanting land of pagan customs
— truly a Polynesian Paradise

BEAUTIFUL MACAWS

THRILL TO THE BRILLIANT COLORS OF
OUR EXOTIC MACAWS, PHEASANTS
AND OTHER SPECIES OF BIRDS
LAUGH AT OUR ENTERTAINING
MONKEYS

"KAHONA" THE WATER GOD

SEE OUR BIG GARDEN
ALIVE WITH BEAUTIFUL PEACOCKS
AND POLYNESIAN LORE

FISHING GOD

HUNDREDS OF COLORFUL
BIRDS FLY IN THE
PARAKEET BELL TOWER

VISIT 7 FASCINATING SHOPS

- Polynesian Shop • Famous Signal House
- Oriental Shop • Basket Mart
- Souvenir Shop • Tahiti Hut • Lotus House

plus Trader Frank's Restaurant and Pier Kahiki

this desire were not easily shed. An alternative world had to be created where one could assume a less restrained persona. The seemingly carefree culture of Polynesia became the escapist counter-reality of choice. Wherever fun could be had, Tiki ruled.

Through the multitude of concepts employed to entertain their customers, Tiki bars had already become little amusement parks in themselves. So it was a natural development to integrate Tiki temples into game parks or to create Tiki parks in their own right. The vacation states of California and Florida offered the right combination of recreation-seekers and climate, and so whole Tiki worlds like Tiki Gardens and The Tikis arose. Of course the Big Kahuna of amusement parks, Walt Disney himself, did not lag behind. A frequent customer in Polynesian supper clubs, he decided to create a Tiki restaurant that

Now completely vanished, Tiki Gardens once included Trader Frank's restaurant and a Bou-Tiki among its shops.

Im „Tiki Gardens"-Park, der heute völlig von der Bildfläche verschwunden ist, gab es ein Trader Frank's-Restaurant und ein Bou-Tiki in der Ladenzeile.

Aujourd'hui totalement disparus, les «Tiki Gardens» offraient jadis parmi leurs commerces un restaurant Trader Frank's et un Bou-Tiki.

would top all existing ones. Walt was an animator, and so to him the logical next step was to make all the usual decor, the flowers, birds, and Tikis come alive. It was the spirit of Tiki that inspired Disney to come up with the concept of "Audio-Animatronics" that later became the heart of many of Disneyland's attractions. But as the project neared completion, the space age technology of 225 robotic performers directed by a fourteen-channel magnetic tape feeding one hundred separate speakers and controlling 438 separate actions had outgrown the space of the restaurant, and so rather than compromising the complexity of the show, Walt decided to eliminate the restaurant and make the show an attraction in its own right. When "The Enchanted Tiki Room" opened in 1963, the New York Times wrote: "POLARIS TAPE AIDS DISNEY ANIMATION—New Synchronizing Device Makes Totem Poles Talk … In the Enchanted Tiki Room scores of brilliantly colored synthetic birds talk, sing or whistle. Carved pagan gods beat drums and chant in weird syllables. Storms are created and fountains play. Artificial parrots hold conversations in several dialects."

An exalted and rather intellectual review by Stanford professor Don D. Jackson, M.D., Director of the Palo Alto Mental Research Institute, compares the Tiki Room to other man-made power places. Speaking of : "PLAY, PARADOX AND PEOPLE: AWE IN DISNEYLAND," he describes having felt "… as great a sense of awe, wonderment and reverence sitting in the synthetic, fabricated, instant-Polynesian Tiki Room at Disneyland, as I have experienced in some of the great cathedrals – Chartres, Rheims, and Notre Dame … In a fake hut, fake parrots play-sang not very estimable tunes, but the colors were a riot of rainbows and the parrots moved their beaks in precision—now this group, now

NOW PLAYING IN ADVENTURELAND...

WALT DiSNEY'S ENCHANTED TiKi ROOM

Introducing—for the first time anywhere—an entirely new dimension in Entertainment! Walt Disney's entertainment magic and the wonders of space-age electronics combine to produce a sit-down theatre show that completely surrounds you, starring a cast of more than 200 birds, flowers and tropical Tikis... all **brought to life** through the wonders of AUDIO ANIMATRONICS! 10 years in research and development at a cost of more than $1,000,000...now in its premiere engagement in Adventureland!

SEE! HEAR! ENJOY!

A "musical fantasy" complete with COMEDY starring those extraordinary Masters of Ceremonies, the fabulous "Four MacAudios"...TROPICAL MELODIES whistled and warbled by exotic Song Birds...the dramatic and surprising "HAWAIIAN WAR CHANT" featuring the wondrous Tikis and Tiki Drummers.. A MUSICAL LUAU brought to life by boatloads of beautiful Orchids...the breath-taking BIRDMOBILE ...the ENCHANTED FOUNTAIN...a new CALYPSO hit plus 5 more special songs...and the ENCHANTED TIKI GARDEN "where fantasy and legend walk, hand in hand with Tiki Talk."

IMPORTANT NOTICE

Admission tickets to the Enchanted Tiki Room and Garden are available at the GATEWAY TO ADVENTURELAND.

* * * * * * * * * * * *

Tickets are NOT included in Disneyland Ticket Books.

3 Shows Every Hour!

UTI

PELE
GOD OF
VOLCANOES

ABOVE: Original renderings by Rolly Crump for the exterior Tiki Garden in front of the "Enchanted Tiki Room"

OBEN: Originaldarstellungen von Rolly Crump für den Tiki-Garten vor dem „Enchanted Tiki Room"

CI-DESSUS: Croquis originaux de Rolly Crump pour le jardin tiki devant le «Enchanted Tiki Room»

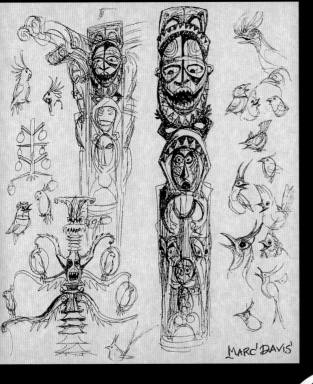

that, never faltering, always surprising. Then the great totems (Tiki) in various corners of the hexagonal room broke into mobile faces, singing and chanting, and soon the songs of men and birds were joined by the songs of flowers. It was like a moment from dimly remembered, complicated dreams." And Jackson goes on to laud the creator: "Disney was a master executive capable of harnessing vast numbers of talented people to work out the details of his childlike vision. Like an innocent, Disney did not recognize the ordinary limitations implied by knowledge. All his creative productions realize the visions of childhood—they reach beyond the stars."

Among the talented people Walt put on the Tiki Room project were artist Rolly Crump, who designed the Tiki tree and statues in the Tiki Garden (the waiting area in front of the hut),

and animator Marc Davis, one of Disney's original "nine old men." Davis had started as an assistant animator for *Snow White and the Seven Dwarfs*, worked on *Bambi,* and drawn the Cruella De Ville character in *101 Dalmations*. His interest in Papuan New Guinea art was mirrored in his designs for the interior of the Tiki Room.

Tiki theme parks appeared in all sizes, from miniature golf courses to complete coaster rides. The Pacific

Ocean Park that once existed at the end of the Santa Monica pier offered a Beachcomber ride that, hovering over the sea and connected by a cable railway above, went around an artificial lagoon and volcano, both constructed on a platform separated from the end of the pier.

Another form of family fun center that took up the Tiki theme was the bowling alley. Mostly the adjacent lounges, but sometimes complete establishments, were dedicated to the god of recreation. Bowling originated in German monasteries, where monks had churchgoers knock down a bottle-shaped object

Ashtrays, matchbooks, towels, and signage are the only evidence remaining of Tiki bowlingalleys today.

Aschenbecher, Streichholzschachteln, Handtücher und Logos sind das einzige, was von Tiki übriggeblieben ist.

Cendriers, pochettes d'allumettes, serviettes et logos sont les seules traces qui restent de tiki aujourd'hui.

197

known as a *Kegel* to prove their devotion to God. The wooden *Kegel* represented the devil, and upsetting it meant complete absolution from sin. We do not know whether Tiki-shaped bowling pins ever existed, but certainly in many places, aloha shirts and bowling shirts mixed freely while tropical libations steadied the aim of the Tiki revellers. One such place was the elaborate *Kapu Kai* (or "Forbidden Sea") in Rancho Cucamonga, an obscure suburb of Los Angeles (see also p. 55). Four jutting A-frame entrances beckoned the believers. The Tikis stationed around the building and between the lanes were carved by Milan Guanko. His relief Tikis at the entrance door welcomed the arriving devotees with a smile, but frowned on the inside at any deserters. Tiki carpeting lined the floors and the Tahititian Fire Room sported amazing Tapacloth fire murals. Still, despite it's inspired designs, the *Kapu Kai* did not survive the end of the 20th century.

Above: Classic Milan Guanko Tikis are grouped under the entrance A-frame.
Below: The tropical materials were provided by Oceanic Arts.

Oben: Klassische Tikis von Milan Guanko sind unter dem A-förmigen Eingang aufgestellt.
Unten: Die tropischen Materialien wurden von Oceanic Arts geliefert.

Ci-dessus: Des tiki classiques de Milan Guanco sont rassemblés sous le porche en A.
Ci-dessous: Les matériaux tropicaux étaient fournis par Oceanic Arts.

199

Tourism and Tikis went hand in hand in 1960s America, and since motel signs were the totem poles of American roadside culture, many utilized the Tiki image as attention-getters. Lighthouses in the urban sea, their neon or gas-fed Tiki torches flickered as beacons for weary travellers and modern traders. Polynesia was now reachable by car. The motel was an American mutation of the hotel, created for that four-wheeled holy cow of the car cult, the symbol of progress and prosperity, the American car of the 1950s. The sky was the limit for American car makers in the 50s, the size and design of their products reaching the dimensions of space ships. These hovercrafts needed easy access harbors, with places for their pilots to rest for the next trip. To mark these space ports in the vast urban universe, giant glowing signs were erected by the trade routes.

Thus the motel sign is a classic symbol of Americana culture. It appears

119

HOTEL, MOTEL...

a true "sign" of ignorance then that the city of Anaheim, home of Disneyland, which caters to international tourists in search of American pop culture, would destroy motel signs like the *Pitcairn* in the course of their "beautification" campaign as recently as 1998. It has been noted that a cultural icon is in it's greatest peril of being destroyed right before it's value gets rediscovered. Consequently we can now look forward to having a bad replica of such signs erected in Disneyland in a couple of years, right next to fake diners equipped with 50's car parts. The *Hanalei* sign in San Diego is a perfect "Before" and "After" example of corporate ignorance, where for the sake of modernization generic

LEFT: Despite being a classic symbol of Tiki Moderne, the Pitcairn Motel sign was toppled as recently as 1998.

LINKS: Obwohl das Pitcairn-Motelzeichen ein klassisches Symbol der Tiki-Moderne war, wurde es erst kürzlich, 1998, abgerissen.

A GAUCHE: Bien qu'étant un symbole classique du modernisme tiki, l'emblème du motel Pitcairn fut détruit en 1998.

Also gone are the Tahitian Village in Downey (above), and the Hawaiian Isle in Miami, Florida (below).

Ebenfalls verschwunden sind das Tahitian Village in Downey (oben) und das Hawaiin Isle in Miami, Florida (unten).

Le Tahitian Village à Downey (en haut) et le Hawaiian Isle à Miami, Floride (en bas), ont également disparu.

blandness replaces individual expression. Just like the iconographic "Stardust" sign in Las Vegas (page 114/115), it has been replaced with bland Helvetica type which has no connection with the theme. Since Polynesian style was identified as "passé", even though the *Islands* restaurant interior at the hotel has been largely left intact, the new entrance bears no trace of the Tiki treasures hidden inside: Many of the artifacts in this eatery and in the highrise atrium of the hotel actually stem from another important Tiki site, the defunct *Luau* in Beverly Hills (page 100). The closing of this Polynesian power spot coincided with the opening of the San Diego hotel's new addition. The original owner was a confirmed Polynesiac and supposedly had the new section blessed by an original Hawaiian Kahuna.

Yet just as with other Tiki temples, Tiki motels not only flourished in the climatically milder zones, but in other American states as well. The Tiki Motor Inn in Lake George, New York State, had artifical palm trees grouped around the main building which greened even in the snow. As of late this "Oasis of Tropical Splendor" was still in operation, although we cannot say in what condition. But the only true Tiki motel chain arose in the desert cities of

The Hanalei Hotel with it's "Islands" restaurant in San Diego, California, is the site of a curious discovery by the author and urban archeologist: Upon studying postcards and menu illustrations (left page, bottom) of the Luau in Los Angeles, it was found that upon closing the so far presumed to be lost Tiki artifacts of the Luau had been traded down south to the Hanalei. Apparently a huge hole was cut into the roof of the restaurant, and not only numerous large Tikis, but the complete entrance hut (left) were lifted out by crane and shipped to San Diego.

Das Hanalei-Hotel mit seinem Islands-Restaurant in San Diego, Kalifornien, ist der Ort einer seltsamen Entdeckung des Autors und Stadtarchäologen: Beim Studieren von Postkarten und Speisekartenillustrationen (unten links) aus dem Luau in Los Angeles fand er heraus, dass bei der Schließung des Luau die bisher als verloren geglaubten Tiki-Artefakte an das weiter südlich gelegene Hanalei verkauft worden waren. Offenbar hat man ein riesiges Loch in das Dach des Restaurants geschnitten und nicht nur etliche große Tikis, sondern die gesamte Eingangshütte (links) mit einem Kran herausgehoben und nach San Diego transportiert.

L'hôtel Hanalei avec son restaurant «Islands» à San Diego, Californie, est le site d'une étrange découverte faite par cet auteur et archéologue urbain. En étudiant les cartes postales et les illustrations du menu (en bas à gauche) du Luau à Los Angeles, on a découvert que peu avant la fermeture de l'établissement, ses objets tiki, que l'on croyait perdus, avaient été transférés plus au sud, au Hanalei. Apparemment la plupart des ornementations du toit du restaurant furent enlevées, et de nombreux grands tikis, ainsi que la totalité de l'entrée de la hutte (à gauche) soulevés avec une grue et transportés à San Diego.

California: Ken Kimes once operated forty motels of which five were decked out with Tikis by the craftsmen from Oceanic Arts: The *Tropics* in Indio, Blythe, Rosemead, Modesto and Palm Springs. Four of them still

OPEN ALL YEAR
Overlooking Beautiful Lake George

ALOHA HOLIDAYS

In an Oasis of Tropical Splendor transplanted to Lake George,
in New York State's Beautiful Adirondack Mountains

AKUA MOTOR HOTEL "At the jungle's edge"
1018 E. ORANGETHORPE • ANAHEIM, CALIF.
Phone TRojan 1-2830 - TWX FULCAL 5340

ABOVE: The Akua Motor Hotel was part of a whole complex that included the Palms Restaurant (page 156) and the Jungle Gardens, where monkeys and exotic birds roamed.

OBEN: Das Akua-Motor Hotel gehörte zu einem größeren Gebäudekomplex, in dem sich auch das Palms-Restaurant (Seite 156) und der „Dschungel"-Park befanden, wo Affen herumsprangen und exotische Vögel zwitscherten.

EN HAUT: Le Akua Motor Hotel faisait partie de tout un complexe comprenant également le restaurant Palms (page 156) et les jardins de la Jungle peuplés de singes et d'oiseaux exotiques.

feature Tikis that have fared well in their dry climate. The Palm Springs *Tropics* is the most elaborate, although the *Reef* bar has recently been renovated in the Mexican motif. Hopefully the rediscovery of Palm Springs as a hub of mid-century modernism will aid the preservation of this rare Tiki Temple.

Right: This rendering is the only evidence left of the Rosemead Tropics in Los Angeles, while the Palm Springs Tropics (all other illustrations) displays several graven images up to this day. The Modesto Tropics also has a Tiki Lounge still in operation, while its pool was once called the Tiki Lagoon.

Rechts: Diese Zeichnung ist das einzige, was von den Rosemead Tropics in Los Angeles übrig geblieben ist, während das Tropics in Palm Springs (alle anderen Abbildungen) bis heute mit etlichen geschnitzten Figuren geschmückt ist. Das Tropics in Modesto verfügt über eine Tiki-Lounge, die noch immer in Betrieb ist; sein Swimmingpool wurde einst „Tiki Lagune" genannt.

A droite : Cette illustration est la seule trace laissée par le Rosemead Tropics à Los Angeles, alors que le Palm Springs Tropics (toutes les autres illustrations) expose encore aujourd'hui plusieurs figures sculptées. Le Modesto Tropics possède également un bar tiki encore en activité, et sa piscine était autrefois appelée le lagon tiki.

Really live it up at the **tropics**, Palm Springs

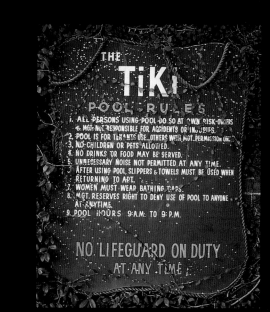

THE
TiKi
POOL RULES

1. ALL PERSONS USING POOL DO SO AT OWN RISK-OWNERS
6. MGT. NOT RESPONSIBLE FOR ACCIDENTS OR INJURIES.
2. POOL IS FOR TENANTS USE...OTHERS WITH MGT. PERMISSION ONLY.
3. NO CHILDREN OR PETS ALLOWED.
4. NO DRINKS OR FOOD MAY BE SERVED.
5. UNNECESSARY NOISE NOT PERMITTED AT ANY TIME.
   AFTER USING POOL SLIPPERS & TOWELS MUST BE USED WHEN
   RETURNING TO APT.
7. WOMEN MUST WEAR BATHING CAPS.
8. MGT. RESERVES RIGHT TO DENY USE OF POOL TO ANYONE
   AT ANYTIME.
9. POOL HOURS 9 A.M. TO 9 P.M.

NO LIFEGUARD ON DUTY
AT ANY TIME

20

UNEQUALLED IN BACHELOR LIVING

"… cross the hand-carved footbridge above the fiery pit of the goddess PELE, where the lava is about to boil and the land is about to tremble, then you're in the region supreme over all—a domain far from stresses, cares and worries, yet merely minutes from public transportation, churches and just seconds from the mainland … In this fantastic setting, PELE knows all. She has been, and shall always be, in the pantheon of Hawaiian worship. You will relax and lounge in the sun around the palm-studded swimming area with the flowing waters of the coral fountain falling into the beautifully contoured lagoon. On the inside footbridge you will find yourself amidst the ruins of her domain, where the remains of Hopoe and Lohiau have been transformed into two large rocks in the turbulent waters cascading down the lava-covered side of a seething

volcano. Here, within the Consolation of the Gods, you can make your home, live among the beautiful palms in a setting unequalled in bachelor living … Just pick up your key and become another of the inhabitants of this exotic little village in the center a bustling city."

ABOVE: The Pomona Polynesia, winner of the 1967 beautification award. Through the entrance we can glimpse the traditional A-frame pool hut.

BELOW, LEFT: The record cover that inspired the apartments; MIDDLE: The Pele, the 1959 all-aluminum "dream car" designed by Kaiser; RIGHT: The interior of the space-age Kaiser Aluminum Dome in Waikiki, where the album was recorded.

OBEN: Das Pomona Polynesia, Gewinner des „Schönheitswettbewerbs" von 1967. Durch den Eingang schaut man auf die Pool-Hütte in traditioneller A-Form. UNTEN, LINKS: Die Plattenhülle, die die Anregung zu der Wohnanlage gab; MITTE: Das Traumauto „Pele" ganz aus Aluminium, 1959 von Kaiser entworfen; RECHTS: Das Innere des Weltraumzeitalter-Kuppelbaus in Waikiki, der Kaiser Aluminum Dome, wo die Platte aufgenommen wurde.

CI-DESSUS: Le Pomona Polynesia, vainqueur du concours d'embellissement. A travers l'entrée, on aperçoit la hutte avec la traditionnelle structure en A. CI-DESSOUS, À GAUCHE: La pochette de disque qui inspira la Résidence; AU CENTRE: La voiture de rêve «Pele» de 1959, tout en aluminium, dessinée par Kaiser; À DROITE: L'intérieur de l'Aluminium Dome de Kaiser à Waikiki, où l'album fut enregistré.

This evocative example of Polynesian pop poetry from the brochure of the *Pele* Apartments gives an idea of the pains developers went through to create these "Polynesian" settlements of the targeted recreation seekers. The architectural concepts employed all hailed from Tiki restaurants and lounges, and in the unique case of the *Pele* Apartments, even the typeface and liner notes of a popular Exotica album were copied as well. Arthur Lyman's *Pele* also inspired the name of a prototype car, built by the same aluminum company

The postcard of the Pomona Polynesia and the rendering on the Pele apartments brochure substantially display all the features that were characteristic of these Tiki islands in the urban sea.

Die Postkarte vom Pomona Polynesia und die Darstellung der Pele-Wohnanlage zeigen alle Elemente, die charakteristisch für diese Tiki-Inseln inmitten des Großstadtozeans waren.

La carte postale du Pomona Polynesia et le dessin de la Résidence Pele présentent toutes les caractéristiques essentielles de ces îles tiki dans la mer urbaine.

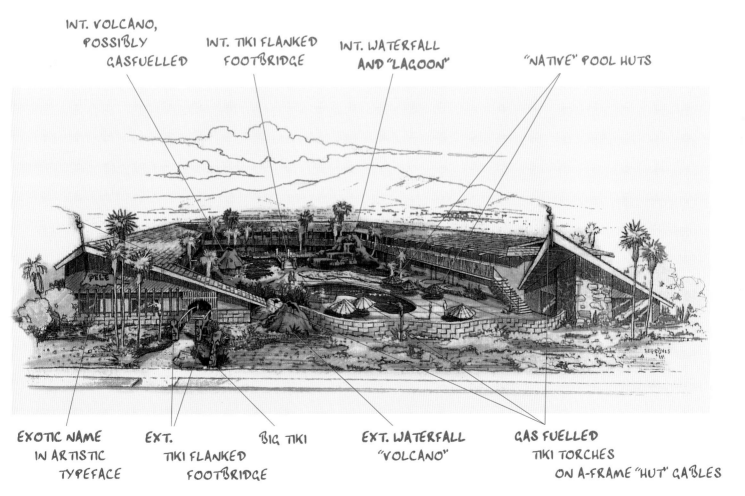

ABOVE: The "abandoned village" installation at the Shelter Isle apartments. Palm trees and Tikis were often planted at oblique angles to enhance the illusion of wilderness.

OBEN: Das „Verlassene Dorf", eine Gartenanlage in dem Shelter Isle-Wohnkomplex. Palmen und Tikis wurden häufig schief und krumm aufgestellt, um die Illusion von Wildnis zu verstärken.

CI-DESSUS: Le «village abandonné» de la Résidence Shelter Isle. Les palmiers et les tiki étaient souvent disposés en biais pour renforcer l'illusion de jungle.

BELOW: A driftwood style sign

UNTEN: Ein Schild im Treibholz-Stil

CI-DESSOUS: Un caractère stylistique en bois flotté

that had constructed the dome where Lyman had recorded his record. Henry J. Kaiser, industrial magnate and owner of the „Kaiser Aluminum Corporation," was a Polynesiac who initially wanted to retire in Hawaii, but once there, built the *Hawaiian Village Hotel* and the *Kaiser Aluminum Dome* as a venue for his favorite music. In 1960, to live in the *Pele* Apartments, drive a *Pele* car, and listen to the jungle jazz of Arthur Lyman's *Pele* album was the dream of every modern primitive.

Another fine concept of apartment living was realized by the same developer at the *Shelter Isle* apartment complex, whose advertising text foreshadowed the demise of its own culture twenty years later: "As one leaves the recreation area and leisurely meanders along the winding pathways he suddenly finds himself amidst the ruins of an abandoned village. Here the remains of a native settlement stand lonely beside a small lake fed by turbulent waters cascading down the lava-covered sides of a seething volcano."

When urban archeologists discovered this installation in the mid-nineties, all that remained of the "remains" were overgrown clumps of lava rock beside a pond. In general though, Tiki villages (Polynesian apartment complexes) today provide the Tiki cultural archeologist with a more rewarding environment, having survived the abolishment of idolatry better then their progenitors, the Tiki temples (restaurants and lounges). Not as dependent on changes in taste as the

Two A-frames house the entrance guardians presenting water and fire.

Zwei A-Formen beherbergen die Eingangswächter, die früher Wasser und Feuer darboten.

A l'entrée de deux maisons en A, les gardiens présentent l'eau et le feu.

restaurant industry, these villages sometimes represent virtual sanctuaries of that endangered species, the Tiki.

Although some owners and managers have tried with missionary zeal to "update" such sites, and many Tikis have rotted away or been stolen

"Streamlined appointments": primitive art and blazing torches

„Stromlinienförmige Anlagen", primitive Kunst und lodernde Fackeln

«Installations aérodynamiques», art primitif et torches flamboyantes

by grave robbers, scanning the urban sea of L. A. for tall palm trees and A-frame structures can still yield spectacular discoveries. At the *Tahitian Village* in the San Fernando Valley, two Gauguinesque native sculptures flanking the entrance bridge represent the archetypes of fire and water. Water once spouted from the mouth of the male, then fell into his hands, and emptied into the moat under the bridge, while the female held an open gas flame in her hand. A seven-foot-tall concrete mask, Tiki support posts, and the ubiquitous crossed spear-and-shield iron railing are among the other features of this settlement.

ABOVE: The main waterfall at the Polynesian Village featured gas jets below the surface of the water. The vegetation was still young just after its planting in 1961.
LEFT AND BELOW: Tiki villages established themselves everywhere.

OBEN: Der zentrale Wasserfall im Polynesian Village hatte Gasfackeln unter der Wasseroberfläche. Kurz nach der Eröffnung im Jahre 1961 war die Vegetation noch jung.
LINKS UND UNTEN: Überall im Land entstanden Tiki-Dörfer.

CI-DESSUS: La cascade centrale du Polynesian Village abritait des torches à gaz sous la surface de l'eau. La végétation était encore jeune en 1961.
A GAUCHE ET CI-DESSOUS: Les villages tiki s'établirent partout.

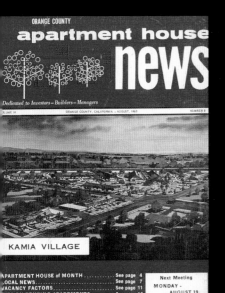

ORANGE COUNTY
apartment house
news
Dedicated to Investors – Builders – Managers

ORANGE COUNTY, CALIFORNIA – AUGUST, 1963   NUMBER 8

KAMIA VILLAGE

APARTMENT HOUSE of MONTH	See page 4
LOCAL NEWS	See page 7
VACANCY FACTORS	See page 11
TIPS ON RENTING APARTMENTS	See page 16
FORCED HOUSING	See page 19

Next Meeting
MONDAY –
AUGUST 19
see page 3

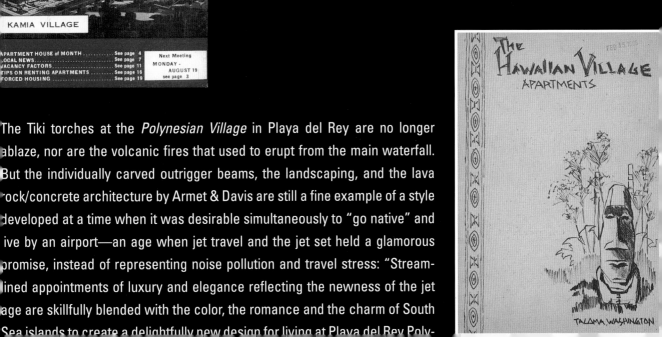

The Tiki torches at the *Polynesian Village* in Playa del Rey are no longer ablaze, nor are the volcanic fires that used to erupt from the main waterfall. But the individually carved outrigger beams, the landscaping, and the lava rock/concrete architecture by Armet & Davis are still a fine example of a style developed at a time when it was desirable simultaneously to "go native" and live by an airport—an age when jet travel and the jet set held a glamorous promise, instead of representing noise pollution and travel stress: "Streamlined appointments of luxury and elegance reflecting the newness of the jet age are skillfully blended with the color, the romance and the charm of South Sea islands to create a delightfully new design for living at Playa del Rey Poly-

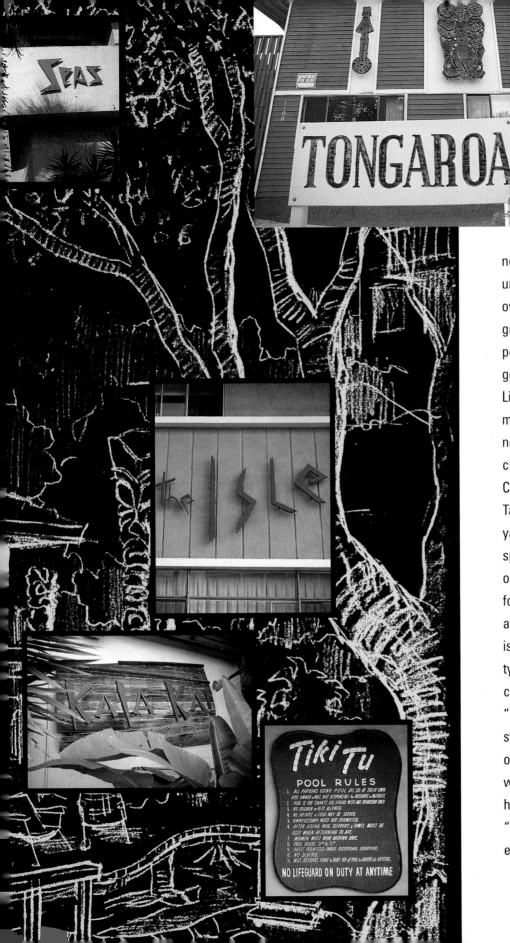

nesian Apartments ... Carved figures of whimsical Tiki gods watch over the lush and lovely landscaped grounds as they cast their charm, portending health, happiness and good fortune."

Like the temples, the villages were most widespread in California and by no means limited to its warmer climes. All the way up the West Coast, around the Seattle area, in Tacoma and Bremerton, a Navy shipyard town, numerous Tiki dwellings sprang up. All across America, more or less elaborate communities formed to hail the godhead of recreation. The names of these suburban islands were as evocative as their type styles. From the "Beachcomber," "Asian," "Primitive," and "Bamboo" to the "Fat Samoan" style, they all represented elements of the Tiki esthetic. Some of the wings or sections of the apartments had their own designations like "Snug Harbor" or "Mauna Loa," taken from Hawaiian sites or hotels.

The Exotic Isle, with its amazing flying rec room,
was still untouched when first rediscovered and
documented for this book, but a recent cleansing
has destroyed much of its charm.
RIGHT PAGE: The yellow tile box is supported by three
strange carvings, while the lettering and wall
masks are lit from behind. The pool Tiki is flanked
by two Tiki-faced torches.

Das Exotic Isle mit seinem schwebenden Erholungs-
raum war unangetastet geblieben, als es wiederentdeckt und für dieses Buch dokumentiert wurde,
doch eine kürzlich erfolgte Renovierung hat viel
von seinem Reiz zerstört.
RECHTE SEITE: Der gelbe Kasten aus Fliesenmosaik
wird von drei seltsamen Schnitzfiguren getragen,
der Schriftzug und die Wandmasken sind von hin-
ten beleuchtet. Der Pool-Tiki wird von zwei tikige-
sichtigen Fackeln flankiert.

Le Exotic Isle, avec son étonnante salle de récréa-
tion volante, était encore intact lorsqu'il fut redé-
couvert et photographié pour ce livre. Mais une récente rénovation a détruit la plus grande partie de
son charme.
PAGE DE DROITE: Les cubes jaunes en mosaïque sont
soutenus par trois figures sculptées à l'aspect bizarre, l'inscription de la façade et les masques
muraux sont éclairés par derrière. La piscine tiki est
flanquée de deux lampadaires en forme de tête tiki.

The *Exotic Isle* Apartments in the Los Angeles suburb of Alhambra, which was named after the Moorish palace in Spain and is now mostly inhabited by Asian immigrants, was until very recently another impressive manifestation of the Tiki faith. Its centerpiece is a recreation room jutting out over the central waterfall, a structure which could be seen as the Tiki equivalent of Frank Lloyd Wright's "Falling Water."

The *Kona Pali* (which is the only complex known to have a look-alike sister apartment, the *Kona Kai*, erected in another part of town) is a treasure-trove of Tiki detail. At the front entrance we are greeted by an inlaid shell "Aloha," and as we investigate the A-frame face, another nice feature appears: in the right corner, four small Tikis stand out against the gold-speckled plaster. Only the trained eye, however, will be able to make out the last traces of yet another exciting aspect of the gable: if viewed at the correct angle to the light, the oval and sloped rectangular panels reveal faint reflections of stenciled Tiki masks that had once been painted on them. This A-

The Kona Pali and the Kona Kai are identical developments. ABOVE RIGHT: Details within the A-frame paneling. BELOW LEFT: Entrance highlights. BELOW RIGHT: Features of the façade and the pool hut mural, which foretells the demise of Tiki style

Das Kona Pali und das Kona Kai sind nach dem gleichen Plan gebaut. OBEN RECHTS: Schöne Details, die sich in der Holzverzierung der A-Form fanden. UNTEN LINKS: Die Besonderheiten im Eingangsbereich. UNTEN RECHTS: Verzierungen an der Fassade und das Wandgemälde in der Hütte des Pools, das den Niedergang der Tiki-Kultur vorausahnte

Le Kona Pali et le Kona Kai sont construits sur le même modèle. CI-DESSUS À DROITE: Détails sur les panneaux de la structure en A. CI-DESSOUS À GAUCHE: Les décorations de l'entrée. CI-DESSOUS À DROITE: Eléments de la façade et la peinture murale de la cabane près de la piscine, qui annonce la fin du style tiki

frame must have been a sight to behold! Partially hidden behind the banana trees and "dutched" Tiki torches, the façade is divided by a collection of individually carved Tiki beams modeled in modernistic streamlined Tiki style. The air conditioning units are hidden by tragicomical Tiki masks. Another outstanding characteristic of this Tiki dwelling is the portal behind the glass door: crossing the entrance bridge over a moat that was once surrounded by tropical plants, we find on our right a tile mosaic map of the Hawaiian Islands. The left side is paneled with wood and guarded by four grotesque Tikis which, carved in various classic styles, alternatively threaten the taboo-breaker with damnation or project good luck and happiness to the initiated.

The Los Angeles suburb of Pico Rivera is worth an intrepid expedi-

A few simple cuts transformed the Kapu Tiki's outrigger beams into Tikis.

Ein paar einfache Einschnitte verwandelten die Einbäume am Kapu Tiki in Tikis.

Quelques entailles de ciseau ont transformé les poutres extérieures du Kapu Tiki en tiki.

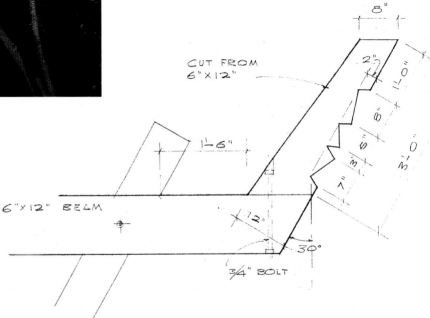

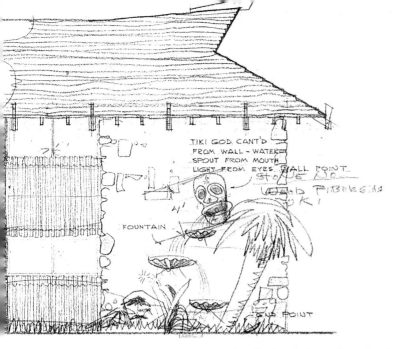

Above: The broken bulb sockets in the eyes and a rubber hose in the mouth are the only evidence of a once-great concept. *Below:* The brochure for Sands West

Oben: Zerbrochene Glühbirnenfassungen in den Augen und ein Gummischlauch im Mund sind die einzigen sichtbaren Beweise einer einst großartigen Idee.
Unten: Die Werbebroschüre des Sands West

Ci-dessus: Des douilles d'ampoules électriques cassées et un tuyau de caoutchouc dans la bouche sont les seules traces d'une grande idée.
Ci-dessous: La brochure de la résidence Sands West

ke aloha no - aloha!
ho'ohelau ı ka hale a piha
ı na makamaka! *

The glamour and romance
of a fabled tropical isle . . .
spice Arizona living today!

Sands WEST

The unique Hawaiian concept of "gracious living in
a friendly clime" is dramatically translated for
discriminating Arizona homebuyers by the distinguished
creative architect, Ragnar C. Qvale, A.I.A., and
Arizona's most trusted home builder, E. T. Wright,
president, American Builders, Inc.

Here you will find the peaceful quiet of suburban
living in a restricted area of unusual homes . . . plus
the conveniences of city services. Long-range planning,
fine design and reliable construction protect your
investment. Shops, schools and churches are nearby,
and all of metropolitan Phoenix is minutes from
your door.

HAWAIIAN GREETING: Welcome! Fill the house full with friends!

tion: here three Tiki settlements are lined up on the 5400 block of Rosemead Boulevard. The local natives eye us with suspicion as we explore the *Aloha Arms*, with its outstanding sloping three-story A-frame (see p. 63). Next to it are the *Samoa* Apartments, and then, after a mysterious empty lot, comes the *Kapu Tiki*, with its handpainted gable Tiki holding a long-extinguished gas torch. The ball-shaped lamps probably used to be hung in fish net to resemble Japanese fishing floats beachcombed on the Hawaiian coast. On the far right of the façade hangs a lonely Tiki mask whose eyes were

225

once equipped with lightbulbs while its monce outh spouted water into a sea-shell waterfall.

In other parts of America there are still more sites to be surveyed, like the *Sands West* in Phoenix, Arizona, whose brochure promised: "In Hawaii, Maori [sic!] traditionally interrupted battles at sundown, retiring to their Hale to enjoy by firelight Awa, Poi and the local delicacy, octopus.

"At Sands West, your family warrior can retire from his daily battle to your private Lanai and find relaxation with his family in a desert evening. Rather than fire-basted octopus or fermented pepper-water however, your Kau Kau may lean more toward an Arizona chuckwagon barbecue enjoyed on your covered patio.

Your home is also protected from Kumumahanahana – the God of Heat— by complete air conditioning and superior installation."

The gods were plentiful on the grounds of the Tiki villages, and although many have decayed and fallen, those who remain stand as sentinels of a forgotten culture, reminding us of the whimsical and creative spirit that pervaded Tiki style.

ABOVE: A Tiki tourist. BELOW: An image reminiscent of Catherwood's "Broken Idol of Copan"

OBEN: Ein Tiki-Tourist. UNTEN: Ein Bild, das an Catherwoods „Broken Idol of Copan" erinnert

CI-DESSUS: Un touriste tiki. CI-DESSOUS: Une image qui rappelle l'«Idole brisée de Copan» du Catherwoods

KONA KAI MOBILE VILLAGE

Numerous mobile-home parks were members of the Tiki cult. Murals, mailboxes, and this strange "Droopy" Tiki are surviving examples of pure folk art at the Kona Kai Mobile Home Village in the San Fernando Valley.

Viele Bewohner der Fertighaus-Siedlungen waren Anhänger des Tiki-Kults. Wandbilder, Briefkästen und dieser seltsame „Droopy"-Tiki sind Beispiele reiner Volkskunst im „Kona Kai Mobile Home Village" im San Fernando Valley.

De nombreux habitants de maisons mobiles participaient au culte tiki. Les peintures murales, les boîtes aux lettres et cet étrange tiki «Droopy» sont quelques-uns des vestiges d'un art populaire authentique au camp des maisons mobiles Kona Kai, dans la San Fernando Valley.

BACKYARD POLYNESIA

In more ways than one, the average American's desire to "go native" was a regression to a simpler period of life: childhood. The responsibilities of work and family were best forgotten at luau-themed garden parties—a sort of "big guys" birthday party—where fun and games were once more allowed. Donning flowery Hawaiian shirts and "muu muus," consuming sweet foods and sweeter drinks that lowered the intellect to child-like consciousness, white grown-ups spent their time Hula dancing and practicing the consonantless sing-song of the Hawaiian language: "All KANES, WAHINES and KEIKIS (men, women and children) will want to WIKI WIKI (hurry) to a Hawaiian LUAU (feast). MALIHINIS (newcomers) will want to know the meaning of the strange words they confront at a luau. Wahines will wear HOLOKUS (Hawaiian princess dresses with a train) or MUU MUUS [loose-fitting flowered garment]. Kanes will wear ALOHA shirts (brightly-colored sport shirts). No PAPALE (hat) is needed. ALOHA (greetings) will be expressed by placing a LEI (flower wreath) about the neck of the malihini. The luau will be served on long tables placed on a LANAI (open porch) or under palm frond awnings in the yard. The luau food is cooked in an IMU (underground oven) made by digging a LUA (hole) in the ground, filling it with POHAKU (rocks) and KUNI (kindling). Imu holes were dug in backyards as if the gold rush days had returned, but the pure desire to go primitive was not enough. Appropriate decor was needed. The necessary paraphenalia to equip these happenings could be found at nurseries and specialty stores like "Sea and Jungle" in the Valley, "Oceanic

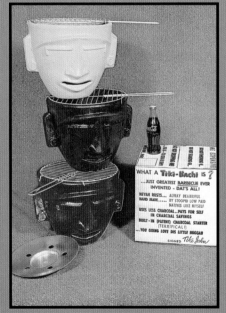

Arts" in Whittier, and "Johnson Products" in Chicago. Tiki torches, grass matting, palm leaves, bamboo poles, fish netting, spears and drums, and Tiki-
shaped items could be found at these suppliers. Thus Tiki huts appeared in
backyards and god-heads were erected by pools and patios, making Tikis the
new garden gnomes of America.

For the hobbist, there were complete kits with instructions on how to build
one's own Tiki bar. In many suburban homes, the basements were turned into
rumpus rooms where grown-ups would gather for cocktails and adult talk.
When rattan and bamboo furniture did not impress enough, Tiki-carved bars
and chairs from the house of Witco (see pp. 44 and 253) did the trick. Always

A Tiki-god fountain

THIS unique fountain, a replica of one of the hand-carved tiki idols of the South Seas, is made of sculptured fiberglass which will last indefinitely. The large bowl is supported by the carved totem pole which also acts as a housing for the pump.

Water circulates from the bowl and cascades over the idol's head, creating a striking effect, especially when used with black light. The entire fountain is painted with several colors of black-ray paint invisible during the day but effective at night when used with a black light fixture in the installation.

Special pellets when dissolved in water give a vivid blue fluorescence to the water curtain. One pellet will last for several weeks.

The tiki god alone is 29 in. high. As a fountain with self-contained pump it is 36 in. high, and can be used inside or outside the house. The fiberglass bowl (34 in. in diameter) is black with a gold fleck. The manufacturer has an inexpensive black-ray paint kit for owners who wish to touch up rocks and shrubbery around the statue.

For where to shop call MAdison 5-2345, Station 1458, or write to Readers' Service Bureau, The Times, Los Angeles 53. Enclose a self-addressed, stamped envelope.

PAGE 230/231: Pagan idolatry at the Orange County Garden Show, 1958. Plastic leis, fish netting, two sea shells, and a skull mug made up this luau kit. LEFT: De rigeur in Backyard Polynesia: Tiki bird houses

SEITE 230/231: Götzenanbetung auf der Orange County Garden Show, 1958. Plastikgirlanden, Fischernetze, zwei Muschelgefäße und ein Totenkopfkrug gehören zu dieser Luau-Ausrüstung.
LINKS: Auch das gab es in Hinterhof-Polynesien: Tiki-Vogelhäuser

PAGE 230/231: Idolâtrie païenne à l'Orange County Garden Show, 1958. Leis en plastique, filets de pêche, deux coquillages et des chopes têtes de mort composaient ce kit de luau.
A GAUCHE: De rigueur dans la Polynésie de jardin: des volières tiki

EXOTIC MATERIALS
BY ORLOFF

FOR CREATIVE USE BY DECORATORS, ARCHITECTS, DESIGNERS, BUILDERS, HOME OWNERS

ABOVE: This shop was the Mecca of Tiki revellers young and old.

OBEN: Dieses Geschäft war das Mekka für junge und alte Tiki-Anhänger.

CI-DESSUS: Cette boutique était la Mecque des noceurs tiki jeunes et vieux.

ABOVE AND LEFT: Examples of rumpus-room decor

OBEN UND LINKS: So sahen die Partykeller aus

CI-DESSUS ET À GAUCHE: Exemples d'un décor pour salle de jeu

a good parameter of popular taste, Elvis Presley equipped his Jungle Room in Graceland with Witco furnishings. Meanwhile, Elvis himself was riding on the crest of the Polynesian wave with movies like *Blue Hawaii*, *Paradise Hawaiian Style*, and *Clambake*, which features the best Florida beach luau scene ever captured on film.

ABOVE: At home and at the prom, the spirit of Tiki prevailed. MIDDLE: Elvis's Jungle Room
BELOW LEFT: A Witco display

OBEN: Ob zu Hause oder auf dem Collage-Ball, der Geist von Tiki herrschte überall.
MITTE: Elvis' „Jungle Room"
UNTEN LINKS: Ein Witco-Ausstellungsraum

CI-DESSUS: A la maison et au bal des étudiants, parpout régnait l'esprit du tiki.
AU CENTRE: La « Jungle Room » d'Elvis
CI-DESSOUS À GAUCHE: Un étalage de chez Witco

BELOW: Publicity still from Paradise Hawaiian Style

UNTEN: Standfoto aus dem Film „Südseeparadies"

CI-DESSOUS: Image publicitaire extraite de « Paradise Hawaiian Style »

TIKI
Surf Club
Monica City

BIG DADDY WUZ HERE

Revell
Authentic Kits

AUTHENTIC 1/25 SCALE READY TO ASSEMBLE P

Surfite
with TIKI HUT
By Ed "BIG DADDY" Roth

CALIFORNIA, the mid-1960s: On the beaches and in their backyards, a generation of middle-class Americans was engaging in rituals called "luaus," where they would intoxicate themselves with Polynesian potions and worship Tiki as the god of recreation. Unbeknownst to them, their children were coming under the alien influence of what was soon to be called the "British invasion." Foreign pop bands with strange names like "The Beatles" inspired a youth culture that, as we all know, started with long hair and ended in psychedelic drugs and the sexual revolution. The parents' attempts to escape the

MODEL KIT

237

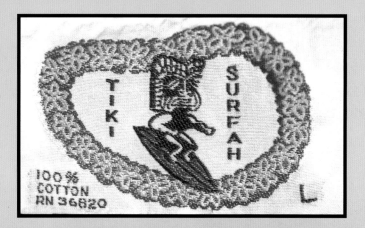

Surfing TIKI

stresses of civilization in a plastic Polynesia were swiftly rated as lame, corny, and outdated. Tiki's spell was soon to be broken. But before this could happen, a local version of that foreign youth culture was to claim Tiki their own: For California's surfers, the Tiki became the hip good-luck fetish guiding them in their search for the perfect wave. As part of beach culture, Tiki amulets were the cool thing to wear among suave urban beachcombers and surfers alike. The inspiration was Hawaii. Not only was it the dream destination because of its amazing surf, but it was here that the first white man laid eyes on the sport. The great explorer Captain Cook discovered many things in Polynesia, and surfing was one of them. Upon entering Kealakekua Bay, where coincidentally he would later find his death at the hands of the natives, he noted in his log: "The boldness and address, with which we saw them perform these difficult and dangerous manouvres, was altogether astonishing, and is scarce to be credited."

In ancient Hawaii, surfing was an activity especially engaged in by the royalty. The carving of a surfboard, like the creation of a Tiki, was accompanied by sacred rituals. In Hawaiian mythology many stories about surfing ancestor-gods have been transmitted, such as that of Mamala the Surf-rider: "Mamala was a female chieftain of *kupua* character. This meant that she was a

Tikis were considered to be good luck charms among surfers. BELOW: This statuette of a female Tiki "Surf God" inspired a T-shirt line in 1966 where Tiki mythology and hippy zodiac consciousness mixed.

Tikis galten bei den Surfern als Glücksbringer. UNTEN: Diese Statuette einer Tiki-Göttin, ein „Surf"-Tiki, war 1966 das Vorbild für eine T-Shirt-Kollektion, bei der sich Tiki-Mythologie und das Interesse der Hippies für Tierkreiszeichen mischten.

Les tiki étaient considérés par les surfeurs comme des porte-bonheur. EN BAS : Cette statuette d'une « Déesse du Surf » tiki inspira une ligne de tee-shirts en 1966, époque où la mythologie tiki se mêlait au zodiaque hippie.

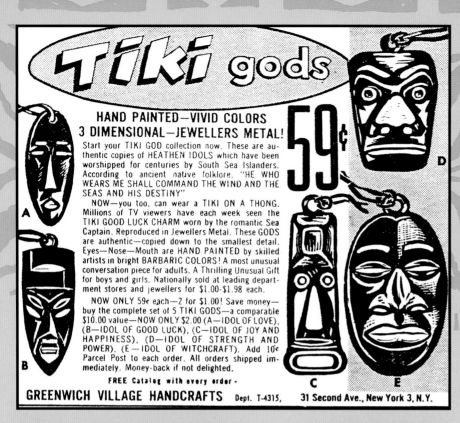

Tiki talismans worn by surfers could be found at beach shops, amusement parks and in bubble gum machines. ABOVE: Four wooden examples, some with rhinestones, and an Tiki amulet made out of green dayglo plastic.

Tiki-Talismane, die von Surfern getragen wurden, konnte man am Strand, in Vergnügungsparks und am Automaten kaufen. Einige waren mit Rheinkieseln verziert, andere bestanden aus phosphoreszierendem Plastik.

Les talismans tiki portés par les surfeurs se trouvaient dans les boutiques de plage, les parcs d'attraction et dans les distributeurs de chewing-gum. Certains étaient incrustés de pierres, d'autres étaient en plastique fluorescent.

mo-o, or gigantic lizard or crocodile, as well as a beautiful woman, and could assume whichever shape she desired. Mamala was a wonderful surf-rider. Very skillfully she danced on the roughest waves. The people on the beach watching her filled the air with resounding applause when they clapped their hands over her extraordinary athletic feats."

As surfing was the Californian surfer's religion, it was only natural that Tiki became his god. As talismans, on T-shirts, and at beachparties, Tikis were valued as icons of cool.

LEFT: Tiki lipstick holder with mirror
BELOW: The "Tiki Tote" clipped on your belt!

LINKS: Tiki-Lippenstifthalter mit Spiegel
UNTEN: Den „Tiki Tote" trug man am Gürtel!

A GAUCHE: Bâton de rouge à lèvres tiki avec miroir
EN BAS: Le « Tiki Toté » en boucle de ceinture !

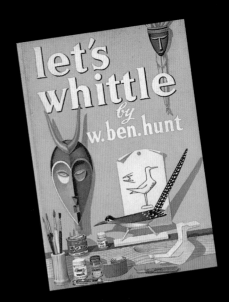

THE ARTISTS 29

The creators of the unrecognized art form of Tiki-moderne, American Tiki sculptors, have never been accepted as artists. Their products were labeled "authentic," a shadowy term denoting genuineness, but not outright claiming that the works were originals. Nobody wanted to draw attention to the fact that the dark complexion of a carver like Vince Buono, for example, derived from his New York Italian immigrant background and not from the South Sea Isles. Tiki style did not seek to betray intentionally; rather, it gently supported the public's need for self-deception, and therefore cloaked itself and its creators in mystery. The power tool Leroy Schmaltz is swinging on this page was taboo at public carving appearances, where hammer and chisel were used. This chapter aims to give several Tiki artists—representative for all who could not be included here—their due recognition.

Leroy Schmaltz and Bob van Oosting founded their decorating firm, Oceanic Arts, in the Los Angeles suburb of Whittier in the late 1950s, just on the crest of the Tiki craze. Beginning on a small scale with Tiki amulets and palm frond masks, Oceanic Arts soon emerged as *the* major manufacturer and supplier countrywide of Tiki art and materials. Schmaltz and van Oosting were contracted by all the major chains, from *Don the Beachcomber* to *Kon-Tiki*; in turn, they themselves employed

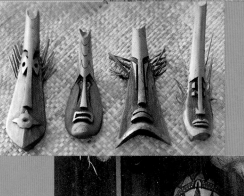

TOP LEFT: Leroy and Bob displaying their earliest works. MIDDLE: The back lot of "Oceanic Arts" at the height of the Tiki craze. LEFT: A corner at the old "Oceanic Arts" warehouse

OBEN LINKS: Leroy und Bob zeigen ihre frühesten Werke. MITTE: „Oceanic Arts"-Hinterhof auf dem Höhepunkt der Tiki-Begeisterung. LINKS: Eine Ecke im alten Lagerhaus von „Oceanic Arts"

CI-DESSUS À GAUCHE: Leroy et Bob montrant leurs premières œuvres. AU CENTRE: L'arrière-cour d'«Oceanic Arts» à l'apogée de la folie tiki. A GAUCHE: Un détail de l'entrepôt d'«Oceanic Arts»

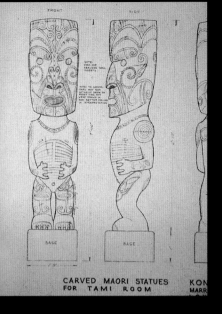

CARVED MAORI STATUES KON
FOR TAMI ROOM MARR

most of the carvers in the business at one point or another. Occasionally the Tikis were designed by the architects or decorators who commissioned them, but mostly the sculptors pursued their own visions, and sometimes became the designers of the Tiki environments, as well.

The list of credits collected by Oceanic Arts is extensive: they have been connected with most of the Tiki temples depicted in this book. Even the honorable Bishop Museum in Honolulu houses some of their carvings—if not in museum display cases, at least on the walls of its cafeteria. The phenomenon of the Tiki style went full circle when idols manufactured by Oceanic Arts were exported to hotels and restaurants in Hawaii, Samoa and Tahiti. Today, Oceanic Arts is the only Polynesian supplier of Tiki decor; having successfully survived the abolishment of Tiki, they are now beckoning a new generation of explorers from all over the world to the shores of Whittier, California.

ABOVE: Blueprint for a god by Irving Weisenberg, created for Armet & Davis. RIGHT: This priapic monument was carved by Ed Crissmann in Whittier, California, and found its final resting place at the Hotel Taharaa in Tahiti (below).

OBEN: Modellzeichnung für einen Gott von Irving Weisenberg für Armet & Davis. RECHTS: Dieses phallische Monument wurde von Ed Crissmann in Whittier, Kalifornien, geschnitzt und fand seinen letzten Ruheplatz am Hotel Taharaa auf Tahiti (unten).

CI-DESSUS: Une idole dessinée par Irving Weisenberg, pour Armet & Davis. A DROITE: Ce monument phallique fut sculpté par Ed Crissmann à Whittier, Californie, et fut installé à l'hôtel Taharaa de Tahiti (en bas).

Community News

Whittier, Calif., Fri., Aug. 30, 1968   The DAILY NEWS—3

'Made In Whittier' Tikis Will Greet Tourists In Tahiti

It may be impractical to send coals to New Castle, but a Whittier firm has encountered great success by sending Polynesian decorations to Tahiti.

Oceanic Arts, 12130 Philadelphia St., has contracted to furnish decorations for the new Hotel Taharra Intercontinental in Papeete, Tahiti.

Leroy Schmaltz and Robert Van Oosting co-owners of the firm, said that one of the items is a 20-foot Tiki, carved from a solid log of Ponderosa Pine weighing five and one-half tons. Schmaltz said that most of the items will be stamped "Made in Whittier".

The co-owner explained that a need for "authentic" Polynesian items has arisen in Tahiti since many of the natives are employed in other jobs, such as at French atomic plants. In addition, there is a shortage of logs there which prohibits the carving of larger items such as Oceanic's 20-foot red Tiki.

Ed Chrissman, an employe of the firm, has been carving the Tiki for several months, but said that such an item could be finished in three weeks if it were the only item being worked on.

He said that the Tiki is valued at approximately $4,000.

Schmaltz said that much of the material other than wood is imported originally from Tahiti, assembled and constructed locally and then sent back. The firm deals in hundreds of types of items, mainly for commercial use.

Other contracts have included Disneyland's Tiki Room and jungle rides and some work at Sea World in San Diego.

"MADE IN WHITTIER" — Ed Crissman of Oceanic Arts in Whittier, gazes up at the 20-foot tall Tiki he has carved for a Tahitian hotel as it is lifted upright by a crane.—(Daily News photo).

TIKI JUNCTION
Sculptor · Barney West

Just across the Golden Gate bridge north of San Francisco, in the quaint yacht harbor of Sausalito, ex-merchant marine Barney West set up camp with his Tiki Junction. He had found his vocation during the Second World War when he was stranded in the Mariana Islands. His Tiki Junction logo was inspired by a book published in conjunction with the first exhibition of South Seas art in America in 1946, the same source that also spawned the Trader Vic logo. Trader Vic, based across the bay in Emeryville, near Oakland, became the main purchaser of Barney's Tikis. Today some of these effigies bearing his unmistakable style can still be found in Trader Vic's franchises all around the world. Meanwhile Barney, who fully fit the role of the hard-drinking, womanizing bohemian, has long since gone to Tiki heaven.

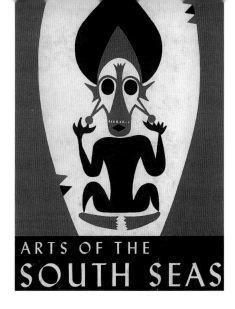
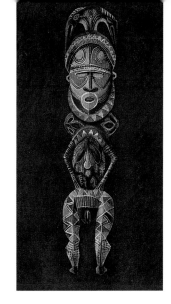

ABOVE: The book "Arts of the South Seas" with color illustrations by Miguel Covarrubias became the bible of many Tiki artists; the female Abelam figure was much copied.

OBEN: Das Buch „Arts of the South Seas" mit farbigen Illustrationen von Miguel Covarrubias war die Bibel vieler Tiki-Künstler, seine weibliche „Abelamfigur" wurde von vielen kopiert.

CI-DESSUS: Le livre «Arts of the South Seas», avec des illustrations en couleur de Miguel Covarrubias, fut la bible de nombreux artistes tiki. La figure feminine «Abelam» fut beaucoup copiée.

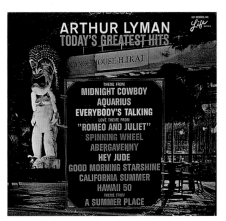

ABOVE: An American Tiki in Waikiki: Barney's work in front of the Canoe House at the Ilikai Hotel, Honolulu.
ABOVE RIGHT: More of his odd idols, lined up at the Tiki Junction, Sausalito
LEFT: A god-head by Barney West at a liquor store in San Mateo, south of San Francisco

OBEN: Ein amerikanischer Tiki in Waikiki: Barneys Werk vor dem Canoe House am Ilikai Hotel in Honolulu
OBEN RECHTS: Weitere eigenwillige Götzenfiguren, die vor dem Tiki Junction in Sausalito aufgestellt sind
LINKS: Eine Götterfigur von Barney West vor einem Spirituosenladen in San Mateo, südlich von San Francisco

CI-DESSUS: Un tiki américain à Waikiki: une œuvre de Barney devant la Canoe House du Llikai Hotel de Honolulu. CI-DESSUS À DROITE: D'autres de ses étranges idoles, alignées devant le Tiki Junction, Sausalito. A GAUCHE: Une idole de Barney West devant un magasin de spiritueux à San Mateo, au sud de San Francisco

Milan Guanko learned carving as a child from his father in the Philippines. After emigrating to the States in 1928 and working in groceries, he found his niche in the emerging Polynesian craze. Eventually becoming one of the most prolific and influential Tiki carvers in America, his style

The garden gnomes of California in the 1960s: Tikis by Milan Guanko at a South Los Angeles garden supply store

Die „Gartenzwerge" der 60er Jahre in Kalifornien: Milan Guankos Tikis in einem Geschäft für Gartenzubehör im Süden von Los Angeles

Les nains de jardin de la Californie des années 1960: les tiki de Milan Guanko dans un magasin de décors de jardin du sud de Los Angeles

ABOVE: In a carving demonstration at Trader Dick's in Nevada, Guanko was announced as "'MILANO', NATIVE OF THE SOUTH PACIFIC", a claim that was not entirely untrue. BELOW: California natives (in customary garb) watch in awe as Guanko wields his chisel.

OBEN: Beim „Schauschnitzen" im Trader Dicks in Nevada wurde Guanko als „,MILANO'". IM SÜDPAZIFIK GEBOREN", vorgestellt, und diese Behauptung war nicht ganz unrichtig.
UNTEN: Kalifornische Eingeborene (in typischer Tracht) sehen andächtig zu, wie Guanko seinen Meißel schwingt.

CI-DESSUS: Exposition de sculptures chez Trader Dick's dans le Nevada. Guanko était présenté comme « ‹MILANO›, NATIF DU PACIFIQUE SUD », ce qui n'était pas entièrement faux. CI-DESSOUS: Des indigènes californiens (en tenue traditionelle) contemplent fascinés Guanko manier son ciseau.

was copied and marketed for the growing needs of Tiki revellers. His credits include pieces at *The Islands* (p. 155) in Phoenix, Arizona; the *Kapu Kai* (p. 199) in Rancho Cucamonga; and Ren Clark's *Polynesian Village* (p. 44) in Fort Worth, Texas, for which Guanko and two Mexican carvers, Juan Razo and Fidel Rodriguez (who had also outfitted the *Mauna Loa* in Mexico City), carved over two hundred Tikis, some as barstools, some as 11-foot-tall giants. A state-of-the-art Polynesian paradise in 1960, nothing remains today of this virtual forest of Tikis, the whereabouts of its many erstwhile inhabitants being unknown. Also a mystery is the fate of one of Milan's giant Anaheim apartment Tikis that, according to the sculptor himself, was mounted on a rotating base.

Milan opened his shop in Anaheim, where he benefitted from the steady supply of palm trees that were being cut down for the expanding Disneyland. Rarely adhering to "authentic" island styles in his work, the artist openly credited "kiddie cartoons" among his influences. Today his work can be appreciated at the Royal Hawaiian in Laguna Beach, one of the oldest Tiki bars still in operation.

Posing with his amazing idols is Bob Lutz, a unique but unrecognized Tiki talent. Too good for this world, he is said to have killed himself after walking in on his girlfriend making love with another man. His only known carving still in situ stands at the *Tiki Spa* in Palm Springs. Another talented creator of highly stylized Tikis was Andres Bumatay, like Milan Guanko also of Filipino heritage. His absurd bug-eyed Tikis were available at the Sea and Jungle store

ABOVE: The late Bob Lutz and his works at an unknown location

BELOW: Among the more unusual artifacts produced by the cult are the Tiki creatures of Andres Bumatay, which inspired the Islander mug on the left.

OBEN: Der inzwischen verstorbene Bob Lutz und seine Werke an einem unbekannten Ort. UNTEN: Die Tiki-Gestalten von Andres Bumatay gehören zu den ungewöhnlicheren Stücken, die von der Tiki-Kultur hervorgebracht worden sind; der "Islander"-Krug ganz links ist von ihnen inspiriert.

CI-DESSUS: Le défunt Bob Lutz et ses œuvres dans un lieu non identifié

CI-DESSOUS: Les créatures tiki d'Andres Bumatay font partie des plus insolites produits par le culte tiki. Elles inspirèrent la chope de l'Islander à gauche.

Creator god (left), "who sees all," is generally set in home or patio. Dramatic figure at gateway is the Home Guardian (center), who protects village from evil. Beyond him you can see the Menahuni, the "little people" who shoulder the blame for all unexplained phenomena. Praying figure (right) is the traditional Rongo, the god of agriculture.

ABOVE: The Royal Tahitian golf club house, for which Charles Rosencrans (left) provided the carvings.

OBEN: Das Golfclub-Haus Royal Tahitian, für das Charles Rosencrans (links) die Schnitzfiguren geschaffen hat.

CI-DESSUS: Le bâtiment du golf Royal Tahitian pour lequel Charles Rosencran (à gauche) réalisa les sculptures.

(p. 234), and provided the inspiration for both a Tiki mug and possibly the *Tahitian* logo Tiki (p. 152).

A construction company foreman, Charles Rosencrans' naive, primitive skill in carving was self-taught. His strange statues adorned *The Reef* in Long Beach, and the *Royal Tahitian*, a modern, slanted A-frame Tiki temple at the Ontario (Los Angeles) Golf Course, which claimed to possess the largest Polynesian grounds in the country by incorporating its golf acreage into the calculation. The A-frame still stands, but all evidence of Rosencrans' odd art is gone. Right next to the A-frame, however, one can find an unnamed apartment building still sporting four Milan Guanko Tikis.

ABOVE: The wonderful world of Witco. How many Tiki faces can you find? BELOW: The young William Westenhaver at work on his modernistic "ID" line

OBEN: Die wundervolle Witco-Welt. Wie viele Tiki-Gesichter sind zu sehen? UNTEN: Der junge William Westenhaver bei der Arbeit an seiner modernistischen „ID"-Serie

CI-DESSUS: Le monde merveilleux de Witco. Combien comptez-vous de visages de tiki? CI-DESSOUS: Le jeune Westenhaver travaillant à sa ligne moderniste « ID »

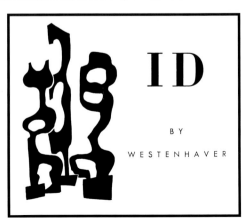

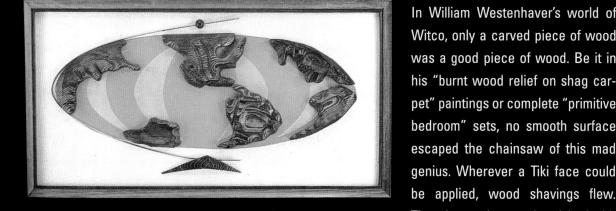

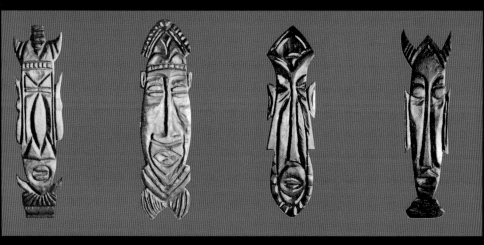

In William Westenhaver's world of Witco, only a carved piece of wood was a good piece of wood. Be it in his "burnt wood relief on shag carpet" paintings or complete "primitive bedroom" sets, no smooth surface escaped the chainsaw of this mad genius. Wherever a Tiki face could be applied, wood shavings flew. Then the carving was burnished with a torch to bring out the grain structure of the wood in thick black veins. Not only Polynesian art, but also modern and Conquistador decor was churned and burned at the Witco plant in Seattle. At one time Witco had showrooms in Chicago, Dallas, Denver, and Seattle. Westenhaver's art can still be found in Florida motels as well as in thrift stores throughout the U.S. His list of customers included Elvis Presley (p. 235) and Hugh Hefner (p. 43). Even several houses of ill repute are rumored to have been clients. Among his most distinguished works are a variety of Tiki bars (p. 6) and Tiki fountains (p. 179). The author is presently working on a monograph on the œuvre of this prolific whittler, hoping that this first book will have opened the eyes of the public to the art of Tiki.

COLLECTABLES
AND
BOOKS

An·tiki

GERMAN

DAS TIKI-BUCH. DER KULT DES POLYNESISCHEN POP IM AMERIKA DER FÜNFZIGER JAHRE

EIN FÜHRER FÜR DEN STADTARCHÄOLOGEN. DIE ENTDECKUNG EINER VERLORENEN ZIVILISATION VOR UNSERER EIGENEN HAUSTÜR

„Die Krankheit der Holzfäulnis verbreitet sich unter den Idolen, die Früchte auf ihren Altären sind nicht mehr wohlgefällig, selbst die Tempel sollten neu gedeckt werden ..."

(Herman Melville: Taipi, 1846)

Diese Bemerkung über das Schicksal der alten polynesischen Zivilisation stammt zwar aus einem Klassiker der Südseeliteratur, scheint jedoch auch auf das Schicksal des amerikanischen Tiki-Stils der 50er und 60er Jahre auf befremdliche Weise zuzutreffen. Seine Symbole, die Tikis, verfallen, die „polynesische" Küche jener Zeit gilt heute als das genaue Gegenteil einer gesunden Ernährung, und die wenigen noch existierenden Zeugnisse der Tiki-Architektur sehen baufällig aus. Schon Paul Gauguin war fasziniert von der melancholischen Atmosphäre des Zerfalls in Papeete, Tahitis Hauptstadt, als er die „verschwommene Oberfläche eines unergründlichen Rätsels" in diesem bereits befleckten Paradies entdeckte; ebenso ergeht es dem Stadtarchäologen von heute, der die Überreste jenes „verlorenen Paradieses", jener amerikanischen Version des Dolce Vita, die wir Tiki-Stil nennen, betrachtet.

Tiki-Tempel, die einst jede größere amerikanische Stadt zierten, sind verschwunden oder umgestaltet worden, die „unbeholfenen, lustig aussehenden Götzenbilder" (Melville) hat man mit missionarischem Eifer hinausgeworfen, um neuen Göttern oder Stilen Platz zu machen. Wasserfälle haben aufgehört zu fließen – ebenso wie die übernatürliche Kraft des „Mana", mit dem sie erbaut wurden; die Tiki-Fackeln sind erloschen und die Auslegerbalken sind abgesägt. Aber die Stadtarchäologen haben eine Sensibilität für verlorene Kulturen und ihre vergessenen Sitten und Gebräuche entwickelt. Unerschrocken reisen sie zu ihren „Grabungsstätten" an so entlegenen und exotischen Orten wie Columbus, Ohio, oder Pomona im städtischen Einzugsgebiet von Los Angeles. Für sie ist es ebenso aufregend, an einem Tag voller Smog über eine öde Schnellstraße in irgendeinen auf keiner Karte verzeichneten Vorort eines Vorortes zu fahren, wie das „Kon-Tiki" durch einen Hurrikan im Pazifik zu steuern. Wie „Stadt-

streicher" im wahrsten Sinne des Wortes durchwühlen sie die Abfälle der Konsumkultur, in Secondhandläden, bei Hinterhofverkäufen und in Antiquariaten, immer auf der Suche nach Puzzlesteinen zu jener versunkenen Kultur, die polynesische Paradiese inmitten der Städte entstehen ließ. Mit seinem wachen Sinn für das Wunderbare erkennt der Stadtarchäologe, dass man nicht immer in die Ferne schweifen muss, um die Geheimnisse vergessener, uralter Traditionen zu erforschen, sondern dass fremdartige Schätze in der unmittelbaren Nachbarschaft begraben liegen können. Das ist es, was wir uns mit diesem Buch, Ihrem Führer zur Tiki-Kultur in Amerika, vorgenommen haben: die Fähigkeit zu erwecken, das Wunderbare im scheinbar so Profanen zu entdecken.

AM ANFANG WAR ...

Seit dem Sündenfall hat der Mensch immer danach gestrebt, wieder in das Paradies zurückzukehren, aus dem er vertrieben worden ist. Als die ersten Berichte von den Südseeinseln die Alte Welt erreichten, glaubte man, diesen verlorenen Ort wiederentdeckt zu haben. Polynesien wurde zur Metapher für das Paradies auf Erden – dessen Strände blieben allerdings für die meisten Sterblichen unerreichbar und so ging die Suche nach anderen mythischen Ländern weiter. Ein solches Land war „California", eine mysteriöse Insel, die man für einen eigenen Kontinent hielt und von der gesagt wurde, dass sie von Amazonen bevölkert sei. Obwohl diese Terra incognita bald besiedelt wurde und derartige Höhenflüge der Fantasie sich als Übertreibung herausstellten, behielt Kalifornien immer seinen Status als goldenes Traumziel. Generationen von Menschen kamen hier an, alle auf der Suche nach der Verwirklichung ihrer eigenen Vorstellung vom Paradies. Eine der vielen Versionen dieses Glücks auf Erden war der tropische Garten der Südseeinseln, und so kam es, dass die erste Palme gepflanzt wurde und sich eine tropische Flora ausbreitete. Da nicht nur die Biosphäre, sondern auch die entsprechende Psycho-Sphäre vorhanden war, bildete sich schon bald ein amerikanisches Polynesien heraus. Tiki-Tempel wurden gebaut und eine Zeit lang waren die Menschen gläubig. Sie kamen zusammen, um dem Kult des modernen Primitivismus zu huldigen, einem Kult, in den sie Alkoholismus, Rassismus, Chauvinismus und Schweinefleischverzehr integrierten – heute absolute Tabus.

Wie die Kalifornier Polynesien nachahmten, so schaute der Rest der Nation auf Kalifornien, um von dort etwas über neue Lebensstile zu erfahren. Schon bald verfügte jede größere Stadt in Amerika über zumindest einen polynesischen Palast.

TIKI – WER WAR DAS?

Am Anfang war das Wort und das Wort lautete: TIK, zumindest nach Angaben des renommierten Spracharchäologen und Linguisten Merrit Ruhlen aus Palo Alto, Kalifornien. Er verfolgte den Ursprung der menschlichen Sprache bis auf dieses magische Dreibuchstabenwort zurück, das sich noch heute in „toe" (Zeh), in „digit" (Finger) und offensichtlich auch in „dick" (Schwanz) erhalten hat. Wenn „Tiki" mit soviel archaischer Kraft ausgestattet ist, darf man sich nicht wundern, dass es zum Schlagwort einer ganzen Generation geworden ist. Aber „Tiki" weist nicht nur diese enge Verwandtschaft mit dem ersten Wort auf, sondern ist in der polynesischen Mythologie auch das Synonym für den ersten Menschen. Schlägt man in A. W. Reeds „Concise Maori Dictionary" nach, findet man die folgenden Erklärungen:

1. TIKI: Erster Mensch oder Personifizierung des Menschen. Durch Ahnenverehrung wurde dieser Maori-Adam zu einem Halbgott und schließlich wurde der Begriff „Tiki" für alle Darstellungen des Menschen verwendet, wie im zweiten Bedeutungsfeld erörtert:

2. TIKI: Groteske Schnitzerei in menschlicher Gestalt an einem Haus – eine präzise Beschreibung der Art von Tiki, wie wir ihn auf diesen Seiten finden. Lesen wir aber weiter, zeigt sich eine noch tiefere Bedeutung des Wortes:

3. TIKI: ein phallisches Symbol. Tatsächlich ist Tiki in den Überlieferungen der Maori der Name für die Zeugungskraft und das Sexualorgan des Gottes Tane, des Schöpfers der ersten Frau. Auf den Tubuai-Inseln südlich von Tahiti war „Tiki-roa" (die lange Ahnengestalt) der Spitzname für den Penis und „Tiki-poto" (die kurze Ahnengestalt) ein Kosewort für die Klitoris.

Da das Wort so schöpferische Kräfte in sich trägt, wird es niemanden überraschen, auf den Marquesa-Inseln noch eine weitere Bedeutung zu finden:

4. TIKI: Gott der Künstler. Es ist ein Anliegen dieses Buches zu zeigen, dass Tiki tatsächlich die Muse vieler Künstler war, ob bekannter oder unbekannter. Möge er sich nun auch als der lang ersehnte Schirmherr der Künstler etablieren.

PRIMITIVE KUNST AN ZIVILISIERTEN ORTEN

„Wer sie je gesehen hat, fühlt sich von ihnen verfolgt wie von einem Fiebertraum." (Karl Woermann über Tikis in seiner *Geschichte der Kunst aller Zeiten und Völker,* 1900–1911)

Die scheinbar naive und ursprüngliche Ästhetik der so genannten primitiven Kunst diente den Urvätern der modernen Kunst als entscheidende Inspirationsquelle – in diesen Anfängen gründet das Prinzip, später diese primitive Kunst in Kontrast zu den glatten Linien des modernen Designs zu setzen, um dessen Wirkung zu verstärken. Im frühen 20. Jahrhundert kamen immer mehr „Kunstkuriositäten", also afrikanische und ozeanische Kunstobjekte, aus den Kolonien in die westeuropäischen Großstädte; eine junge Künstlergeneration, zu der Pablo Picasso, Joan Miró, Paul Klee und Max Ernst gehörten, benutzte den Primitivismus, um den bis dahin gültigen Kunstbegriff in Frage zu stellen. Das Studium der etablierten klassischen Kunst, sagte Gauguin damals, „stieß mich ab und entmutigte mich, denn es gab mir so ein unbestimmtes Gefühl, zu sterben, ohne wieder geboren zu werden". Pablo Picasso hatte sein Erweckungserlebnis, als er die Sammlung primitiver Kunst im Musée d'Ethnographie du Trocadéro in Paris sah: „Plötzlich wusste ich, warum ich Maler geworden war!" Schon 1919 wurde er als „alter Anhänger von Tiki" begrüßt. Das lag wahrscheinlich daran, dass Picasso schon um 1910 stolzer Besitzer eines Tiki von den Marquesa-Inseln war, von dem er sich für den Rest seiner einzigartigen Karriere nicht mehr trennte (Seite 26).

Während die primitive Kunst in den 20er und 30er Jahren vorwiegend von der Avantgarde geschätzt wurde, interessierte sich nach dem Zweiten Weltkrieg auch der wohlhabende Mittelstand für diese Objekte: Man verband mit ihnen einen künstlerischen, bohemehaften Lebensstil und eine originelle, spielerische Lebenseinstellung. In den späten 50er Jahren war es ein absolutes Muss, irgendeine hinreißende Plastik aus dem Busch zu besitzen und so die Monotonie der damaligen Wohnzimmereinrichtungen ein wenig aufzulockern. Die Zeit des Tiki war gekommen.

PRÄ-TIKI UND DIE GEBURT DES POLYNESISCHEN POP

„Man sollte oft wünschen, auf einer der Südseeinseln als so genannter Wilder geboren zu sein, um nur einmal das menschliche Dasein ohne falschen Beigeschmack, durchaus rein zu genießen." (Goethe zu Eckermann, 12.3.1828)

Der Wunsch, die Segnungen der Zivilisation gegen ein einfacheres, natürliches Leben einzutauschen, ist so alt wie die Zivilisation selbst. Eskapistische Träumer und ernsthafte Philosophen waren der Ansicht, dass in den frühen Reiseberichten von den Südsee-Expeditionen James Cooks und Louis-Antoine de Bougainvilles die perfekte Alternative zu den Lebensbedingungen der affektierten Gesellschaft im alten Europa beschrieben sei. Melville pries in „Taipi" die Natürlichkeit der eingeborenen Mädchen: „Ich hätte gern für einen Augenblick eine Galerie Krönungsschönheiten aus Westminster/Abbey dieser Schar Inselmädchen gegenübergestellt, ihre Steifheit, Förmlichkeit und Geziertheit mit der ungekünstelten Lebhaftigkeit und der unverhüllten natürlichen Anmut dieser wilden Geschöpfe verglichen."

Angenehmes Klima, natürliche Schönheit, leidenschaftliche Eingeborene und exotische Nahrungsmittel im Überfluss versprachen ein Leben frei von allen Einschränkungen und Belastungen der modernen westlichen Gesellschaft. Abenteuergeschichten über Polynesien wurden so populär, dass 1921 bei G. P. Putnam's Sons eine Parodie auf derartige Südsee-Expeditionen mit dem Titel „The Cruise of the Kawa" herauskam. Obwohl das Werk schon durch seine Fotos eindeutig als Satire erkennbar war, erwies sich die Nachfrage nach dieser Art von literarischer Kost als so groß, dass man die Berichte als authentisch betrachtete und der Autor sogar zu einem Vortrag vor der National Geographic Society eingeladen wurde. Wenn es um die Darstellung des Paradieses auf Erden ging, war man nur allzu leicht geneigt, der Fiktion gegenüber den nüchternen Tatsachen den Vorzug zu geben. Mit diesem Buch etablierte sich auch der Sinn fürs Humorvolle, der von da an den polynesischen Pop beherrschte. Ursprünglich aber waren es viel archaischere Bedürfnisse, die durch die Berichte aus Polynesien angesprochen worden waren. „Auf der Insel Otaheite (Tahiti), wo Liebe die Hauptbeschäftigung ist, der bevorzugte Luxus, oder genauer gesagt, der einzige Luxus der Einwohner, sind die Körper und Seelen der Frauen perfekt geformt." (Joseph Banks, 1743–1820, Naturforscher auf Cooks „Endeavour")

Bemerkungen wie diese machten aus dem nackten Eingeborenenmädchen, der Wahine, die Eva im polynesischen Garten Eden. Sie wurde die erste und wichtigste Ikone des polynesischen Pop, verkörperte sie doch die Verheißung bedingungsloser Liebe. Bald kamen andere Sinnbilder hinzu, zum Beispiel die Palme, die Eingeborenenhütte, das Einbaumkanu und alle Arten exotischer Tiere und Pflanzen, die eine ganze Galerie populärer Symbole der ozeanischen Kultur bildeten. Tiki war bislang lediglich eine von vielen Figuren, die das Märchenland „Polynesia-Americana" bevölkerten.

Als in den 20er Jahren im ganzen Land eine riesige Begeisterung für hawaiische Musik ausbrach, wurde auch die Hawaiigitarre, die Ukulele, immer beliebter. Nachtclubs rissen sich um hawaiische Entertainer und die Clubs legten sich zunehmend ein tropisches Ambiente zu. Bambus und Rattan vom Boden bis zur Decke, üppige tropische Pflanzen und Wandschmuck von den Inseln gehörten für diese frühen Stadtflüchtigen zur Grundausstattung, mit der sie sich die Illusion verschafften, in die Südsee entkommen zu sein.

Und bald richtete sich die allgemeine Aufmerksamkeit auf ein neues Symbol: In Europa entstanden die ersten Zoos und zu ihrer Attraktionen wurden auch „wirkliche Wilde" hinzugenommen, *das* Faszinosum für die Damenwelt, worüber sich die Journalisten immer wieder mokierten. Das ambivalente Verhältnis von Attraktion und Aversion, mit dem man den „Wilden" begegnete, die Anziehungskraft des „exotischen Anderen" fand Eingang in das kollektive Bewusstsein der westlichen Welt. In der Polynesischen Popkultur nahm diese Faszination die Form des Tiki an.

TIKI: EINE GENERATION SPANNT AUS

„Das ganze Wesen der Götzenanbetung, welches von einem Volk gepflegt wurde, das von der Mehrheit seiner Artgenossen durch das unendliche Meer getrennt war, aber in ungewöhnlichem Masse über die Mittel verfügte, sich nicht nur selbst zu erhalten, sondern sogar im Überfluss zu leben, ist eine höchst bewegende Zurschaustellung von Dummheit, Absurdität und Entwürdigung."

(Reverend William Ellis: Polynesian Researches, 1831)

In den 50er Jahren waren die Amerikaner bereit, die Früchte ihrer harten Arbeit, die ihnen wirtschaftliche Unabhängigkeit und Wohlstand gebracht hatte, zu ernten. Sie waren als Helden aus dem Zweiten Weltkrieg hervorgegangen und sonnten sich in internationalem Erfolg und Anerkennung. Doch dasselbe puritanische Arbeitsethos, durch das sie es so weit gebracht hatten, zog auch ein ganzes Bündel sozialer und moralischer Einschränkungen nach sich, die es ihnen erschwerten, ihren Wohlstand zu genießen.

Polynesische Partys gestatteten dem Mann im grauen Flanellanzug, sich in einen von allen Regeln befreiten Wilden zu verwandeln: In bunte Hawaii-Hemden gekleidet (die nicht in die Hose gesteckt werden mussten!), leicht berauscht von exotischen Drinks mit noch exotischeren Namen, die an Babysprache erinnerten (Lapu Lapu, Mauna Loa Puki), während sie mit bloßen Händen von dem Luau-Schwein aßen und sich an Hula- und Limbo-Wettbewerben beteiligten – endlich durften sie sich vergnügen und sich gehen lassen, und das in einer Gesellschaft, in der es ansonsten ausgesprochen konservativ zuging.

Eine weitere Freiheit, die man als „Vorstadtwilder" genoss, war die Erlaubnis, sich Bilder von barbusigen eingeborenen Frauen anzusehen, solange dies etwas mit einem anthropologischen Interesse zu tun hatte, man also eine Art National Geographic-Erotik praktizierte. Doch als die Wahine und all die anderen Klischee-Ikonen des Südsee-Märchenlandes wieder hervorgeholt wurden, tauchte eine neue Gallionsfigur des polynesischen Volksbrauchtums auf: das geschnitzte Götzenbild der Eingeborenen, das gemeinhin Tiki genannt wurde. Obwohl es diesen Begriff weder in der hawaiischen noch in tahitischen Sprache gab und die Steinskulpturen auf den Osterinseln immer noch „Moai" hießen, wurden im polynesischen Pop alle ozeanischen Schnitzereien Mitglieder einer großen glücklichen Familie: der Tikis. Diese primitiven Götzen waren ein Antidot gegen die moderne Welt aus Plastik und Chrom, phallische Monumente der menschlichen Triebe. Zwar richteten sich die amerikanischen Tikis in ihrer Form weitgehend nach ihren polynesischen Vorbildern, waren aber doch meistens frei nachempfundene Interpretationen von Stilen, die sich aus mehreren Inselkulturen zusammensetzten, gemischt mit einer guten Dosis Comics-Fantasie und einem Touch moderner Kunst. Selbst die Figuren, die als „authentisch" bezeichnet werden konnten, waren lediglich Kopien von den wenigen Originalen, die den fanatischen „Bildersturm" der Missionare überlebt hatten. Diese liberale Einstellung gegenüber Nachbildungen hatte sich auf den hawaiischen Inseln schon bei den frühesten westlichen Kontakten abgezeichnet, wie man aus dem folgenden Dokument von 1825 ersieht: „Die Offiziere des königlich britannischen Schiffes ‚Blonde' wollten, als sie sich hier aufhielten, unbedingt ein paar alte Götzenbilder haben, um sie als Andenken mit nach Hause zu nehmen. Durch die große Nachfrage waren die verfügbaren Vorräte bald erschöpft: Um den Mangel zu beheben, fertigten die Hawaiianer neue Figuren und schwärzten sie mit Rauch, um ihnen ein antikes Aussehen zu geben, und tatsächlich gelang ihnen diese Täuschung" (W.S.W. Ruschenberger: Extracts from the Journal of an American Naval Officer, 1841). Mehr als ein Jahrhundert später erklärte Pablo Picasso, ein Sammler primitiver Kunst und begeisterter Flohmarktbesucher: „Man braucht kein Meisterwerk, um die Idee zu verstehen. Die Grundidee oder das Wesentliche eines Stils wird auch bei einem zweitklassigen Exemplar und sogar bei Fälschungen völlig plausibel." Also hatten auch amerikanische Künstler, die ganz vom Geist des Tiki erfüllt waren, keine Hemmungen, die Götzenköpfe auf ihre bizarre Art neu zu kreieren.

Ein perfektes Beispiel für diesen Stil ist der Tiki, den Alec Yuill-Thornton für Tiki Bob's Bar in San Francisco schuf. Diese Skulptur, ein bisschen George Jetson, ein bisschen moderner Primitivismus, hat nur noch sehr wenig mit den ozeanischen Artefakten zu tun. Sie markiert aber, gemeinsam mit dem Tiki-Signet von Stephen Cranes Luau den Beginn des Tiki-Stils. Zum ersten Mal wurde ein Tiki als Logo verwendet; er stand als Wächter am Eingang, war auf den Speisekarten und Streichholzheftchen abgebildet und tauchte auch als Krug und als Salz- und Pfefferstreuer wieder auf.

„Sneaky" Bob Bryant hatte als Trader Vics Barkeeper gearbeitet, aber als sie sich 1955 überwarfen, zog Bob vom Traders am Cosmo Place einen Block weiter und eröffnete seine eigene Bar. Sein Versuch, dieses Konzept als Franchise an das Capitol Inn in Sacramento zu verkaufen, hatte nur kurzfristigen Erfolg. Bob eröffnete außerdem Tiki Bobs Mainland an der Bush Street, wo er Dessous-Modenschauen veranstaltete, um die Geschäftsleute zur Mittagszeit anzulocken.

Tiki wurde zum Star im polynesischen Pop-Theater und so taufte man mit seinem Namen viele Lokale quer durch die U.S.A., von Alabama bis Alaska, wobei er in seinen vielfältigen Erscheinungsformen unzählige Bars schmückte, die den zivilisationsmüden Zeitgenossen Erfrischung versprachen. Tiki-Darstellungen erreichten den Höhepunkt ihrer Beliebtheit, als in der TV-Serie „Hawaiian Eye" ein Tiki als Logo benutzt wurde; diese Serie wurde von 1959 bis 1963 ausgestrahlt, und das archaische Logo grub sich fast unmerklich in die hypnotisierten Mittelstandsgemüter ein.

Aber als das Tiki-Fieber gerade auf seinem Höhepunkt angekommen war, setzte ihm der schwere Generationenkonflikt der 60er Jahre ein Ende. Die Kinder der Tiki-Schwärmer beschlossen, sich ihr eigenes Nirwana zu erschaffen, wo die freie Liebe und exotisches Glück zur Realität wurden. Alkohol gehörte nicht länger zu den bevorzugten Rauschmitteln, Marihuana und psychedelische Drogen wurden zum neuen Freizeitvergnügen, und gleichzeitig schien die sexuelle Revolution alle puritanischen Begriffe von Monogamie hinwegzufegen. Die tropischen Cocktails gerieten ebenso in Konflikt mit dem wachsenden Gesundheitsbewusstsein wie die fettige und süße pseudo-chinesische Küche.

Die „britische Invasion" verlagerte das Interesse der jungen Generation auf einen weiteren merkwürdigen Kult aus Übersee: The Beatles. Und in ihrem Song „Holiday in Waikiki" klagten The Kings über ein Plastikpolynesien: „... and even all the grass skirts were PVC!" Genau wie die Polynesier zwei Jahrhunderte zuvor festgestellt hatten, dass die weißen Forscher keine Götter waren, als sie Captain Cook in einem Scharmützel in der Kealakekua Bay töten konnten, erlebten die Amerikaner mit dem Kennedy-Attentat 1963 einen traumatischen Zusammenbruch ihres Selbstbewusstseins. Das war der Anfang vom Ende, der Verlust ihrer jungenhaften Unschuld, sowohl in der Selbstwahrnehmung als auch in dem Bild, das die Welt von Amerika hatte.

Exotica und Tiki-Style wurden als Rituale denunziert, die vom imperialistischen Establishment erfunden worden seien, und das zu einer Zeit, da die Erkenntnis sich durchzusetzen begann, dass der Vietnamkrieg von Beginn an ein grauenvoller Fehler gewesen war – sah man doch im Fernsehen Eingeborenenhütten und Palmen brennen. Junge Rebellen zogen im Protestmarsch zum Capitol in Washington, während Richard Nixon in seinem Stammlokal, dem Washington Trader Vic's, Mai-Tais schlürfte.

Zusätzlich wurde der für die jüngere Generation diskreditierte polynesische Stil in den 70er Jahren durch die Einführung eines generalisierten Tropenthemas verwässert, das keine eindeutige Identität, keine Inselmerkmale mehr aufwies. Ob Karibik, Mexiko oder Polynesien, überall war „Margharita-Ville". Die populäre Fernsehshow „Fantasy Island" war ein typisches Beispiel für diese politisch korrekte Abgrenzung von kultureller Komplizenschaft und kreierte stattdessen eine Welt im Kolonialstil aus Korbgeflecht, durchmischt mit exotischen Pflanzen. Die mit Farnen dekorierte Bar trat nun an die Stelle der Tiki-Bar.

Die 80er Jahre waren das Jahrzehnt des Niedergangs der Tiki-Kultur. Die polynesischen Paläste wurden entweder dem Erdboden gleichgemacht oder so umgebaut, dass man sie nicht wieder erkannte; sie verschwanden, ohne dass man sie je als eine besondere Facette der amerikanischen Popkultur anerkannt hatte. In den 80er Jahren stellten sie nur noch eine peinliche Geschmacksverirrung dar. Unbemerkt und unbetrauert verschwand eine ganze kulturelle Tradition.

DER BAU EINES TIKI-TEMPELS

Der Bau eines „Hale Tiki" (Tiki-Hauses) war ein kompliziertes Unterfangen, nicht nur wegen der diversen exotischen Materialien, die dafür benötigt wurden, sondern auch wegen der außergewöhnlichen Entwürfe, mit denen man die Tiki-Anhänger, die sich hier exotischen Trinkritualen hingaben, verblüffen und begeistern wollte.

Dieses Kapitel möchte einen bisher kaum gewürdigten Aspekt der amerikanischen Popkultur vorstellen und befaßt sich mit den für den Tiki-Stil charakteristischen architektonischen Ausdrucksformen. Obwohl es eine klare Traditionslinie gibt, der man sich seit *Don the Beachcomber* anschloß und man bestimmte Entwürfe immer und immer wieder aufgriff und variierte, so ist es doch kennzeichnend für den Tiki-Stil, dass ihn jeder, der vom Tiki-Fieber erfasst war, auf seine Weise neu interpretierte. Vom künstlichen Dschungel bis zu bestimmten Ritualen, mit denen die Drinks serviert wurden, die Fantasie kannte keine Grenzen, als die Amerikaner einmal beschlossen hatten, dem Ruf von Tiki zu folgen und ihre ganz persönlichen Versionen eines Südsee-Refugiums zu entwerfen.

Der beliebteste architektonische Entwurf war der einer A-Form. War es bloßer Zufall, dass gegen Ende der 50er Jahre der neue Primitivismus des Tiki-Stils auf sein genaues Gegenteil traf, den futuristischen Stil des Düsenzeitalters, oder bedingte das eine das andere? Wie auch immer, beide vereinten sich ruhmvoll unter der A-Form. Mit Eero Saarinens TWA-Terminal und Frank Lloyd Wrights First Unitarian Church wurden spitz aufragende Giebel zum Lieblingsspielzeug moderner Architekten. Wie in der Heckflosse des Cadillac drückte sich auch in ihm der optimistische Glaube an das Raketenzeitalter aus.

Zufällig waren die meisten traditionellen ozeanischen Wohnhäuser Palmenhütten und daher in A-Form errichtet. Doch da die Eingeborenenhäuser der Polynesier mit Ausnahme der kunstvoll geschnitzten Maori-Versammlungshäuser gänzlich ungeschmückt waren, bediente man sich der Südseekultur. Das neuguineische Kulthaus oder „Haus Tambaran" mit seinem geschwungenen Giebel und der mit Masken geschmückten Vorderfront und das zeremonielle Versammlungshaus aus Palau, Mikronesien, mit seinen bunten Frontbemalungen waren die Vorbilder für viele amerikanische Tiki-Tempel. Als moderne Primitive der Mittelklasse trafen die Jetsons auf die Feuersteins, parkten ihre Shuttle-Maschinen vor diesen Raumschiffen vom Planet Tiki und überschritten nur allzu gern die Grenze zu einer anderen Dimension, einer anderen Welt, um für eine gewisse Zeit zu Mitgliedern des Tiki-Stammes zu werden.

A-Formen waren einfach zu bauen, und so wurden herkömmliche Bauten wie Wisconsin-Blockhütten oder klassische Geschäftshäuser in heidnische Paläste umgestaltet, indem man sie um eine spitz zulaufende Eingangshalle erweiterte. Chinarestaurants modernisierten ihr Interieur und übernahmen den Hüttenlook, um von der polynesischen Welle zu profitieren. Doch was spielte sich hinter dem großen A ab? Um die Schwelle zu einer anderen Realität zu symbolisieren, musste häufig eine Brücke überquert werden, die über einen Fluss führte; dieser wurde von einem Wasserfall gespeist, der über einen Lava-Felsen herabfiel. Das Element des Feuers wurde mit gasgetriebenen Tiki-Fackeln ins Spiel gebracht, die manchmal auch als Leuchtfeuer die Spitzen der Giebel zierten, und auch drinnen gab es Wasserfälle, die für ein Plätschern im Hintergrund sorgten. Imponierende

Tikis flankierten den Eingang, glotzten zwischen dem Dschungel-Blattwerk hervor und dienten als Pfosten oder hatten andere architektonische Zwecke.

Im Inneren befand sich eine Erlebniswelt, die alle Sinne ansprach. Die verschiedenen Räume trugen malerische Namen wie „Schwarzes Loch von Kalkutta" oder „Salon der sieben Freuden" und waren vom Boden bis zur Decke mit exotischen Hölzern, Bambus, Rattan, Tapa-Stoffen und anderen organischen Materialien ausgekleidet. Primitive Waffen und Masken schmückten die Wände und unter der Decke hingen Beachcomber-Lampen und ähnliches Strandgut. Wandbilder vom Inselleben und dreidimensionale Dioramen verstärkten darüber hinaus die Illusion, sich in einem fernen Teil der Welt zu befinden.

Ein weiteres wichtiges Material war die menschliche Haut: Viele Etablissements rühmten sich ihrer spärlich bekleideten exotischen Kellnerinnen; sie waren die lebendigen Gegenstücke zu den Akten in schwarzem Samt, die ebenfalls zum üblichen Dekor von Tiki-Lokalen gehörten. Für die Krieger im weißen Kragen bedeutete diese Fleischbeschau eine besondere Attraktion, die durch die polynesischen Varieteevorführungen zum üblichen Unterhaltungsprogramm in vielen Südsee-Nachtclubs gehörten. Dass die samoanischen Feuertänzer oder die tahitischen Hula-Mädchen häufig aus Südamerika oder Asien stammten, war dabei nicht wichtig. Die Kostüme und die Musik, die exotischen Materialien, die tropische Ausstattung und die starken Drinks – das alles ergab ein wirksames Gemisch, um alle kleinlichen Bedenken, ob dies nun authentisch war oder nicht, in Luft aufzulösen; stattdessen durfte sich der Tiki-Nachtschwärmer ganz dem unwirklichen Zauber des städtischen polynesischen Paradieses hingeben.

DON THE BEACHCOMBER – AHNHERR DES POLYNESISCHEN POP

Hollywood 1934: Amerikas „nobles Experiment" mit der Prohibition war gerade beendet worden. Hochprozentiges war gefragt, und ein aus New Orleans zugezogener Gastronom namens Ernest Beaumont-Gantt beschloss, mit Rum ein Experiment zu wagen. Vielleicht war es die Vergangenheit seiner Heimatstadt als Piratennest, vielleicht auch die Tatsache, dass sein Vater, Hotelier in New Orleans, ihn mit auf Reisen nach Jamaika genommen hatte – wie auch immer: Ernest kam auf die Idee, eine kleine Bar am McCadden Place in Hollywood zu eröffnen, die er mit ein paar künstlichen Palmen schmückte und *Don the Beachcomber* nannte. Hier mixte er das flüssige Gold wie ein Alchimist auf der Suche nach dem Stein der Weisen und kreierte dabei hochprozentige Cocktails, mit denen seine Gäste eine Zeit lang an ferne Küsten entfliehen konnten, während draußen das Großstadtleben vorbeirauschte. Ernest identifizierte sich so sehr mit der Figur des Beachcomber, des „Strand-Streichers", dass er seinen Namen offiziell in Don Beach änderte. Seine besonderen Fähigkeiten als Barkeeper zogen schon bald die nach Alkohol und exotischer Atmosphäre lechzende Filmwelt an, und 1937 baute er seine Bar zu einem Südsee-Refugium aus, das zum Vorbild für viele weitere Gastronomen werden sollte: Don gestaltete sein polynesisches Paradies wie eine Insel im Stadtozean, als Zufluchtsort vor der brodelnden Großstadt.

Die Grundausstattung bestand aus exotischen Materialien wie Bambus, Lahaula-Matten und importierten Hölzern. Tropische Pflanzen, frische Blumengirlanden und Gebinde aus Bananen und Kokosnüssen sorgten für die Dschungel-Atmosphäre, während Waffen von Eingeborenen und andere ozeanische Artefakte eine Stimmung primitiver Zivilisationen heraufbeschworen. Strandgut und Krimskrams aus allen Ecken und Enden der Welt hing von der Decke und verstärkte die Illusion, dass man irgendwo in einem Hafen der Freuden gelandet sei. Ein regelmäßig wiederkehrender künstlicher Regenschauer erweckte den Eindruck, dass man gerade einem tropischen Wolkenbruch entgangen sei, während die sanften Töne der ununterbrochen laufenden Hintergrundmusik die Gäste in ihre exotischen Träumereien einlullte. Das Ganze wurde durch Dons hochwirksame Cocktail-Kreationen verstärkt, die bisweilen in ausgehöhlten Ananasfrüchten serviert wurden. Doch was Don Beach an Showtalent und Fantasie besaß, fehlte ihm an Geschäftstüchtigkeit. Um diesen Part kümmerte sich seine Frau Cora Irene „Sunny" Sund. Die geschäftliche Teilhaberschaft mündete 1937 in der Ehe, die aber schon drei Jahre später geschieden wurde. Geschäftlich hielt Sunny die Zügel fest im Griff, so fest, dass Don, als er von seiner Verpflichtung im Kriegsdienst als Oberst der Luftwaffe aus dem Zweiten Weltkriegs zurückkehrte, feststellen musste, dass sie ihn aus seinem eigenen Lokal ausgebootet hatte. Sunny hatte 1940 die Eröffnung des ersten Franchise-Betriebs in Chicago eingeleitet und das Unternehmen war jetzt fest in ihrer Hand; sie brauchte Don nicht mehr, nur noch seinen Namen.

Da Don aber von jeher eher ein Ideengeber denn ein Manager gewesen war, erklärte er sich einverstanden, dem *Don the Beachcomber* in beratender Funktion zur Seite zu stehen, gleichzeitig aber steckte er all seine kreativen Energien in sein Traumprojekt: ein eigenes Lokal auf Hawaii.

Don hatte aber auch einen Prototyp geschaffen: den urbanen Beachcomber, eine Person irgendwo zwischen weit gereistem Connaisseur, Strand-Beatnik und Jachthafen-Playboy. In der Hochzeit des polynesischen Pop kamen andere Beachniks zum Vorschein, der bemerkenswerteste unter ihnen Ely Hedley, der auch als der „Original-Beachcomber" bekannt war.

Ehemals ein erfolgloser Lebensmittelhändler in Oklahoma, war er dem Ruf des Pazifischen Ozeans gefolgt und mit seiner Familie nach Whites Point, einer kleinen Bucht in der Nähe von San Pedro bei Los Angeles, gezogen. Dort baute er mit seiner Frau und seinen vier Töchtern ein Haus aus Treibholz und begann einen florierenden Handel mit Lampen und Möbeln, die sie aus dem Treibgut und Fundsachen herstellten, der ihnen vors Haus gespült wurde. Ely wurde so bekannt für seinen Stil, „Beachcomber modern" genannt, dass er Aufträge zur Einrichtung von Tiki-Tempeln wie *Trader Dick's* und *Harvey's* in Nevada bekam. Als das Tiki-Fieber ausbrach, fing er an, Tikis zu schnitzen, und eröffnete seinen *Island Trade Store* zuerst in Huntington Beach und dann im *Adventureland* in Disneyland. Nachdem Ely Hedley den Tiki-Stil entscheidend mitgeprägt hatte, zog er sich in die *Islander*-Apartments in Santa Ana zurück, die er selbst eingerichtet hatte.

In der Zwischenzeit war *Don the Beachcomber* zu einem kommerziellen Markenzeichen geworden und das Geschäft war schon zweimal in andere Hände übergegangen, um schließlich im Besitz der Getty-Corporation zu landen. Die Logo-Figur ähnelte nun nicht mehr dem leibhaftigen Don, sondern war modernisiert worden und sah wie irgendein x-beliebiger, freundlicher Lebenskünstler aus. Das Franchise-Unternehmen war auf 16 Lokale angewachsen, von denen einige, etwa das in Dallas und in Marina Del Rey, wie braune Ufos aussahen. Andere Polynesienbegeisterte überall in den Staaten hatten sich von dem Beachcomber-Vorbild beeinflussen lassen, aber keiner kam an Dons Flair heran. Wenige Jahre nach Dons Tod im Jahre 1987 wurden auch die Überreste der Restaurantkette, die seinen Namen trug, aber schon lange ohne sein „Mana" existiert hatte, geschlossen. Sein prägender Einfluss auf das Phänomen des polynesischen Pop jedoch bleibt unvergessen.

TRADER VIC – DER BOTSCHAFTER DES GUTEN GESCHMACKS

Die Amerikanisierung von Tiki als einem Freizeitgott war ein allmählicher Prozess. Einer seiner wichtigsten Propheten war ein Mann namens Victor Bergeron, besser bekannt als Trader Vic. Zwar stellte er die Gottheit nicht ins Zentrum seiner Religion – er benutzte vielmehr seine eigenen mythologischen Figuren, die „Menehune", das „kleine Volk" aus den polynesischen Legenden –, doch seit Beginn der 50er Jahre war Tiki immer um ihn. Und der Trader war eine jener überlebensgroßen Figuren, ein Original, Angehöriger einer aussterbenden Spezies von einzigartigen Charakteren, wie man sie heute im öffentlichen Leben nicht mehr findet.

Er war Patriarch, Gentleman und Chauvinist zugleich; ein erfolgreicher Gastronom und Genussmensch, der eine ganze Generation von kultivierten Wilden dazu anregte, der Zivilisation den Rücken zu kehren, und sich in Bars und Res-

taurants, in Gärten, Hinterhöfen und auf Bowlingbahnen ein eigenes Polynesien zu schaffen. Er erhob das Essen und Trinken nach Südseeart zu einer Kunst – „chow and grog", wie er es in seiner rauen Art zu nennen pflegte. Mehr noch als Don the Beachcomber, der angeblich auf den Namen „Rumaki" für seine Vorspeisenkreation gekommen ist, indem er mit seinem Finger in die Seiten eines Lexikons von den Cook-Inseln stach, war Trader Vic ein richtiger kulinarischer Erneuerer. Nach seinem Erfolg mit dem „Nouveau Polynesian"-Stil gehörte er zu den ersten, die die mexikanische Küche in Amerika populär machten.

Es begann alles in einem Lokal namens *Hinky Dinks* in Oakland auf der anderen Seite der Bucht von San Francisco. Dies war Vics erster eigener Laden, eine Holzhütte, die er 1934 mit seinen letzten 500 Dollar errichtet hatte. In der Geschichte des polynesischen Pop gab es bestimmte „Energiezentren" wie das *Beachcomber* in Hollywood, das *Luau* in Beverly Hills, das *Lanai* in San Mateo oder das *Bali Ha'i* in San Diego, die das Mana der Tiki-Kultur ausstrahlten. *Hinki Dinks*, das bald *Trader Vic's* heißen sollte, gehörte dazu. Victor Bergeron war ein ehrgeiziger Mann mit einer Vorliebe für fantasievolle Cocktails, und genau danach hatten die Leute Sehnsucht, nachdem die Prohibition endlich aufgehoben war. Er ging auf eine „Forschungsreise" nach Kuba und Louisiana und experimentierte an Ort und Stelle mit den Top-Barkeepern. Aber ein Besuch in Los Angeles hatte den entscheidenden Einfluss. In seiner Biografie verrät er: „Wir fuhren zu einem Lokal namens *South Seas*, das es heute nicht mehr gibt, und besuchten auch das *Don the Beachcomber* in Hollywood. Ich habe sogar ein paar Flaschen im *Don the Beachcomber* gekauft. Als ich wieder in Oakland war und meiner Frau erzählte, was ich gesehen hatte, waren wir uns einig, den Namen unseres Restaurants zu ändern und auch die gesamte Einrichtung. Wir fanden beide, dass *Hinky Dinks* ein blöder Name war und das Lokal nach jemandem benannt werden sollte, über den wir etwas zu erzählen hatten. Meine Frau schlug *Trader Vic's* vor, weil ich ständig mit irgendjemandem Geschäfte machte. So war es, ich wurde also Trader Vic." Daraufhin bekam das Holzbein, das die Folge einer Tuberkuloseerkrankung in seiner Kindheit war (und das schon manchmal dazu gedient hatte, seine Gäste zu unterhalten, indem er völlig überraschend einen Eispickel hineinstach), eine neue Geschichte: Er habe es der Begegnung mit einem Hai zu verdanken – eines der vielen Märchen, die auf Vics neue Rolle zugeschnitten waren.

Das freimütige Geständnis den Ursprung des *Trader Vic* betreffend kam von einem Mann, der nicht nur genauso viel wie sein Kollege und Vorgänger erreicht, sondern ihn sogar übertrumpft hatte. Vic musste nie verheimlichen, wo seine Ursprünge lagen, denn er hatte nie die Leitung seines Unternehmens verloren, wie es Don passiert war, und als der polynesische Trend in den 50er Jahren richtig los ging, war er in der Lage, ihn voll zu nutzen. Nachdem er 1949 seine erste Filiale in Seattle gegründet hatte, die er *The Outrigger* nannte, folgten Lokale in San Francisco (1951), Denver (1954), Beverly Hills (1955), Chicago (1957), New York und Havanna (1958) und Portland (1959); später in Boston, Houston, Dallas, Detroit, Atlanta, Kansas City, St. Louis, St. Petersburg, Washington, Vancouver, Scottsdale, London, München und in vielen anderen Städten im Ausland.

Vic weitete seinen Einfluss noch weiter aus, indem er Cocktail- und Rezeptbücher veröffentlichte, in denen er bevorzugt Produkte aus seiner neuen „Trader Vic's Food Products Company" verwendete. In diesen Veröffentlichungen breitete er seine Ansichten über gesellige Zusammenkünfte und Essgewohnheiten der Mittelklasse aus, und zwar in seinem charakteristischen Trader Vic-Tonfall, der sich deutlich von der blumigen Prosa unterschied, die er in seinen Speisekarten verwendete: „Es gibt ein paar Sachen, die mir besonders sauer aufstoßen, wenn ich sehe, was da zusammengekocht wird, wenn man mal bei jemandem eingeladen wird, wo's ein bisschen was zu Essen und zu Trinken geben soll. Ich bin dafür, dass die durchschnittliche amerikanische Gastgeberin einen leichten Tritt in ihr kulinarisches Hinterteil vertragen kann, legen wir also los. Die Leckerbissen, die üblicherweise auf Cocktailpartys serviert werden, bringen mich ganz einfach um. Nachdem ich mir nun viele Jahre lang Hunderte von Silbertabletts und ihren Inhalt angeguckt habe, bin ich zu dem Schluss gekommen, dass irgendjemand einen jährlichen Pulitzerpreis für das absolut tödlichste Hors d'œuvre ausgeschrieben hat." Der Trader spielte ein grantiges Rauhbein, und die Leute liebten ihn dafür.

Als Hawaii Amerikas Ferientraumziel Nummer eins wurde, engagierte man Vic, um als Ernährungsberater für die United Airlines und die Hotels der Matson-Reederei zu fungieren, die die beiden wichtigsten Reiseunternehmen zwischen den Inseln und den USA waren. Schon früher, um 1940, war er eine Partnerschaft eingegangen, um ein Lokal in Honolulu zu eröffnen, doch aufgrund von Meinungsverschiedenheiten zog er sich daraus zurück und überließ der anderen Seite das Recht, seinen Namen auf den Inseln zu benutzen. Die Tatsache, dass ein ursprünglich aus Kalifornien stammendes *Trader Vic's* auf Hawaii eröffnet wurde, dem später auch ein *Don the Beachcomber*, Stephen Cranes *Kon-Tiki* und *Christian's Hut* folgten, stützt die Behauptung, der polynesische Pop sei tatsächlich eine Facette der amerikanischen Popkultur und nach Hawaii importiert worden, um die Erwartungen der Touristen zu erfüllen.

Die Ausweitung des Trader-Imperiums wurde durch die Zusammenarbeit mit finanzstarken größeren Hotelketten ermöglicht. Sie hatten die finanziellen Mittel, so raffinierte Bauten hinzustellen, wie ein Tiki-Lokal der Extraklasse es erforderte, und *Trader Vic's* war Extraklasse. Andere Südseekneipen, die häufig seinen Spitznamen kopierten, waren eher für das gemeine Fußvolk gedacht, während *Vic's* der Offiziersclub war. Aber nicht etwa, weil Vic ein Snob war, sondern weil er Geld damit verdienen wollte. Doch letztlich war dies einer der Gründe für den Untergang der Kette, denn als die Oberschichtenklientel, die diese Genusstempel aufzusuchen pflegte, ausstarb, suchte die jüngere Generation nach erschwinglicheren und weniger gekünstelten Lokalitäten.

Bedauerlicherweise sind in den 90er Jahren noch die Filialen in Seattle, Washington, Vancouver, Portland und sogar in San Francisco geschlossen worden. Aber in Übersee hält sich *Trader Vic's* gut und ist die einzige Kette mit Tiki-Lokalen, die bis heute überlebt hat. Trotz der misslungenen Renovierungen in den 80er Jahren, bei denen die charakteristischen Vogelkäfiglampen und andere traditionelle Einrichtungsstücke als „Staubfänger" hinausgeworfen wurden, gibt es immer noch *Trader Vic's* in Chicago und München, die als seltene Beispiele für den Tiki-Stil erhalten geblieben sind.

STEPHEN CRANE – DER MANN, DER DIE FRAUEN LIEBTE

In polynesischen Legenden von der Insel Mangareva und den Marquesa-Inseln wird Tiki, der erste Mann, als Gauner und Frauenheld dargestellt. Schließlich war er es, der die erste Frau aus Lehm schuf und sogleich daranging, alle Kinder dieser Welt mit ihr zu machen. Daher scheint es nur recht und billig, dass der nächste, der die Tiki-Fackel übernahm, ein Mann war, der für seine Geselligkeit bekannt war und Frauen im Nu eroberte. Er war ein erfolgloser B-Picture-Schauspieler („Cry of the Werewolf"), und sein einziger Anspruch auf Ruhm gründete darin, mit Lana Turner verheiratet gewesen zu sein. Die Ehe hielt nur fünf Monate, aber sie hatten eine gemeinsame Tochter, Cheryl, die später als Teenager in die Schlagzeilen geriet, weil sie Lanas Mafioso-Liebhaber Johnny Stompanato erstochen hatte (was damit zu tun hatte, dass sie zuvor schon von einem anderen Verehrer ihrer Mutter, dem Film-Tarzan Lex Barker, vergewaltigt worden war). Stephen aber blieb mit Lana befreundet, während er daranging, weitere Filmstars zu verführen. Der Besitzer von *Ciro's*, Hollywoods bekanntestem Ausgehlokal in den 40er Jahren, bemerkte staunend, nachdem er Steve an drei aufeinander folgenden Abenden mit Ava Gardner, Rita Hayworth und Lana Turner gesehen hatte: „Mit den drei absoluten Königinnen der Stadt! Ich hab noch nie jemanden kennengelernt, der das geschafft hat."

Glücklicherweise konzentrierte Stephen Crane seine Energie schon bald auf sein anderes Talent, Geselligkeit zu organisieren und zu unterhalten. 1953 eröff-

nete er das Restaurant *Luau* in Beverly Hills am 421 Rodeo Drive. Dort war vorher das Südseelokal *The Tropic* beheimatet gewesen, und Stephen baute die thematische Ausrichtung des Lokals weiter aus, wobei er im Sinn hatte, die Klientel aus der „Filmkolonie" anzuziehen. Er tat dies auf seine Weise, wie sich seine Tochter Cheryl in ihrer Biografie „Detour – A Hollywood Story" erinnert: „Er überlegte sich, dass Männer besonders gern in solche Lokale gingen, die auch für Frauen attraktiv waren, und darum wollte er den Ort so verführerisch machen wie eine Honigfalle … Das Herzstück von Daddys Honigfalle war eine wenig bekannte und nie hinausposaunte Regel, dass er nämlich ausgewählten und sehr teuren Callgirls erlaubte, sich diskret an der Bar aufzuhalten. Es waren häufig erfolglose Starlets, aufregend und geschmackvoll gekleidet, die die Männer anzogen, für weibliche Gäste jedoch kein Störfaktor waren, da diese nur selten erkannten, um wen es sich dabei wirklich handelte."

Um das Prinzip „Die Schöne und das Biest" voll zum Tragen kommen zu lassen, bevölkerte Crane sein Paradies mit Tikis und stellte sie in seiner Speisekarte vor: „Von besonderem Interesse sind die Tikis, die großen und wunderbar ungraziösen Holzfiguren, die Sie um sich haben. Ein Tiki ist ein heidnischer Gott, ein Götze. Obwohl heute die meisten Bewohner der Südseeinseln Christen sind, bringen sie den Göttern ihrer Vorfahren immer noch Respekt und Verehrung entgegen, und hier bei uns im *Luau* haben wir Tikis u. a. als Regengott, Sonnengott und Kriegsgott. Der Tiki mit dem besonders großen Mund ist der Gott des Trinkens, der Großmäulige. Der Tiki mit dem größten Bauch ist unser Lieblingsgott, vielleicht weil er der Gott des guten Essens ist." Dieser humorvolle und naive Umgang mit der erloschenen Religion eines anderen Volkes sollte fortan für den Tiki-Stil charakteristisch sein. Zum ersten Mal wurde ein Tiki, der den beiden holzgeschnitzten Eingangsposten ähnlich sah, als Sinnbild auf der Speisekarte, den Streichhölzern und Postkarten sowie für den Fuß einer Keramiklampe und als Salz- und Pfefferstreuer verwendet.

Für die übrige Einrichtung hatte Stephen kräftig Anleihen beim *Beachcomber* und *Trader Vic* genommen. Artdirector Florian Gabriel erinnert sich, dass Stephen Crane and Associates für seinen Job von ihm erwarteten, ins *Trader Vic's* im Beverly Hilton (das sich einst rühmen konnte, fünf Tikis von 4,5 Meter Höhe vor dem Lokal stehen zu haben) zu gehen um eine Ecke des Restaurants zu skizzieren, was ihm auch gelang. Er bildete gemeinsam mit George Nakashima, der zuvor für Welton Becket, den Architekten des *Beverly Hilton*, gearbeitet hatte ein Einrichtungsteam. Sie wirkten auch daran mit, die Filialen aufzubauen, die Stephen Crane am Ende der 50er Jahre in anderen amerikanischen Städten errichtete.

Die Sheraton Corporation, die unbedingt mit dem *Hilton* gleichziehen wollte, hatte Crane gebeten ein Lokal wie sein *Luau* in ihrem Hotel in Montreal einzurichten; es wurde 1958 unter dem Namen *Kon-Tiki* eröffnet und präsentierte sich dem begeisterten Publikum mit „von den Maoris handgeschnitzten Wandtäfelungen mit speziellen Mustern, um böse Geister fernzuhalten, mit Speeren aus Neuguinea, deren Fledermausflügel-Spitzen von den Jägern in Gift getaucht wurden, und einem Opferaltar". In den nächsten Jahren folgten dann Portland (mit drei Wasserfällen!), Chicago, Dallas, Cleveland und Honolulu. Das *Kon-Tiki Ports* in Chicago und das *Ports of Call* in Dallas entwickelten das Konzept des Westentaschen-Abenteurers weiter und gestalteten jeden Speisesaal nach einem anderen Motto: Papeete, Singapur, Macao und Saigon. Ihre Geschichten waren reinste polynesische Pop-Poesie: „*Papeete* – einer von vier exotischen Aufenthaltsräumen im Ports o' Call Restaurant im Penthouse des Southland Center, Dallas, Texas. Für dieses tropische Lokal ist die Natur domestiziert worden. Ein Wasserfall plätschert zu ihrem Vergnügen, während einheimische Wildtiere bewegungslos verharren, damit sie sich so richtig wohlfühlen. Doch Speere und Felle erinnern den Gast daran, dass auch das einfache Leben seine aufregenden Seiten hat."

Aber die Kluft, die sich schon bald zwischen der Tiki-Generation und ihren gegen den Vietnamkrieg protestierenden Kindern auftat, ist wohl am besten in der

Beschreibung des Saigon-Raums zum Ausdruck gebracht: „Orientalische Pracht und Opulenz bestimmen diesen Hafen der Sinnenfreuden. Seine glücklichen Bewohner sind umgeben von echtem Blattgold, seltener Seide, feinstem Kristall und einst verbotenen Tempelschnitzereien". Was 1960 noch als poetische Phantasie erlaubt war, hatte sich 1968 in schmerzlichen Sarkasmus verwandelt. Ende der 70er Jahre bot ein iranisches Konsortium Stephen Crane 4,1 Millionen Dollar für das *Luau*. 1979 wurde es bis auf die Grundfesten niedergerissen, ein deutliches Signal für das Ende der Tiki-Ära.

DANNY BALSZ – DER VERLORENE SOHN

Die Gestalt des Danny Balsz lässt sich nicht nahtlos in die Reihe der Ahnherren des polynesischen Pop einordnen. Weder begründete er eine Restaurantkette, noch glänzte er mit kulinarischen oder alkoholischen Neuerungen. Er befasste sich weniger mit Qualität denn mit Quantität. Für Danny Balsz lautete die Devise „Größer ist besser", und somit baute er den größten Vulkan auf dem ausgedehntesten polynesischen Luau-Gelände des Landes. Hier wurde jede Nacht eine Tiki-Jungfrau als Opfer in seinen gefräßigen Schlund geworfen, während tahitische Tänzerinnen, deren Kostüme eher aus Las Vegas als von den Südseeinseln zu stammen schienen, sich nach den Rhythmen verschiedener Bands wiegten. Als er herausfand, dass die Hawaiianer angeblich daran glaubten, dass das Glück von der Anzahl der Tikis abhänge, die man in seinem Hause habe, umgab er sich mit Holzfiguren aller Größen und Formen und nannte den Ort *The Tikis*. Mehr Götter, mehr Tänzer, mehr Essen und Trinken für mehr als 3000 Gäste pro Nacht. Das war Tiki für die Massen, und Danny war Mr. Tiki!

The Tikis stellt den Höhepunkt der gesamten Tiki-Ära dar, die sich noch einmal mit einer nie da gewesenen Grandiosität und Dekadenz präsentierte, bevor sie aus dem kulturellen Leben verschwand und in Vergessenheit geriet. Als ich über die Ruinen dieses vergessenen Disneylands der Götter stolperte, wusste ich, dass seine Geschichte eines Tages erzählt werden müsste. Vor mir lag der verlorene Planet der Tikis, der Elefantenfriedhof einer erloschenen Spezies. Was hatte zum Niedergang dieser einst so großartigen Zivilisation geführt?

Danny Balsz war der Sohn eines Nachtclubbesitzers aus der Grenzstadt Mexicali. Eines Tages ging er nach East Los Angeles, im Kopf die Erinnerungen an einen zwielichtigen Glanz. Zehn Jahre lang arbeitete er als Metzger in einem Schlachthaus, bis er beschloss, in die Landschaftsgärtnerei zu wechseln; dort spezialisierte er sich auf Wasserfälle. 1958 holte Danny Pflanzmaterial aus einer japanischen Baumschule in Monterey Park, einem ländlichen Vorort von Los Angeles, der eingeklemmt zwischen vier Schnellstraßen lag. Als er an einer benachbarten Hühnerfarm hielt, traf er die Besitzerin Doris Samson. Vier Monate später waren sie verheiratet. Während er Doris bei der Hühnerhaltung half, baute er sein Können in der Landschaftsgestaltung aus und verwandelte den halben Hektar Grundbesitz in einen tropischen Garten. 1960 fragten zwei College-Studenten bei Danny an, ob sie auf seinem Grund eine Luau-Party veranstalten dürften. Zu jener Zeit schossen Luau-Anlagen, die man für Partys mieten konnte, in Südkalifornien wie Pilze aus dem Boden. Danny und Doris beschlossen, ihre sämtlichen Hühner zu schlachten und im polynesischen Party-Geschäft ihr Glück zu versuchen. Sie kamen genau zur richtigen Zeit, ihre Anlage wuchs und gedieh, und Jahr für Jahr goss und formte Danny mehr Beton zu Lava-Tunneln, Tropfsteinhöhlen und Wasserfällen und schuf eigenhändig sein persönliches Xanadu. In den 60er Jahren wurde seine Kundschaft, die vor allem aus der Arbeiterklasse stammte, in Bussen von den Flugzeugfabriken und Speditionsunternehmen herbeigekarrt. Die nötigen Vorräte, zum Beispiel 50 000 hawaiische Blütenkränze aus der Plastikblumenfabrik in Hughestown, Pennsylvania, und tonnenweise Ananas wurden bar bezahlt, und wenn noch Geld übrig war, kaufte Danny noch mehr Tikis. „Ich kann dir sagen, ich hatte alles: Geld, Autos, Ringe!" erinnert sich Danny. Aber er wollte mehr. Dannys Glückssträhne ging zu Ende, als er die Ursünde beging: Er verliebte sich in Leilani, eine mormonische hawaiische Tän-

zerin im *The Tikis*. Die Verbindung zwischen dem Haole und der Wahine wurde von den Göttern nicht gutgeheißen, und noch viel weniger von Dannys Frau und seinen Kindern, die das Rückgrat seines Familienunternehmens gewesen waren. Unter dem Druck von Nachbarn, die ohnehin seit langem die Nase voll hatten, widerrief der Stadtrat seine Lizenz für das Unterhaltungsgeschäft. Der polynesische Affenzirkus war vorüber, so schien es. Aber Danny Balsz war ein ehrgeiziger Mann. Er packte seine Tikis ein und baute ihnen in Lake Elsinore, noch weiter südlich von Los Angeles gelegen, eine neue Heimat. Dort arbeitete er jahrelang am Aufbau eines völlig neuen Lavalandes. Geduldig wachten seine Tikis über seine Arbeit und warteten auf die große Neueröffnung. Aber die Zeiten hatten sich geändert, und der große Tag kam nie.

„Das Licht, das doppelt so hell brennt, brennt halb so lang, und du hast doch so hell, so leuchtend hell gebrannt. Du bist der verlorene Sohn! – Aber ich habe zweifelhafte Dinge getan … Auch großartige Dinge, du hast deine Zeit in vollen Zügen genossen …" (aus Ridley Scotts „Bladerunner")

KON-TIKI, AKU AKU UND THOR

„Die ungelösten Rätsel der Südsee hatten mich in ihren Bann gezogen. Es muss eine rationale Lösung dafür geben, und ich setzte mir zum Ziel, die Sagengestalt Tiki zu identifizieren." So sprach ein junger norwegischer Zoologe namens Thor Heyerdahl im Jahre 1937, während er auf Fatu Hiva, einer zur Marquesa-Gruppe gehörenden Insel im zentralen Pazifik, ums Überleben kämpfte. Heyerdahl führte dort mit seiner Frau eine Art „Hippie-Leben". Thor und Liv hatten beschlossen, die Zivilisation hinter sich zu lassen und „zurückzukehren zur Natur". Wie Primitive lebten sie auf ihrer Insel, deren Fauna sie für die Universität Oslo untersuchten. Doch als Thor den alten Tei Tetua, den letzten Eingeborenen, der ein „Long Pig" (einen Menschen) gekostet hatte, am abendlichen Feuer ein altes Volksmärchen erzählen hörte, änderte sich alles. „Tiki war Gott und Häuptling zugleich. Tiki war es, der unsere Vorväter auf die Inseln gebracht hat, auf denen wir heute leben. Früher lebten wir in einem großen Land, weit hinter dem Meer."

Thor kam auf die Idee, seinen Forschungsgegenstand von Schnecken und riesigen giftigen Tausendfüßlern auf den Ursprung der polynesischen Rasse zu verlagern. Ihm war die Ähnlichkeit der marquesischen Stein-Tikis und Felszeichnungen (Petroglyphen) mit den Götzenbildern der Inkas in Peru aufgefallen, und während der nächsten zehn Jahre arbeitete er an seiner Theorie, dass der Prä-Inka-Hohe Priester und Sonnengott Kon-Tici Viracocha, der von einem kriegerischen Häuptling gezwungen worden war, aus Peru zu fliehen, identisch mit dem polynesischen Gott und Stammesvater Tiki war. Da Thor nur auf erbitterten Widerstand seitens der Archäologen, Ethnologen, Linguisten und Soziologen stieß, ging er daran, seine Theorie in der Praxis zu beweisen. Er baute ein präkolumbianisches Floß aus Balsaholz, für das er nicht einen einzigen Eisenstift, Nagel oder Draht verwendete, nannte es „Kon-Tiki" und ließ sich und seine fünf Mann Besatzung auf dem Humboldtstrom von Peru nach Polynesien treiben.

Nach nur drei Monaten auf hoher See erreichte das Floß leicht versehrt die polynesischen Küstengewässer. Der Reisebericht erschien 1948 unter dem Titel „Die Kon-Tiki-Expedition" zuerst in Norwegen und erhielt ziemlich schlechte Besprechungen: Das ganze Unternehmen sei damit vergleichbar, „in einem Fass die Niagarafälle hinunterzufahren". Doch das große Interesses des breiten Publikum blieb von diesen Kritiken unberührt.

Als das Buch 1950 in England und Amerika veröffentlicht wurde, stellte sich schnell heraus, dass die Verleger einen Bestseller im Programm hatten. Schließlich wurde „Kon-Tiki" in sechzig Sprachen übersetzt, nur die Bibel hatte weltweit größere Verbreitung gefunden. Die Verfilmung der Reise erlitt ein ähnliches Schicksal: Von amerikanischen Verleihern zunächst wegen technischer Schwächen abgelehnt, erhielt der Film 1951 dennoch den Oscar als bester Dokumentarfilm, und Millionen von Menschen haben ihn gesehen. Die Welt begann gerade, sich vom Trauma des Zweiten Weltkrieges zu erholen und sehnte sich nach friedfertigen Abenteuern.

Die beispiellose weltweite Kon-Tiki-Begeisterung heizte das Interesse der Amerikaner an der polynesischen Kultur weiter an. Obwohl „Tiki-Stil" in den 50er und 60er Jahren kein gängiger Begriff war, sprach man doch gemeinhin vom „Kon-Tiki-Stil" wenn man die polynesischen Architektur meinte. Thor und Tiki, der nordische Gott des Donners und der polynesische Gott der Sonne, hatten sich verbündet um Pophelden zu werden. Heyerdahls Buch „Aku Aku" von 1955 über seine Osterinsel-Expedition erwies sich als ebenso einflussreich für den polynesischen Pop. Der Buchumschlag wurde zu einer so populären Ikone, dass die riesigen Steinstatuen, die eigentlich „Moai" heißen, als „Aku Aku-Köpfe" oder eben als „Aku-Tikis" bekannt wurden, und zu einem weit verbreiteten Motiv im amerikanischen Tiki-Kult wurden.

JAMES MICHENER UND BALI HA'I

„Bali Hai wird dich vielleicht rufen, Tag und Nacht.
Mit deinem Herzen wirst du es hören, komm her, komm her.
Bali Hai säuselt im Wind, rauscht im Meer,
Ich bin hier, deine eigene geheime Insel, komm her, komm her.
Deine geheimsten Wünsche, deine geheimsten Träume,
Umspielen hier die Gipfel und glitzern dort im Flüsschen.
Wenn du suchst, wirst du mich finden, wo Himmel und Meer sich treffen
Ich bin hier, deine geheime Insel, komm her, komm her."

(aus Rodgers & Hammerstein's „South Pacifc")

Thor Heyerdahl war nicht der einzige Bestseller-Autor, der einen Beitrag zum polynesischen Pop leistete. Während des Zweiten Weltkriegs kam eine ganze Generation amerikanischer Wehrpflichtiger in direkten Kontakt mit der Kultur der Pazifik-Inseln, darunter auch James Michener. Sein fiktionaler Bericht über ihre schrecklichen Erlebnisse („Tales of the South Pacific", dt. „Im Korallenmeer") erhielt 1948 den Pulitzerpreis und wurde ein riesiger Publikumserfolg. Ein Broadway-Musical und ein Breitwandfilm romantisierten die tatsächliche Härte und Unerbittlichkeit des Krieges so erfolgreich, dass ein neuer Begriff für das „exotische Paradies" erfunden wurde: das fiktive „Bali Ha'i", die Insel der Frauen. Es wurde das neue Shangri-La, die Trauminsel schlechthin.

Dort erlebte die Hauptfigur des Romans, Leutnant Cable, die jahrhundertealte Männerfantasie einer zwanglosen Liebe zu einer jungen exotischen Schönheit. Dem Protagonisten wird das Privileg zugestanden, die Insel, „ein Juwel im weiten Ozean", zu besuchen, auf der „die Franzosen mit gallischem Weitblick und Kennerschaft in diesen Dingen, alle jungen Frauen von den umliegenden Inseln untergebracht hatten. Jedes Mädchen, egal welcher Hautfarbe und ob hübsch oder hässlich, das sonst von amerikanischen Soldaten vergewaltigt worden wäre, wurde auf Bali Ha'i versteckt." (Michener)

Als Leutnant Cables Boot dort vor Anker geht, wird er wohl von jedem männlichen Leser in den 50er Jahren beneidet: „Zum ersten Mal in seinem Leben hatte er so viele Frauen gesehen, ja überhaupt Frauen, die bis zur Hüften hinunter völlig unbekleidet waren … Wie im Dschungel, wie die Früchte des Dschungels schien es hier junge Mädchen in unglaublicher Fülle zu geben." (Michener)

Cable wird schon bald von der eingeborenen Matrone Bloody Mary vor den Heerscharen junger Mädchen gerettet und Mary bringt ihn unverzüglich mit ihrer hübschen, jungfräulichen Tochter Liat zusammen. Im Film betritt unser Held eine romantische Palmenhütte, wo Liat ihn erwartet, eine hinreißende Schönheit, die für die Liebe bereit ist. Es wird kein Wort gesprochen, nur sehnsüchtige Blicke, zitternde Lippen, sie verlieben sich auf der Stelle und die Liebe ist tief. Offenbar sind die Urbilder aus der Südsee doch wahr.

Der Umstand, dass Amerikaner aus allen Lebensbereichen plötzlich aus erster Hand mit einer völlig fremden Kultur bekannt gemacht wurden, hinterließ einen unauslöschlichen Eindruck auf Amerika: „Was mache ich hier? Wie bin ich, Joe Cable aus Philadelphia, ausgerechnet hier gelandet? Dies hier ist Bali Ha'i, und vor einem Jahr hatte ich noch nie davon gehört. Was mache ich hier?" (Michener) Die Soldaten reagierten mit kindlichem Staunen und da sie als Retter vor den verhassten Japanern herzlich empfangen worden waren, kehrten sie mit eher heiteren und aufregenden Erinnerungen in die U.S.A. zurück. Die Folge war, dass überall kleine Bali Hai's aus dem Boden schossen, die nicht nur bei denen beliebt waren, die einmal dort gewesen waren.

Das tatsächliche Bali Ha'i auf der kleinen Insel Mono in der Nähe von Guadalcanal hatte Michener kennen gelernt und obwohl er es als „einen dreckigen, unangenehmen Ort" empfand, machte er sich eine Notiz zu seinem Namen, weil sein „musikalischer Klang" ihm gefiel. Dies bewahrte den polynesischen Pop-Mythos von Bali Ha'i nicht davor, schließlich nach Französisch-Polynesien reimportiert zu werden. Im Jahre 1961 beschlossen ein Börsenmakler, ein Rechtsanwalt und ein Sportartikelverkäufer, die offenbar vom Tiki-Fieber erfasst waren, ihr zivilisiertes Leben im Küstenvorort Newport Beach vor Los Angeles hinter sich zu lassen und sich nach Tahiti aufzumachen. Dort eröffneten sie ein Hotel und nannten es selbstverständlich „Bali Ha'i". Die Fiktion hatte über die Wirklichkeit gesiegt, wie so oft im polynesischen Pop.

WEITERE MAGISCHE TIKI-TEMPEL

Wie an anderer Stelle bereits erwähnt, hatte der Tiki-Stil, wie jeder andere Kult, seine „magischen Plätze", bestimmte energiegeladene Orte, wo sich die Macht des Tiki ungehemmt entfalten konnte. In diesem Kapitel werden einige Lokalitäten beschrieben, die noch heute existieren, darunter das *Mai Kai* und das *Kahiki*, die wohl zu den bemerkenswertesten und schönsten Beispielen dieser inzwischen untergegangenen Kultur gehören. In einem bis heute nicht da gewesenem Akt seltener Erleuchtung wurde das *Kahiki* erst kürzlich in das National Register of Historic Places, also in die Liste nationalen Kulturdenkmäler aufgenommen, für ein Gebäude von 1961 ein höchst ungewöhnliches Ereignis, das auf eine positive Neubewertung des Tiki-Stils hinweist. Das Eingangsfoto für dieses Kapitel zeigt ein „Mystery Girl", die uns am Tiki-Brunnen vor dem *Kahiki* in Columbus, Ohio, empfängt. Das Mystery Drink-Ritual ist wahrscheinlich vom *Mai Kai* ausgegangen, wo es eingeführt wurde, da sich der exotische Flair der Kellnerinnen als so publikumsträchtig erwies.

Der erste „magische Ort", dem unser Besuch gilt, war einst eine ganze Insel voller Tiki-Tempel. Passenderweise war es eine künstliche Insel, aufgeschüttet mit Sand, den die Navy aus der San Diego Bay ausgehoben hatte, um die Passage für ihre Kriegsschiffe zu erleichtern. Es konnte wohl kaum einen besseren Platz für ein künstliches Polynesien geben als eine von Menschen erschaffene Insel.

DAS *BALI HA'I*, SHELTER ISLAND, SAN DIEGO, KALIFORNIEN

Der erste Tiki-Tempel, der auf Shelter Island gebaut wurde, war das *Bali Ha'i*, das ursprünglich *The Hut* hieß und ein Ableger von *Christian's Hut* in Newport Beach war. Nur zwei Jahre nach seiner Eröffnung übernahm der Geschäftsführer Tom Hamm das kränkelnde Unternehmen und wandelte es in eines der beliebtesten Lokale der Stadt um. Das *Bali Ha'i* bot einen überwältigenden Blick auf den Hafen von San Diego, hatte einen eigenen Yachthafen, und seine polynesischen Nachtclubdarbietungen waren berühmt. Es war nicht nur bei Südkaliforniern beliebt, sondern ebenso bei Exil-Polynesiern, die im Gegensatz zu Akademikern, die über Tiki die Nase rümpften, ganz einfach glücklich waren, einen Platz zu haben, der sie an ihre heimische Kultur erinnerte.

Der Mr. Bali Ha'i-Tiki, das Logo, begrüßte die Gäste am Eingang als Skulptur, und er kam in Form von Bechern daher, die ein bis heute einmaliges Beispiel für Kopfjäger-Skurilitäten bieten. In einem Ausstellungskasten, der nach Art der Covarrubias-Tiki-Karte gestaltet und mit echten Skulpturen ausgestattet war, die die verschiedenen Tiki-Stile der einzelnen polynesischen Inseln repräsentieren, zeigte auch der Bali Ha'i-Krug anschaulich, woher er stammt.

Doch woher stammte der seltsame Kopf auf dem Dach des *Bali Ha'i*? Der Ursprung dieser Kreation, und das ist ein einschlägiges Beispiel für Stadtarchäologie, kann durch Nachforschungen auf Streichholzheftchen nachgewiesen werden: *Christian's Hut* hatte seinen Namen von Fletcher Christian, dem berühmten Meuterer auf der „Bounty". 1935 wurde die Geschichte mit Clark Gable verfilmt, der die Rolle des mutigen Offiziers spielte. Catalina Island vor der kalifornischen Küste wurde als Drehort ausgesucht und in Tahiti verwandelt. Man baute ein ganzes tahitisches Dorf, und irgendwann bewohnten sechshundert Statisten und Mitglieder des Filmstabs die Insel. Die Bar, die unterhalb von Clark Gables Übernachtungsquartier eingerichtet wurde, erhielt den Namen „Christian's Hut". Als die Dreharbeiten beendet waren, wurde die Hütte nach Newport Beach verlagert, wo sie zu einem Prominentenlokal wurde, in dem Leute wie John Wayne und Howard Hughes zu den Stammgästen gehörten. Es wurden dann auch mehrere Filialen eröffnet, doch keine wurde so berühmt wie das Original, das 1963 abbrannte. Die ursprüngliche Bedeutung des Kopfes, der „Goof" genannt wurde, bleibt ein Rätsel.

Das Mana des *Bali Ha'i* zog weitere Tiki-Tempel auf die Insel. Die seltsamste A-Form entstand gegenüber dem *Bali Ha'i* und nannte sich *Half Moon Inn*. Das Restaurant, das sich darin befand, sollte eigentlich *Tahiti* heißen, wurde dann aber zum *L'Escale*. Weitere Etablissements im polynesischen Stil folgten, darunter das *Shelter Isle Inn*, der *Kona Kai Club* und das *Kona Inn*. Heute ist vom Tiki-Stil nichts mehr zu spüren, entweder ist er durch Renovierung verschwunden oder, wie im Fall des *Kona Kai Clubs*, völlig vom mediterranen Stil verdrängt worden.

DAS *MAI KAI*, FORT LAUDERDALE, FLORIDA

In den frühen 50er Jahren beschlossen zwei Brüder aus Chicago, Bob und Jack Thornton, den eisigen Wintern der „windigen Stadt" den Rücken zu kehren und ins tropische Florida zu entfliehen. Hier bauten sie sich nach dem Vorbild der *Don the Beachcomber*-Filliale in ihrer Heimatstadt ihre eigene polynesische Traumwelt, der sie den Namen *Mai Kai* gaben. Seit seiner Eröffnung im Jahre 1956 ist das *Mai Kai* von einer bescheidenen Hütte mit vier Räumen zu einem verzweigten Dorf mit acht Speisesälen, üppigen tropischen Gärten mit Wasserfällen und einer Vielzahl von Tikis angewachsen. Bob Thornton suchte immer professionelle Künstler des polynesischen Pop aus, um sein Reich auszubauen, engagierte George Nakashima und Florian Gabriel von Stephen Crane and Associates als künstlerische Leiter und verwendete Ausstattungen von Oceanic Arts in Whittier, um dem *Mai Kai* das begehrte „authentische" Aussehen zu geben.

Das *Mai Kai* hatte nie ein spezielles Tiki-Logo, benutzte aber, wo immer möglich, die geschnitzten tahitischen Kannibalen-Tikis, die zuerst auf der Speisekarte von *Don the Beachcomber* zu sehen waren. Ein anderer gern benutzter Fetisch war der Gott der Fischer der Cook-Inseln, dessen Gestalt im Design einer Rumflasche wiederkehrte. Das bemerkenswerteste Artefakt ist wohl die „Mai Kai Mystery Bowl". Die drei hawaiischen Kriegsgötter, die sie tragen, öffnen ihre Münder, um die Strohhalme darin aufzunehmen. Doch neben seiner großen Sammlung an Schnitzereien war das *Mai Kai* stolz darauf, der weiblichen Schönheit zu huldigen, und ließ seine Gäste von einer Schar hübscher Mädchen in Bikinis verwöhnen. Diese Schönheiten wurden in der *Mai Kai*-Hauszeitschrift, „Happy Talk" (nach einem Song aus „South Pacific"), als Starlets und Models vorgestellt, im jährlich erscheinenden Kalender und in Filmen gezeigt, in denen das Ritual des Mystery Drinks vorgeführt wurde.

Heute wird das *Mai Kai* von einem solchen Exotica-Mädchen geleitet, von Mireille Thornton, der Frau des verstorbenen Bob Thornton, die als Tänzerin aus Tahiti hierher kam. Sie ist auch die Choreografin der polynesischen Mai Kai-Revue, der am längsten laufenden Show dieser Art. Das Mana des *Mai Kai* hat entscheidend dazu beigetragen, den Tiki-Kult in Florida zu verbreiten, wo der Tiki-Archäologe bis heute Bars und Motels finden kann, die diesem Image nacheifern.

DAS *KONA KAI*, PHILADELPHIA, PENSYLVANIA

Die *Kona Kai*-Kette war Marriots Antwort auf Hiltons *Trader Vic's* und Sheratons *Kon-Tikis*. An der Küste von Kona auf Hawaii wurde in den 60er Jahren ein neues Waikiki aufgebaut und viele Tiki-Etablissements auf dem Festland, sowohl Restaurants als auch Motels und Apartmenthäuser, schmückten sich mit dem Namen dieses hawaiischen gelobten Landes.

Das *Kona Kai* in Philadelphia, das von Armet & Davis gestaltet worden war, wurde zum Flaggschiff der Kette, weitere Dependancen wurden in Chicago und Kansas City eröffnet. Es war ein richtiger Tiki-Tempel mit allem, was dazu gehörte, mit Wasserfällen, Brücken und Dioramen. Das klassische *Kona Kai*-Tiki-Logo lässt sich bis zu einer frühen Zeichnung des Designers Irving Weisenberg zurückverfolgen, der bei Armet & Davis beschäftigt war (Seite 54). In diesem frühen Stadium hieß es noch „Hale Tiki" und hatte nur entfernte Ähnlichkeit mit dem Endergebnis, aber die Zeichnung des Tiki am Eingang stand sicherlich Pate für das Emblem des *Kona Kai*.

DAS *KAHIKI*, COLUMBUS, OHIO

Das städtische Tiki Island-Konzept funktionierte nicht nur in Staaten mit hohem Freizeitwert wie Florida und Kalifornien, wo das Klima das Wachstum von Palmen und Dschungelpflanzen begünstigte, sondern auch in kälteren Zonen. Wenn man aus der Unwirtlichkeit draußen in ein tropisches Ambiente kam, war die Wirkung nur umso stärker. Das *Kahiki*, wie man auf der Zeichnung von Seite 61 sehr gut sehen kann, ist ein perfekt erhaltenes Beispiel für solch ein Tiki-Heiligtum. Die Hauptstraße zwischen den Restaurant-Hütten des „Quiet Village" wird von zwölf Meter hohen, künstlichen Palmen gesäumt, und von einigen der Essnischen aus hat man einen Blick auf den Regenwald, in dem richtige Vögel leben. In regelmäßigen Abständen bricht hier ein tropisches Gewitter los, während draußen die Eiszapfen von den Einbaumbalken hängen. Eine riesige Götterstatue von den Osterinseln wacht über die ganze Szenerie.

Das *Kahiki* wurde von Coburn Morgan für Lee Henry und Bill Sapp entworfen und (erstaunlich nah am Entwurf) im Jahre 1961 gebaut; es ist eine Schatztruhe voller Tiki-Kunst. „Der Besucher wird von authentischen Repliken primitiver Wandbilder über der Tür empfangen. Diese Zeichnungen verhindern, dass böse Geister Einlass finden." Die schwarzen Samtgemälde sind mit „La Visse" signiert, offenbar einer der vielen „Schüler" von Edgar Leeteg. Die Tiki-Kacheln rund um die im Maya-Stil gebauten Eingangstüren tragen die Bezeichnung „Tectum Pan-L-Art". Unglücklicherweise wird dieses Kleinod durch das Kaufangebot einer der führenden Drogerie-Ketten bedroht – also nichts wie hin, solange es noch geht!

DIE TIKI-KUNST DER SPEISEKARTEN

Die Umschläge der Speisekarten sind die in Öl gebannte Ahnengallerie des Tiki-Stils, Bildnisse von Tikis und ihren Tempeln, die es längst schon nicht mehr gibt, zum Beispiel *Dorian's* in Whittier, Kalifornien. Hier gab es viele geschnitze Bildwerke und eine „Happy Talk"-Cocktailbar, die ihren Namen von einem Song aus dem Musical „South Pacific" hatte. In der naiven Eingeborenensprache Liats, Lieutnant Cables Inselmädchen, bedeutete „Happy Talk" „flirten". Die Darstellung auf der Speisekarte zeigt offenbar zwei männliche Tikis, die einen weiblichen Tiki in solch einen „Happy Talk" verstricken. Leider existiert von dieser Figurengruppe kein Foto mehr.

Speisekarten überlieferten außerdem die Mythologie des polynesischen Pop, denn sie erwiesen seinen Urvätern Reverenz, erzählten die abenteuerlichen Geschichten der Besitzer oder die Legenden von Tiki, dem Gott des Müßiggangs. Trader Vic begründete diese Tradition auf der Rückseite seiner Speisekarte von 1947, wo zu lesen stand: „Ich grüße Don the Beachcomber aus Hollywood, den Erfinder so außergewöhnlicher Drinks wie dem *Zombie* und dem *Missionary's Downfall*." Das *Tahitian*, auf dessen Karte 68 tropische Drinks zu finden waren, zollt Don noch mehr Respekt: „Das *Tahitian* zieht den Hut vor Don the Beachcomber, einem der ersten Rumexperten der Welt. Don hat einige der besten Rumdrinks kreiert, am berühmtesten aber ist er für seinen *Zombie*. Er verdient den Applaus aller Liebhaber guten Essens und Trinkens, denn er hat einen völlig neuen Restauranttypus geschaffen. Das *Tahitian* grüßt auch Trader Vic, der so viele köstliche Drinks und Gerichte im polynesischen Stil beigesteuert hat. Wir wollen nicht behaupten, dass wir diese Großmeister übertreffen, aber wir sind fest davon überzeugt, dass das *Tahitian* weltweit eines der Top-Restaurants seiner Art ist."

So viel schwärmerische Höflichkeit brachte Dick Graves, den Besitzer von *Trader Dick's*, dazu, alle Poesie beiseite zu lassen und folgendes auf seine Speisekarte zu schreiben: „Leute, ich bin nie in der Südsee gewesen ... keines dieser Rezepte stammt von mir ... nicht eines hat dieses Lokal berühmt gemacht. Wie könnten sie auch? *Trader Dick's* ist brandneu. Für all die Ideen und Rezepte, die ihr hier findet, habe ich gelogen, betrogen, geborgt und gebettelt ... Es ist das Feinste, das ich aus kantonesischen und polynesischen Top-Restaurants zwischen Honolulu und New York stehlen konnte. ... Ich habe bei allen herumgeschnüffelt ... habe Speisekarten geklaut, Barkeeper und Köche bestochen und ausgefragt und alles, was es an Gutem zu finden gab, kopiert." Mit dieser untypischen Aufrichtigkeit beschrieb Dick Graves den Konkurrenzgeist, der im polynesischen Pop herrschte, sehr viel wahrheitsgemäßer. Das *Kona Kai* in Philadelphia erzählte in seiner Speisekarte das folgende Märchen, mit dem es dem Gast das Gefühl gab, er sei am Ziel seiner Träume angekommen: „DAS GEHEIMNIS VON *KONA KAI*. Nach der Legende suchte Tiki, der Südseegott des Überflusses und freudigen Genusses, einst nach der perfekten Umgebung für ein zeitloses Paradies voller Lachen und Glück. Er gab sich große Mühe und verbrachte viel Zeit damit, seine Sinne zu schärfen, um sich ganz sicher sein zu können, wenn er seinen Garten Eden tatsächlich gefunden hätte. Er bereiste sein ganzes Land ... Schließlich kam er ans Meer ... in eine herrliche Lagune namens Kona Kai. Dort fand er die Vollkommenheit, nach der er gesucht hatte. In dieser unglaublichen Bucht wehten laue Winde, sie war in sanftes Sonnenlicht getaucht und abgeschirmt vor Stürmen und Mittagshitze. Farbenprächtige Blumen wuchsen in Hülle und Fülle und das Plätschern der Wasserfälle hörte sich an wie tröstliche Musik – Tiki ist bis heute in Kona Kai geblieben. Dort sonnt er sich in der makellosen Vollkommenheit und segnet alle, die ihm nachgefolgt sind, mit überschwänglicher Freude und Glück."

In der Speisekarte des *Luau 400*, einem New Yorker Tiki-Tempel, betete man das Tiki-Evangelium in sehr viel einfacherer Form vor: „Tiki ist der traditionelle Gott alles Guten ... gute Gesundheit, Glück, gutes Leben und, oh ja, gutes Essen, dies alles gehört zu den Segnungen, die uns von Tiki, dem polynesischen Gott, zuteil werden."

BAR-KÜNSTLER UND KREATIONEN von Jeff Berry

Welches Restaurant könnte es sich leisten, Konservenobst auf einem Löffel Hüttenkäse „Ports of Desire" zu nennen? Das *Luau* konnte – vor allem darum, weil es die besten exotischen Rum-Drinks in ganz Beverly Hills servierte. Solche Drinks waren das Öl im Getriebe der polynesischen Restaurants, sie hielten das Geschäft am Laufen. Sie waren mehr als nur Cocktails. Von Anfang an wurden sie als farbenprächtige Fantasiegebilde angeboten, die ebenso das Auge wie die Zunge erfreuen sollten, und sie wurden mit ausgefallenen Garnierungen und in ebenso ausgefallenen Gefäßen serviert. Sogar das Eis, das sie kühl halten sollte, war in ungewöhnliche Formen gegossen, zum Beispiel als ein gefrorener Zylinder, in dem der Strohhalm steckte, oder als Iglu, so dass der Drink „in einer Eishöhle schlummernd" am Tisch serviert wurde. Aber genauso gut konnte der Drink rauchend, Flammen sprühend oder mit einer Gardenie verziert, in der eine versteckte Perle auf ihre Entdeckung wartete, beim Gast ankommen.

Das war der Cocktail als Konversationsstück. Wenn man ein polynesisches Restaurant verließ, sprach man nicht über das Essen, sondern über den „Mystery Drink" oder den „Penang Afrididi" oder „Peles Bucket of Fire". Und der Service begann meistens mit einem Hinweis auf die Karte, auf der die Drinks in poetischen Beschreibungen mit detailbesessenen, bunten Illustrationen dargestellt waren. So nannte *The Islander* seinen „Mount Kilauea" „eine Eruption feinsten Rum-Imports, gekrönt mit dem heiligen Nektar der Tiki-Götter".

Wie Sie sich wohl denken können, haben diese teuflischen Mischungen nicht immer so gut geschmeckt, wie sie aussahen. Aber die besten tropischen Drinks konnten sehr komplex und nuancenreich sein, zugleich fein und sinnlich, in einer heiklen Balance von süß und sauer, stark und leicht, fruchtig und trocken. Die besten tropischen Drinks wurden im *Don the Beachcomber* kreiert.

Als Don 1934 seine erste Bar eröffnete, galt Rum als indiskutabel. Alkoholiker hießen „Rummies". Nur Seemänner und Säufer tranken Teufelsrum; die bessere Gesellschaft trank Bourbon und Gin. Warum hat Don also keine Whiskey- und Gin-Drinks kreiert? Weil Rum billiger war! Als die Prohibition beendet wurde, konnte man das Zeug kistenweise für gerade mal siebzig Cents den Liter kaufen. In Dons Fall war Sparsamkeit die Mutter des Gedankens.

Aber Don erfand seine „Rum-Rhapsodien" nicht aus dem Nichts heraus. Nash Aranas, früher für die „Authentizitätskontrolle" in der Beachcomber-Restaurantkette zuständig, verriet 1989, dass Don „eine Zeit lang in Westindien gewesen war, wo ihm die Rum-Idee gekommen war". Wahrscheinlich lernte Don dort den jamaikanischen Planter's Punch und den kubanischen Daiquiri kennen; diese beiden Drinks sind eine einfache Mischung aus Limettensaft, Zucker und Rum – drei Zutaten, die zu den Grundbestandteilen der meisten von Dons Kreationen wurden. Zu den Limetten fügte er Ananas, Papaya und Passionsfrucht hinzu; zum Zucker gab er Anis, Vanille und Mandelextrakt; zum Rum mischte er Schnäpse, parfümierte Brandies ... und noch mehr Rum, sehr viel mehr Rum! Don hatte nämlich entdeckt, dass die Mischung dunkler und heller Rumsorten einen völlig neuen, komplexeren Basisgeschmack erzeugte, der seinen Kompositionen ganz neue Akzente verlieh. „Don konnte den ganzen Tag mit seinen alten Freunden dasitzen und Drinks mixen", erinnert sich Aranas. „Er probierte und probierte und probierte wie ein verrückter Wissenschaftler." Die Kombinationen waren endlos und wurden endlos variiert, und dabei kamen so populäre Kreationen heraus wie seine frühen Erfindungen *Vicious Virgin*, *Shark's Tooth*, *Cobra's Fang*, *Dr. Funk* und *Missionary's Downfall*.

MISSIONARY'S DOWNFALL

4 frische Minzeblätter
½ Scheibe frische Ananas
3 cl frischer Limettensaft
1 cl Peach Brandy
½ cl Zuckersirup*
2 cl leichter puertoricanischer Rum

Die Minzeblätter vom Stengel pflücken. Die Blätter mit allen anderen Zutaten und 30 cl gestoßenem Eis in den Mixer geben. Alles gut mixen. (*Zur Herstellung von Zuckersirup 1 kg Zucker mit zwei Tassen Wasser zum Kochen bringen, dann abkühlen und in eine Flasche füllen.)

Der Legende zufolge soll Dons berühmtester Drink, der *Zombie*, entstanden sein, als man einem verkaterten Gast, der einen wichtigen geschäftlichen Termin durchzustehen hatte, wieder auf die Beine zu helfen versuchte. Als dieser Gast später gefragt wurde, wie die Kur geholfen habe, sagte er: „Ich fühlte mich wie ein lebender Toter – sie hat einen Zombie aus mir gemacht." Doch eine Speisekarte aus dem *Beachcomber* von 1941 erzählt eine andere Entstehungsgeschichte: „Der *Zombie* ist nicht durch Zufall entstanden. Er ist das Ergebnis eines langen und teuren Entwicklungsprozesses. Für die Experimente, die schließlich zum *Zombie* führten, wurden dreieinhalb Kisten ausgesuchten Rums verbraucht, damit Sie jetzt dieses starke ‚Heilmittel für zerbrochene Träume' genießen können."

Kurz vor seinem Tod erzählte der alte Barkeeper Ray Buhen, einer der Angestellten im Original-*Beachcomber* im Jahre 1934, die Geschichte noch anders. „Don war ein netter Typ", erinnerte sich Buhen, der 27 Jahre später seine eigene Bar, das *Tiki Ti*, eröffnete. „Aber er erzählte viel, wenn der Tag lang war. Er hat gesagt, er habe den *Zombie* erfunden, hat er aber nicht. Und auch kaum einen der anderen Drinks." Buhen war der Meinung, dass die meisten Erfindungen von den „vier Jungs" stammten, einem Filipino-Quartett, die bei Don hinter der Bar arbeiteten. Sicherlich eine ketzerische Behauptung, aber Rays Glaubwürdigkeit ist ziemlich unantastbar: 62 Jahre als Barkeeper in den berühmtesten polynesischen Palästen, von den *Seven Seas* und dem *Luau* bis zum *China Trader* und seiner eigenen Bar, wo er Leute wie Clark Gable, Charlie Chaplin, Buster Keaton, die Marx Brothers und Marlon Brando bediente.

Wie auch immer sie nun entstanden sind, Dons Drinks wurden schnell so populär, dass die „vier Jungs" bald nicht mehr ausreichten. Schließlich hatte er sieben Barmänner, die hauptberuflich bei ihm arbeiteten und alle auf besondere Drinks spezialisiert waren. Hinter ihnen standen noch mehr Filipino-Mitarbeiter, die Ananas mit Stahldraht schälten und zerlegten, riesige Eisblöcke abschabten, bis ihnen die Arme schmerzten, und Limetten auspressten, bis ihnen die Zitronensäure die Fingernägel zerfraß. Und um die Sache auf die Spitze zu treiben, führte er auch noch strikte Sicherheitsmaßnahmen ein, um zu verhindern, dass sich diese Assistenten Dons Geheimrezepte merkten. Statt der Etiketten waren die Flaschen nur mit Nummern und Buchstaben gekennzeichnet. Wie einem Artikel in der Saturday Evening Post von 1948 zu entnehmen ist, „sind die Rezepte codiert und die Barkeeper folgen einem vorgegebenen Muster codierter Symbole, mit denen vorgemixte Ingredienzien bezeichnet sind, nicht aber die eigentlichen Namen von Fruchtkonzentraten und Rumsorten. Selbst wenn sich also ein konkurrierender Barbesitzer einen der *Beachcomber*-Mitarbeiter unter den Nagel reißt … kann der Abtrünnige Dons Rezepte nicht mitnehmen." Trotzdem wurde dieses Zombie-Rezept bereits 1941 abgedruckt:

ZOMBIE
2 cl dunkler Jamaika-Rum
4 cl goldener Barbados-Rum
2 cl weißer puertoricanischer Rum
1 cl Apricot Brandy
1½ cl ungesüßter Ananassaft
1½ cl Papaya-Nektar
Saft einer großen Limette
1 Barlöffel fein zerstoßener Zucker

Den Zucker im Limettensaft auflösen, alles im Shaker auf Eiswürfeln schütteln und in ein großes geeistes Becherglas geben. 2 cl Mineralwasser hinzufügen und ausreichend Eis, um das Glas zu füllen, dann einen Spritzer 151 proof Demerara-Rum darüber fließen lassen. Mit einem Minzezweig und mit einem zwischen einer roten und einer grünen Cocktailkirsche aufgespießten Ananaswürfel garnieren, dann alles mit Puderzucker bestäuben.

Wenn Don der große weiße Vater des tropischen Drinks war, so hatte er viele verlorene Söhne. Kaum hatte Don sein Lokal eröffnet, waren die Nachahmer schon zur Stelle. In Harry Sugerman's Nachtclub *Tropics* in Beverly Hills wurde aus dem *Zombie* der *Zulu*. „One drink, you're important! Two drinks, you're impatient! Three drinks, you're impotent!" Während sich einige damit begnügten, Don zu imitieren, hatte sich Trader Vic Größeres vorgenommen. „Ich hatte nicht die geringste Ahnung von diesem ganzen Zeug", schreibt er in seiner Autobiografie, „aber ich dachte, dass ich es gern lernen würde." Er reiste in alle Him-

melsrichtungen, um international bekannte Barmänner kennen zu lernen, zum Beispiel Constantine Ribailagua in Havanna (der den Papa Dobles Grapefruit-Daiquiri für Ernest Hemingway kreierte) und Albert Martin in New Orleans (durch Ramos Fizz berühmt). Als er in seine Bar in Oakland zurückkehrte, war Trader Vic längst kein Imitator mehr. Er war ein Erfinder und Erneuerer.

Als Vic den *Scorpion*, den *Samoan Fog Cutter* und den *Mai Tai* erfand, war er plötzlich derjenige, dem man die Ideen klaute. „Davon bekomme ich Magengeschwüre", schnaubte er, wenn er hörte, dass sich Bars von Tahiti bis Tulsa als die Ursprungsorte des *Mai Tai* ausgaben. „Wer behauptet, ich hätte diesen Drink nicht erfunden, ist ein mieses Stinktier." Mit der folgenden für ihn typischen Geschichte rückte er die Legende zurecht: „Eines Tages 1944 stand ich hinter meiner Bar und redete mit meinem Barkeeper, und ich erzählte ihm, dass ich den besten Rumdrink der Welt machen wollte. In dem Augenblick kamen Ham und Carrie Guild, ein paar alte Freunde aus Tahiti, herein. Carrie probierte, hob ihr Glas und sagte, ‚Mai Tai – Roa Ae', was auf tahitisch bedeutet, nicht von dieser Welt – einfach der Beste!' Das ist der Name, sagte ich, wir nennen den Drink Mai Tai." Vic's Rezept:

MAI TAI
2 cl alter Jamaika-Rum
2 cl St. James Martinique-Rum
1 cl Curaçao
Saft einer Limette
½ cl Orgeatsirup*
½ cl Zuckersirup

Im Shaker auf gestoßenem Eis schütteln. Ausgepresstes Limettenviertel ins Glas geben und mit Minzezweig garnieren. (*Orgeat ist ein im Handel erhältlicher Mandelsirup.)

Der Streit darüber, wer den *Mai Tai* erfunden habe, zog sich hin, bis Trader Vic die Angelegenheit vor Gericht brachte und 1970 einen Prozess gegen die Sun-Vac Corporation führte. Zu der Zeit brachte Sun-Vac eine Produktlinie von vorgefertigten Mix-Sirupen heraus, die den Namen „Don the Beachcomber" trug. Ironischerweise behauptete Sun-Vac, dass Don selbst – der Mann, dem Vic, wie er ehrlich zugab, vor mehr als dreißig Jahren die Idee geklaut hatte – den Mai Tai erfunden habe. Der Prozess wurde schließlich außergerichtlich zu Vics Gunsten entschieden.

Als die exotischen Rum-Cocktails immer beliebter wurden und die polynesischen Lokale, in denen sie serviert wurden, immer besser liefen, wurde der Wettbewerb natürlich noch erbitterter. Im Gegensatz zu Don und Vic hatten die neuen Emporkömmlinge noch keine Ruhmestaten vorzuweisen und suchten darum nach irgendeinem Etikett, das ihrem Restaurant das spezielle Markenzeichen verlieh, zum Beispiel indem sie ihre Mitarbeiter zu Cocktail-Wettbewerben schickten, die von Rum-Firmen gesponsert waren. Das Restaurant durfte dann mit seinem eigenen, preisgekrönten Cocktail werben, den sein legendärer Barkeeper kreiert hatte, und die Rum-Firma konnte damit werben, dass das preisgekrönte Rezept mit ihrem Rum gemixt war.

1953 nahm ein anonymer Kellner aus dem *Luau* namens Popo Galcini an einem solchen Wettbewerb teil, der von Ron Rico gesponsert war; er gewann und stieg sofort zum Star der Branche auf, obwohl Gerüchte umgingen, dass der Wettbewerb, wie die meisten seiner Art, manipuliert worden sei. Trotzdem wurde Galcini schon bald aus dem *Luau* abgeworben: Im *Kelbo's* in West Los Angeles hatte er den ersten einer Reihe lukrativer Auftritte als Barkeeper, bis er schließlich im *Outrigger* in Laguna Beach auf dem Gipfel seiner Karriere angekommen war. Auf der Getränkekarte im *Outrigger* prangte stolz „preisgekrönte Cocktails von POPO".

„Preisgekrönte" Drinks waren aber nicht die einzige Möglichkeit, Tiki-Bars ins Gespräch zu bringen. Wenn man schon nicht die Urheberschaft ins Feld führen konnte, dann zumindest die Kennerschaft.

Nicht länger als minderwertig abgetan, hatte Rum Mitte der 50er Jahre ein völlig neues Image bekommen, was hauptsächlich dem missionarischen Eifer von Vic und Don zu verdanken war, die inzwischen ihre eigenen Marken herstellten und verkauften. Die bessere Gesellschaft ließ ihren Whiskey und Gin stehen für einen Teufelsrum, der plötzlich zum Drink der „Abenteurer der Meere" und zum „meist diskutierten und sagenumwobenen Getränk aller Zeiten" erklärt und romantisch verbrämt wurde. Wahre Genießer strömten zu den polynesischen Palästen mit der größten Auswahl an seltenen, alten oder sonst wie bemerkenswerten Marken aus allen Teilen der Welt; Restaurantbesitzer rühmten sich ihrer „Rumkeller" oder stellten ihre Riesenauswahl hinter der Bar zur Schau. In seinen Glanzzeiten bot *Don the Beachcomber* 120 verschiedene Rumsorten an. Einige Lokale boten nicht nur eine enorme Auswahl an Rum an, sondern auch ein ebenso gigantisches Angebot an Rum-Cocktails. „Es stehen 36 tropische Drinks zur Auswahl", war in einer Restaurantkritik aus jener Zeit von dem *China Trader* in Burbank zu lesen, „und ein Professor von der Technischen Universität Kalifornien stellte einen Rekord auf, indem er sechzehn Drinks schaffte, danach aber vollständig betäubt war". Wir können nur hoffen, dass er das niemals im *Luau* probiert hat, wo nicht weniger als 74 exotische Drinks auf der Karte standen – darunter auch der Martiki, die „polynesische Antwort auf einen trockenen Martini".

In den 60er Jahren strömten selbst die abgehobensten Nachkriegsintellektuellen in Tiki-Bars. Die Regisseure Bob Fosse und Stanley Kubrick waren Stammgäste in New Yorks *Trader Vic's* – wo Kubrick 1964 zum ersten Mal die Idee verlauten ließ, aus der vier Jahre später sein Film „2001: Odyssee im Weltraum" werden sollte. (Wir wissen nicht, was er getrunken hat, aber er muss jenem Professor von der Technischen Universität harte Konkurrenz gemacht haben.) In seiner Autobiografie erzählt Gore Vidal, dass er den bekannten Historiker Arthur Schlesinger und den Wirtschaftswissenschaftler und Nobelpreisträger John Kenneth Galbraith mit ins *Luau* genommen habe, wo sie, „reichlich mit Rum abgefüllt" mehrere Speichen aus dem riesigen Schiffsrad, das im Eingangsbereich stand, herausbrachen und dabei riefen: „Dies ist das Staatsschiff!" Frank Sinatra war ein großer Fan des *Navy Grog*, den man in *Don the Beachcomber* in Palm Springs servierte. Er war sehr großzügig mit Trinkgeld, erinnert sich Barkeeper Tony Ramos, „aber er kriegte einen Tobsuchtsanfall, wenn er nicht schnell genug bedient wurde".

Als die 70er Jahre zu Ende gingen, änderte sich auch der allgemeine Geschmack. An die Stelle des *Missionary's Downfall* trat jetzt der *Screaming Orgasm* und die besten und erfolgreichsten Barkeeper des goldenen Zeitalters verstreuten sich in alle Winde und nahmen dabei ihr Können, ihre Erfahrung und ihre „geheimen Zutaten" mit. Bittet man heute einen Barkeeper, einen tropischen Drink zu mixen, wird das unangenehm süße Ergebnis leider Tony Ramos' Behauptung bestätigen, dass das Mixen dieser Drinks eine „verlorene Kunst" sei.

Doch auch heute gibt es noch eine Handvoll Lokale, die sich auf gute exotische Drinks verstehen. Das *Mai Kai* in Fort Lauderdale, Florida und das *Kahiki* in Columbus, Ohio, servieren noch immer Mystery Drinks in verzierten Schalen, die von spärlich bekleideten Eingeborenenmädchen zum Klang von zeremoniellen Gongs serviert werden. Und das *Tiki Ti* des verstorbenen Ray Buhen, das heute von seinem Sohn Mike geführt wird, bietet den Einwohnern von Los Angeles immer noch 72 einwandfrei gemixte exotische Drinks.

Wie könnte man dieses Kapitel über die Geschichte amerikanischer Drinks besser schließen als mit Rays Worten: „Es ist Eskapismus. Es ist nicht real. Es ist ein Riesen-Tam-Tam", sagte er über die so genannten polynesischen Cocktails. Und dann: „Oh ja, das waren noch Zeiten!"

SCORPION BOWL

1½ l Orangensaft
0,8 l frisch gepresster Zitronensaft
3 cl Orgeatsirup
1,2 l leichter puertoricanischer Rum
1 cl Weinbrand

Mit zwei Tassen gestoßenem Eis vermengen und in einen Tiki-Krug geben, anschließend drei Eiswürfel hinzugeben und mit einer Gardenie garnieren. Mit Strohhalm servieren.

JÄGER UND SAMMLER

„Zunächst dienen die Objekte zur Illustration einer einfachen Geschichte, doch dann entfalten sie nach und nach ihre tiefere Bedeutung, bis sie schließlich das Herz anrühren."   (Henry Mercer, Sammler, 1898)

So wie eine alte Tonscherbe den Makrokosmos einer ganzen Kultur in sich birgt, ist der Tiki-Krug die Verkörperung des Tiki-Stils. Schon so mancher Stadtarchäologe geriet bei der Entdeckung eines solch eigenartigen Gefäßes in helle Aufregung, denn häufig stellte es den ersten Hinweis auf einen vergessenen Tiki-Tempel dar. Waghalsige Expeditionen zu entlegenen Orten sind häufig durch die kryptischen Inschriften, die bisweilen Hinweise auf weitere verborgene Schätze in sich tragen, angeregt worden, und manchmal brachten sie weitere Fundstücke zum Vorschein. Auf diese Weise konnte die Geschichte dieser großartigen polynesischen Paradiese vor dem Vergessen bewahrt werden.

Die unendliche Vielfalt und einfallsreiche Gestaltung des Tiki-Krugs verrät den kreativen Geist, von dem die Tiki-Anhänger erfüllt waren. Seine rituelle Verwendung als Trinkgefäß, um durch pseudo-polynesische Getränke einen anderen Bewusstseinszustand zu erreichen, unterstreicht die Verbindung des Tiki mit der Cocktailkultur.

Viele Tiki-Bars erfanden eigene Logo-Krüge, die von ihre rumseligen Gästen häufig als Souvenir ihres kurzen Ferienaufenthalts auf der städtischen Insel mitgebracht wurden. Doch waren die Krüge erst einmal zu Hause gelandet, endeten sie nach einer gewissen Zeit auf dem Dachboden, weil sie doch eher als Ausrutscher des guten Geschmacks betrachtet wurden, ästhetische One-Night-Stands, die man am nächsten Morgen nach dem Nüchternwerden bedauerte. Wenn auch die Herkunft des ersten echten Tiki-Krugs (wahrscheinlich Ende der 50er Jahre) im Dunkeln bleibt, ist doch der Gebrauch eines menschlichen Kopfes als Gefäß schon recht alt und verbindet moderne Krugsammler mit einer weit zurückliegenden, düsteren Tradition: Andreas Lommel, der Direktor des Münchner Museums für Anthropologie, beschreibt in „Vorgeschichte und Naturvölker" wie der Glaube daran, dass der menschliche Kopf den größten Anteil an „Mana" (Lebenskraft) enthalte, zur Verehrung desselben und letztlich auch zum Brauch des Kopfjagens geführt habe. Lommel schreibt: „In weit auseinanderliegenden Gebieten des Pazifik waren Gefäße, die wie menschliche Köpfe geformt waren, eindeutig Substitute für erbeutete Trophäen." Man kann wohl die heutigen Tiki-Krugsammler als Kopfjäger des zwanzigsten Jahrhunderts bezeichnen, die ihre Trophäen wie Stammesreliquien auf dem Schädelbord in dem zeremoniellen „Haus Tambaran" aufreihen. (Auch das Sammeln von Köpfen als Souvenirs ist nicht ganz ohne Vorgeschichte. Selbst wenn das Sammeln von Tiki-Krügen erst seit kurzem für manche zur Obsession geworden ist, wird es wohl kaum in jene Grenzbereiche vorstoßen, die Generalmajor Robley aus Neuseeland in seinem „Traffic in Heads" 1896 beschrieben hat: „Bis die Europäer nach Neuseeland kamen und anfingen, sich hier niederzulassen, waren die ‚Mokomai' (getrocknete und tätowierte Köpfe) der Maoris nur von sentimentalem Interesse und hatten keinen kommerziellen Wert. Doch als das Bedürfnis aufkam, sie als Kuriositäten in Museen und Privatsammlungen auszustellen, schnellte die Nachfrage in die Höhe. Die Maori ihrerseits waren ganz wild auf Feuerwaffen, Munition und Eisenwerkzeuge. Ihr Unwille, sich von den Köpfen zu trennen, war schnell überwunden und es begann ein so sprunghafter Handel, dass die Nachfrage weit größer war als der Vorrat. Dadurch wurde die Bevölkerung Neuseelands erheblich reduziert, doch die Museen Europas waren mit barbarischem Gesichtskult versorgt; als kommerzielles Unternehmen brachte der Handel erheblichen Profit. Frisch erlegte und minderwertige Köpfe traten an die Stelle der alten und ursprünglichen. Man fand sogar, dass ein frisch tätowierter Kopf nach seiner Konservierung genauso gut aussah wie ein alter." Die Häuptlinge hatten schnell begriffen, dass sie Gewinn aus dieser Entdeckung ziehen könnten, und machten sich daran, die am wenigsten wertvollen ihrer Sklaven zu töten, tätowierten aber zunächst deren Köpfe, damit sie aussahen, als wären sie Männer von hohem Rang gewesen, trockneten sie dann und verkauften sie. Der Geistliche J.S. Wood sagt: „Grundsätzlich war kein Mann, der gut tätowiert war, auch nur für eine Stunde sicher, wenn er nicht ein großer Häuptling war, denn er stand jederzeit unter Beobachtung, um den Moment abzupassen, da er unbewacht war, um ihn dann niederzuschlagen und zu töten, und dann wurde sein Kopf an die Händler verkauft. Man ließ alte Fehden wieder aufleben, unternahm lokale Kleinkriege, um den Nachschub sicherzustellen. Der Handel nahm ständig an Umfang zu, und als die Qualität immer schlechter wurde, zeigten die Händler ihre Unzufriedenheit; und einige von ihnen, die persönlich angereist kamen, um sich lebende Sklaven anzusehen und diejenigen auszuwählen, deren Köpfe sie kaufen wollten, wurden von einem Schicksal ereilt, das wenig Mitleid verdient.")

Moderne Tiki-Krüge wurden hauptsächlich in Japan hergestellt, dem billigsten Herstellerland für Werbegeschenke. Der führende Hersteller war O.M.C., Otagiri Merchandising. Restaurants schickten ihre Entwürfe, und O.M.C. formte daraus keramische Trinkgefäße. Doch das Tiki-Fieber führte dazu, dass neben Krügen noch eine erstaunliche Vielzahl von anderen Artikeln mit den Zügen des Südsee-Götzen hergestellt wurden: Tiki-Schalen, Flaschen, Aschenbecher, Feuerzeuge, Kerzen, alles, was als Partyutensilien oder Hausbarschmuck verwendet werden konnte. Die stilistischen Einflüsse reichten von polynesischer Volkskunst bis zu moderner Kunst. Authentizität und kulturelle Konkordanz waren nebensächlich, solange die Gegenstände den Geist Tikis verkörperten, eine Mischung aus Wildheit, naiver Kunst und Witz. Masken zum Beispiel waren in Polynesien sehr unüblich, und doch war der grimassierende Wandschmuck mit rotglühenden Augen ein klassisches Element des amerikanischen Tiki-Stils.

Als der städtische Tiki-Kult seine Anhängerschaft verlor, wurden die Götzenköpfe auf den Müll getragen oder versteckt, genau wie es ihren alten polynesischen Gegenstücken ergangen war, als es den missionarischen Bemühungen auf den Inseln gelungen war, mit der Ahnenverehrung und dem Götzenkult Schluss zu machen. Heute werden diese Relikte von Stadtarchäologen in Trödelläden, auf Flohmärkten und bei Haushaltsauflösungen ans Tageslicht befördert. Leider hat das Internet der Tiki-Jagd ein wenig das Abenteuerliche genommen, denn nun können sich auch Lehnstuhlabenteurer, die über die notwendige Zeit und das Geld verfügen, mit wenigen Mouseclicks Raritäten verschaffen, für die sonst waghalsige Anstrengungen vonnöten gewesen wären. Das Ergebnis sind besessene Preiskämpfe auf Auktions-Websites wie e–bay, die den Preis für einen *Mainlander*-Krug aus St. Louis auf absurde 103 Dollar in die Höhe treiben. Diese Art gieriger Trophäenjagd ist ziemlich unsportlich. Andererseits müssen wir auch dringend davon abraten, Kultgegenstände von den wenigen Tiki-Orten, die noch existieren, mitzunehmen, denn deren ohnehin schon gebrechliches „Mana" wird durch solche Plünderei nur weiter geschwächt.

... UND DIE GÖTTER WAREN GUTER DINGE

Hawaii, 1820, ein Tanzfest. Der Missionar Hiram Bingham beobachtet die Eingeborenen bei einem Hula-Marathon, wie sie einem Götterkopf Leis (Blumengirlanden) zum Geschenk machen, und er versucht, sie zu verstehen. „Wozu dient euch euer Gott, wofür ist er gut?" Ihre einfache Antwort verwirrt ihn: „Zum Spielen!" Ein Konzept, das damals für den Puritaner noch völlig unzugänglich war, aber über ein Jahrhundert später bei den Amerikanern auf fruchtbaren Boden fallen sollte. Ihre Rechtschaffenheit und Bescheidenheit hatte ihnen geholfen, die Depression durchzustehen und den Zweiten Weltkrieg zu gewinnen. Ein gesicherter Lebensstandard schien für jeden erreichbar zu sein, und nun war die Zeit gekommen, zu spielen. Doch die unerschütterlichen Moralvorstellungen der Väter, die diesem Bedürfnis im Wege standen, waren schwer abzuschütteln. Es musste eine alternative Welt geschaffen werden, in der man in eine freizügigere Rolle schlüpfen konnte. Die scheinbar sorglose Kultur Polynesiens wurde zum Vorbild einer eskapistischen Gegenwelt. Wo immer man Spaß haben konnte, da herrschte Tiki.

Durch die vielfältigen Konzepte, die zur Unterhaltung der Gäste verwirklicht wurden, waren Tiki-Bars richtige kleine Vergnügungszentren geworden. Daher war es eine natürliche Entwicklung, Tiki-Tempel in Spielparks zu integrieren oder eigene Tiki-Parks zu bauen. Die Ferienparadiese Kalifornien und Florida boten die richtige Kombination aus Erholungswert und Klima, und so entstanden ganze Tiki-Welten wie *Tiki Gardens* und *The Tikis*. Der Big Kahuna der Vergnügungsparks, Walt Disney, wollte dem natürlich in nichts nachstehen. Als häufiger Gast in polynesischen Nachtclubs hatte er beschlossen, ein Tiki-Restaurant zu eröffnen, das alle bisher existierenden in den Schatten stellen sollte. Walt war ein Animationskünstler und daher war für ihn der nächste logische Schritt, den ganzen üblichen Schmuck aus Blumen, Vögeln und Tikis lebendig werden zu lassen. Der Geist Tikis inspirierte Disney, das Konzept der „Audio-Animatronics" zu entwickeln, das später zum Herzstück vieler Disneyland-Attraktionen wurde. Doch als das Projekt sich seiner Vollendung näherte, war die Raumzeitaltertechnologie von 225 Roboterdarstellern, die von einem Vierzehnkanal-Magnetband gesteuert wurden, das an hundert separate Lautsprecher angeschlossen war und 438 separate Handlungen kontrollierte, über den zur Verfügung stehenden Raum des Restaurants hinausgewachsen, und anstatt einen Kompromiss einzugehen und die ganze Show etwas zu reduzieren, beschloss Walt, den Gastronomiebereich zu streichen und aus der Show eine eigenständige Attraktion zu machen. Als *The Enchanted Tiki Room* 1963 eröffnet wurde, schrieb die New York Times: „POLARIS-TONBAND HILFT DISNEY-ANIMATION – Neues Synchronisiergerät lässt Totempfähle sprechen ... Im *Enchanted Tiki Room* reden, singen und pfeifen Dutzende von leuchtend bunten synthetischen Vögeln. Geschnitzte heidnische Götter schlagen Trommeln und singen in fremdartigen Lauten. Stürme brausen und Quellen plätschern. Künstliche Papageien führen in verschiedenen Dialekten Gespräche."

In seiner begeisterten, wenn auch recht intellektuellen Besprechung „SPIEL, PARADOX UND MENSCHENMENGEN: EHRFURCHT IN DISNEYLAND", in der er den *Enchanted Tiki Room* mit anderen von Menschen gebauten „Kraft-Zentren" verglich, schrieb Stanford-Professor Don D. Jackson, Direktor des Palo Alto Mental Research Institute: „... und zwar weil ich behaupte, ebenso viel Ehrfurcht, Verwunderung und Verehrung empfunden zu haben, als ich in dem synthetischen, technisch konstruierten, instant-polynesischen Tiki-Room in Disneyland saß, wie ich es in einigen der großen Kathedralen – Chartres, Rheims und Notre Dame – erlebt habe ... In einer falschen Hütte sangen und spielten falsche Papageien recht erbauliche Melodien, es war ein Feuerwerk der Farben, und die Papageien bewegten ihre Schnäbel mit Präzision – einmal diese Gruppe, einmal jene, niemals versagend, immer überraschend. Dann bewegten die großen Totems (Tiki) in verschiedenen Ecken des sechseckigen Raums plötzlich ihre Gesichter, stimmten Chorgesänge an und schon bald vermischten sich die Lieder der Menschen und Vögel mit den Liedern der Blumen. Es war wie eine Szene aus einem schwach erinnerten, komplizierten Traum." Auch der Schöpfer des Ganzen erhält von Jackson ein Lob: „Disney hat es hervorragend verstanden, eine große Zahl von talentierten Leuten einzuspannen, um die vielen

Einzelheiten dieses kindlichen Traums zu verwirklichen. Wie ein ahnungsloses Kind ignoriert Disney die von der Erkenntnis auferlegten üblichen Grenzen. Mit seinem gesamten kreativen Schaffen verwirklicht er Kindheitsträume – er greift nach den Sternen."

Zu den talentierten Leuten, die Walt im *Tiki Room* einsetzte, gehörte auch der Künstler Rolly Crump, der den Tiki-Baum und die Statuen im Tiki-Garten (dem Eingangsbereich der Hütte) entworfen hat, und der Trickfilmzeichner Marc Davis, einer von Disneys „nine old men", seinen ursprünglichen Mitarbeitern. Davis hatte als Assistenz-Trickfilmzeichner bei „Schneewittchen" begonnen, bei „Bambi" mitgearbeitet und die Figur der Cruella De Ville aus „101 Dalmatiner" gezeichnet. Sein Interesse für Papua Neuguinea-Kunst spiegelte sich in seinen Entwürfen für die Innenausstattung des *Tiki Room*.

Tiki-Vergnügungsparks entstanden in allen Größen, angefangen bei Minigolf-Plätzen bis zu ganzen Jahrmärkten. Am Ende des Santa Monica-Piers gab es früher den *Pacific Ocean Park*, in dem auch eine Beachcomber-Rundfahrt stattfand, die um eine künstliche Lagune und einen Vulkan führte; diese waren auf einer Plattform errichtet, die am Ende der Mole lag, über dem Meer schwebend und durch eine Kabelbahn verbunden.

Eine andere Form des Familienvergnügungscenters, die mit dem Tiki-Thema zu tun hatte, war die Bowlingbahn. Meistens war es die angrenzende Cocktailbar, manchmal aber auch das gesamte Etablissement, das dem Gott der Erholung gewidmet war. Bowling hatte seinen Ursprung in deutschen Klöstern, wo Mönche die Kirchgänger einen flaschenförmigen Gegenstand umhauen ließen, um dadurch ihre fromme Ergebenheit zu Gott zu bekunden. Der hölzerne Kegel stellte den Teufel dar, und ihn umzustürzen bedeutete völlige Erlösung von den Sünden. Es ist nicht bekannt, ob je tikiförmige Bowlingkegel existiert haben, doch in vielen Lokalen wurden Aloha-Hemden und Bowling-Hemden beliebig gemischt und tropische Getränke sorgten dafür, den Tiki-Nachtschwärmern ihr Ziel klarer vor Augen zu führen. Einer dieser Orte war das extravagante *Kapu Kai* (Verbotenes Meer) in Rancho Cucamanga, einem Vorort von Los Angeles (siehe auch Seite 55). Vier Eingänge in dynamisch aufragender A-Form lockten die Gläubigen an. Die Tikis zwischen den Kegelbahnen und um das Gebäude herum waren von Milan Guanko geschnitzt. Die Relief-Tikis auf der Eingangstür begrüßten die ankommenden Gäste mit einem Lächeln, innen aber zeigten sie den Hinausgehenden einen Schmollmund. Die Böden waren mit Tiki-Teppichen ausgelegt und der „tahitische Feuerraum" stellte beeindruckende Tapa-Wandbehänge zur Schau. Und doch war alles schnell vorbei – trotz seines bemerkenswerten Designs überlebte das *Kapu Kai* nicht das Ende des 20. Jahrhunderts.

HOTEL, MOTEL

Im Amerika der 60er Jahren gingen Tourismus und Tikis Hand in Hand, und da die Motel-Leuchtreklamen die Totempfähle der amerikanischen Straßenrandkultur waren, wurden Tikis oft als Blickfang eingesetzt. Sie waren Leuchttürme im Stadtozean und ihre Tiki-Fackeln, mit Neon oder Gas betrieben, dienten als Leuchtfeuer für müde Reisende und moderne Kaufleute – Polynesien war nun mit dem Auto erreichbar. Das Motel war eine amerikanische Variante des Hotels, das eigens für die vierrädrige heilige Kuh geschaffen worden war. Der Himmel war die Grenze für amerikanische Autobauer jener Zeit, Größe und Aussehen Ihrer Produkte erreichten die Dimensionen von Raumschiffen. Für diese mussten leicht zugängliche Anlegeplätze geschaffen werden, mit einem dazu passenden Ort, an dem sich ihre Kapitäne bis zum nächsten Auslaufen ausruhen konnten. Um diese Raumschiffhäfen im unübersichtlichen Stadtuniversum kenntlich zu machen, wurden riesige Leuchtreklamen am Rande der Hauptverkehrsadern errichtet.

Seither ist die Motel-Leuchtreklame ein klassisches Symbol amerikanischer Kultur. Es ist daher ein wirkliches Zeichen von Ignoranz, dass Anaheim, Heimatstadt Disneylands, Anziehungspunkt für Touristen aus aller Welt auf der Suche nach amerikanischer Popkultur, noch 1998 die Motel-Leuchtreklame des *Pitcairn* im Rahmen ihrer „Verschönerungskampagne" abreißen ließ. Es scheint, dass Kulturikonen am ehesten dann Gefahr laufen, abgerissen oder zerstört zu werden, wenn ihr Wert gerade kurz vor der Wiederentdeckung steht. Folglich ist absehbar, dass es bald schlechte Imitationen solcher Leuchtreklamen geben wird, die dann in einigen Jahren in Disneyland aufgestellt werden, direkt neben den nachgebauten Diners, ausgestattet mit Autoteilen aus den 50er Jahren. So ist das *Hanalei*-Zeichen in San Diego ein perfektes Beispiel für „vorher" und „nachher" und die Ignoranz einer Firma, die der Modernität zuliebe den individuellen Ausdruck durch eine alles beherrschende Unverbindlichkeit ersetzen lässt. Genau wie bei dem ikonenhaften *Stardust*-Zeichen in Las Vegas (Seite 114/115), das auch durch eine fade Standard-Schrifttype ersetzt wurde, die nichts mehr mit dem Weltraumthema zu tun hat. Seit der polynesische Stil als überholt gilt, hat man zwar trotzdem das Innere des *Islands*-Restaurants im *Hanalei* weitgehend unverändert erhalten, doch von den tatsächlichen Tiki-Schätzen im Inneren ahnt man vor dem neuen Eingangsbereich nichts. Viele Einrichtungsgegenstände in diesem Restaurant und auch im hohen Atrium des Anbaus stammen aus einem anderen wichtigen Tiki-Lokal, dem abgerissenen *Luau* in Beverly Hills (Seite 100). Die Schließung des beliebten polynesischen „Kraft-Zentrums" fiel mit der Eröffnung des Anbaus des San Diego Hotels zusammen. Der ursprüngliche Besitzer war ein überzeugter Polynesien-Fan und hat den Anbau angeblich durch einen original hawaiischen Kahuna segnen lassen. Florida war bestens geeignet für die touristische Tiki-Kultur, und selbst heute noch kann der aufmerksame Stadtarchäologe Motels finden, die den Geist der Gottheit beschwören.

Tiki-Tempel und Tiki-Motels waren in ganz Amerika, nicht nur in klimatisch milderen Zonen, beliebt. Um das Hauptgebäude des *Tiki Motor Inn* in Lake George im Staat New York standen künstliche Palmen, die selbst im Schnee noch grün waren. Die einzig wahre Tiki-Motelkette jedoch entstand in den kalifornischen Wüstenstädten: Ken Kimes betrieb einst vierzig Motels, von denen fünf mit Tikis aus der Werkstatt von Oceanic Arts ausgestattet waren: Die *Tropics* in Indio, Blythe, Rosemead, Modesto und Palm Springs. Vier davon beherbergen noch immer Tikis, die durch das trockene Klima gut erhalten sind. Das *Tropics* in Palm Springs ist Tiki-Stil in Vollendung, wenngleich seine „Reef"-Bar erst kürzlich im mexikanischen Stil umgestaltet worden ist. Die Wiederentdeckung von Palm Springs als Zentrum der Moderne in der Mitte des 20. Jahrhunderts wird hoffentlich dazu beitragen, dass dieser außerordentliche Tiki-Tempel erhalten bleibt.

FÜR DEN JUNGGESELLEN EINE BEISPIELLOSE UMGEBUNG

„Überquere die handgeschnitzte Fußgängerbrücke, die über den Abgrund der Göttin Pele führt, wo die Lava kurz vor dem Ausbruch steht und die Erde gleich zu beben beginnen wird, dann befindest du dich in der besten Gegend aller Welten, fern von Stress, Sorgen und Nöten; und doch nur Minuten entfernt von öffentlichen Verkehrsmitteln, Kirchen, und nur Sekunden entfernt vom Festland … In dieser fantastischen Umgebung weiß Pele alles. Sie gehörte und wird immer in den Pantheon der hawaiischen Götter gehören. Du kannst dich entspannen und in der Sonne liegen, es gibt dafür einen palmenbestandenen Schwimmbereich mit Wasser, das aus der Korallenquelle in die schön geformte Lagune sprudelt. Auf der Fußgängerbrücke im Inneren stehst du dann inmitten der Ruinen ihres Reiches, wo die Überreste von Hopoe und Lohiau, in zwei riesige Felsen verwandelt, im wilden Wasser stehen, das in Kaskaden von dem lavabedeckten Hang eines brodelnden Vulkans herabstürzt. Von den Göttern getröstet kannst du hier dein Heim aufschlagen, in der herrlichen, palmenbestandenen und für den Junggesellen beispiellosen Umgebung leben …"

Dieses eindrückliche Beispiel für polynesische Pop-Poesie aus der Werbebroschüre der *Pele*-Apartments gibt eine gute Vorstellung davon, wie viel Mühe sich die Erbauer gegeben haben, diese „polynesischen" Wohnblöcke zu gestalten. Die architektonischen Entwürfe griffen auf alles zurück, was Tiki-Restaurants und Freizeitlokale bisher geboten hatten. Im speziellen Fall der *Pele*-Apartments wurde der Broschürentext vom Cover einer beliebten Exotica-Platte kopiert. Arthur Lymans „Pele" stand auch Pate bei der Namensgebung eines Auto-Prototyps, der von derselben Aluminiumfirma entworfen worden war, die die Konzerthalle, in der Lyman seine Platte eingespielt hatte, gebaut hatte. Henry J. Kaiser, Industriemagnat und Besitzer der Kaiser Aluminum Corporation, war ein begeisterter Polynesien-Fan, der sich eigentlich auf Hawaii zur Ruhe setzen wollte, dort angekommen aber das *Hawaiian Village Hotel* baute und auch die Kaiser-Aluminumkuppel errichten ließ, wo Veranstaltungen mit seiner Lieblingsmusik stattfinden sollten. In den 60er Jahren in den *Pele*-Apartments zu wohnen, den „Pele"-Wagen zu fahren und den Jungle Jazz von Arthur Lymans „Pele"-Album zu hören, das gehörte zu den Träumen, nach denen sich jeder moderne Primitive sehnte.

Der Erbauer des *Pele*-Apartments entwickelte ein weiteres ansprechendes Konzept für Apartmentwohnungen in seinem *Shelter Isle*-Wohnkomplex, das in dessen Werbebroschüren den bevorstehenden Niedergang der Tiki-Kultur zu erahnen schien: „Wenn man den Erholungsbereich verlässt und gemächlich die gewundenen Pfade entlang schlendert, findet man sich plötzlich in den Ruinen eines verlassenen Dorfes wieder. Hier stehen die Überreste einer Eingeborenensiedlung einsam an einem kleinen See, der von wilden Wassern gespeist wird, die von den lavabedeckten Hängen eines brodelnden Vulkans herabstürzen."

Als Stadtarchäologen Mitte der 90er Jahre diese Einrichtung entdeckten, waren von diesen „Überresten" nur einige überwachsene Lava-Felsen neben einem Teich übrig geblieben. Zumeist bieten Tiki-Dörfer dem Archäologen der Tiki-Kultur allerdings ergiebigere Einsichten, denn im allgemeinen haben sie die Abschaffung der Götzenverehrung besser überlebt als ihre Vorfahren, die Restaurants und Lounges. Da sie nicht so abhängig von Veränderungen des Geschmacks sind wie die Restaurantkultur, stellen sie manchmal regelrechte Refugien jener bedrohten Spezies der Tikis dar.

Auch wenn manche Besitzer und Pächter versucht haben, sie mit missionarischem Eifer in einen zeitgemäßen Zustand zu versetzen, und viele Tikis verrottet oder von Grabräubern gestohlen worden sind, kann man beim Durchforschen des Stadtgebiets von Los Angeles nach hohen Palmen und A-Form-Bauten noch immer spektakuläre Entdeckungen zutage fördern. Im *Tahitian Village* im San Fernando Valley sind die Archetypen für Feuer und Wasser durch zwei Eingeborenenskulpturen im Stile Gauguins dargestellt, die die Eingangsbrücke flankieren. Die männliche Figur spie einst Wasser aus dem Mund in ihre Hände und ließ es von dort in den Graben unter der Brücke fließen; die weibliche Figur hielt eine offene Gasflamme in der Hand. Eine über zwei Meter hohe Betonmaske, Tiki-Stützpfosten und überall Eisengeländer mit einem Dekor aus gekreuzten Speeren mit Schild sind weitere Besonderheiten dieser Wohnanlage.

Die Tiki-Fackeln im *Polynesian Village* in Playa del Rey brennen nicht mehr und ebenso wenig die Vulkanfeuer, die aus dem großen Wasserfall hervorbrachen. Aber die eigenwillig geschnitzten Einbaumbalken, die tropische Landschaftsgestaltung und die heterogene Lavafelsen- und Betonarchitektur von Armet & Davis geben immer noch ein hervorragendes Beispiel für einen Stil ab, der sich entwickelte, als es erstrebenswert erschien, wie ein Primitiver, aber in der Nähe eines modernen Flughafen zu wohnen, als Flugreisen noch bezaubernd waren und mit dem Jetset gleichgesetzt wurden, anstatt mit Lärm, Luftverpestung und Reisestress: „Stromlinienförmige Einrichtungen, luxuriös und elegant, ein Spiegel des Düsenzeitalters, sind kunstvoll mit dem Kolorit, der Romantik und dem Zauber der Südseeinseln angereichert, um eine verführerische Umgebung nach neuestem Design in den *Playa del Ray Polynesian*-Apartments zu schaffen … Geschnitzte Tiki-Götter wachen über der üppigen, herrlich gestalteten Gartenlandschaft und lassen ihren Zauber wirken, um Gesundheit, Glück und Zufriedenheit zu bringen."

Wie die Tempel waren auch die Dörfer am weitesten in Kalifornien verbreitet, blieben jedoch nicht auf wärmere Gegenden beschränkt. Entlang der ganzen Westküste, rund um Seattle in Tacoma und Bremerton, einer Navy-Werftstadt, wurden viele Tiki-Wohnanlagen gebaut. Über ganz Amerika verstreut bildeten sich mehr oder weniger exquisite Gemeinschaften, die dem Gott der Erholung huldigten. Die Namen dieser Vorstadtinseln waren genauso vielsagend wie der Schriftstil ihrer Schilder. Ob sie *Beachcomber*, *Asian*, *Primitive*, *Bamboo* oder *Fat Samoan* hießen – all diese Schriften waren Teil der Tiki-Ästhetik. Bestimmte Flügel oder Bereiche der Wohnanlagen hatten spezielle Bezeichnungen wie „Snug Harbour" oder „Mauna Loa", benannt nach Orten oder Hotels auf Hawaii. Die *Exotic Isle*-Appartements in Alhambra, einem Vorort von Los Angeles, die heute überwiegend von asiatischen Emigranten bewohnt werden, waren bis vor kurzem noch sehr eindrucksvolle Dokumente des Tiki-Kultes. Ein Entspannungsraum, der sich über den Hauptwasserfall erstreckt, bildet das Zentrum und könnte als Tiki-Entsprechung für Frank Lloyd Wrights *Falling Water* angesehen werden.

Das *Kona Pali*, der einzige bekannte Wohnkomplex, zu dem es ein identisches Schwester-Apartmenthaus, das *Kona Kai*, gibt, das sich in einem anderen Stadtteil befindet, hat kürzlich sogar die Beschädigungen durch das Northridge-Erdbeben überstanden. Es ist eine Fundgrube für herrliche Tiki-Details. Am Vordereingang wird man von einem in Beton eingelassenen und aus Muscheln geformten „Aloha" begrüßt. Betrachtet man die A-Form-Fassade genauer, kommt ein weiteres eindrucksvolles Element zum Vorschein: In der rechten Ecke ragen vier kleine Tikis aus dem goldgesprenkelten Verputz heraus. Doch nur ein geübtes Auge wird die letzten Spuren eines weiteren aufregenden Aspekts am Giebel ausfindig machen: Blickt man im richtigen Winkel zum Licht hinauf, zeigen die ovalen und geschwungenen rechteckigen Holztafeln schwache Spuren von Tiki-Masken, die mit Schablonen aufgemalt worden waren. Dieses Gebäude muss eine Sehenswürdigkeit gewesen sein! Teilweise hinter Bananenbäumen und „modernen" Tiki-Fackeln verborgen, ist die Fassade durch eine Reihe unterschiedlich geschnitzter Tiki-Balken unterteilt, die in einem modernistischen, stromlinienförmigen Tiki-Stil gestaltet sind. Die Aggregate für die Klimaanlage sind hinter Tiki-Masken, in der Tradition des Tragikomödie-Dekorums, verborgen. Eine andere Besonderheit in dieser Tiki-Wohnanlage ist das Portal hinter der Glastür: Überquert man die Eingangsbrücke, die über einen Graben führt, der einst von tropischen Pflanzen bestanden war, findet man rechter Hand eine Karte der hawaiischen Inseln aus Keramikmosaik. Die linke Seite ist mit Holz verkleidet und wird von vier grotesken Tikis bewacht, die in unterschiedlichen klassischen Stilen geschnitzt sind.

Pico Rivera, ein weiterer Vorort von Los Angeles, ist ebenfalls einen Ausflug wert, denn am Rosemead Boulevard im Block 5400 befinden sich drei Tiki-Wohnanlagen hintereinander. Die Anwohner beobachten uns argwöhnisch, als wir das *Aloha Arms* durchforsten, das eine großzügige dreigeschossige A-Form hat (Seite 61). Gleich daneben befinden sich die *Samoa*-Apartments, und dann, nach einem mysteriösen unbebauten Grundstück, kommt das *Kapu Tiki* mit seinem handbemalten Giebel-Tiki, auf dem eine Gasfackel thront, die schon lange erloschen ist. Die kugelförmigen Lampen waren wahrscheinlich früher in Fischernetzen aufgehängt, sodass sie aussahen wie japanische Fischernetzglaskugeln, die an der hawaiischen Küste auf dem Wasser trieben. Ganz rechts an der Fassade hängt eine einsame Tiki-Maske, in deren Augen früher Glühbirnen eingeschraubt waren, und aus deren Mund sich ein Wasserfall in eine Seemuschel ergoß.

Auch in anderen Teilen Amerikas gibt es noch Orte, die zu erforschen sich lohnt, zum Beispiel das *Sands West* in Phoenix, Arizona, dessen Werbebroschüre folgendes versprach: „In Hawaii war es Tradition, dass die Maori [sic!] bei Sonnenuntergang ihre Kämpfe unterbrachen und sich in ihr Hale zurückzogen, um bei Feuerschein Awa, Poi und die lokale Delikatesse Tintenfisch zu genießen. Im

Sands West kann ihr Familienkrieger sich von seinem täglichen Kampf in sein privates Lanai zurückziehen und mit seiner Familie einen Abend in völliger Entspannung erleben. Doch statt mit über dem Feuer geröstetem Tintenfisch oder fermentiertem Pfefferwasser wird ihr Kau Kau wohl eher an einem verschwenderischen Arizona-Barbecue im überdachten Innenhof stattfinden. Im *Sands West* wird ihnen dank der Annehmlichkeiten unserer automatisierten Heime die Arbeit wie von den Menehunen [den Angehörigen des „kleinen Volkes"] abgenommen erscheinen. Ihr Zuhause steht auch unter dem Schutz von Kumumahanahana, dem Gott der Hitze – durch die komplette Ausrüstung mit Klimaanlage und Heißwasserversorgung."

Götter gab es in Hülle und Fülle in den Tiki-Dörfern, und obwohl viele zerfallen und umgestürzt sind, stehen die verbliebenen immer noch als Wächter einer vergessenen Kultur und erinnern uns an den wundersamen und kreativen Geist, der dem Tiki-Stil innewohnte.

POLYNESIEN VOR DER EIGENEN HAUSTÜR

In mehr als einer Hinsicht war das Bedürfnis des Durchschnittsamerikaners, „den Wilden zu spielen", eine Regression in die Kindheit. Die Verantwortung bei der Arbeit und in der Familie ließ sich am besten bei „Luau"-Gartenpartys, vergessen; einer Art Geburtstagsparty für „große Jungs", wo Spaß und Spiele wieder erlaubt waren. Erwachsene Weiße in blumigen Hawaiihemden oder „Muu Muu"-Kleidern konsumierten süßes Essen und noch süßere Drinks, die weiter dazu beitrugen, den Intellekt auf Kinderniveau herabzuschrauben, übten sich im Hula-Tanz und im melodiösen, konsonantenlosen Singsang der hawaiischen Sprache: „Alle KANES, WAHINES und KEIKIS (Männer, Frauen und Kinder) wollen WIKI WIKI (eilen) zu einem hawaiischen LUAU (Fest). MALIHINIS (Neuankömmlinge) wollen die Bedeutung der seltsamen Wörter kennen lernen, die sie auf einem Luau hören. Wahines tragen HOLOKUS (hawaiisches Prinzessinnengewand mit Schleppe) oder MUU MUUS (flatternde Gewänder mit Blumenmuster). Kanes tragen ALOHA-Hemden (fröhliche Sporthemden). Ein PAPALE (Hut) ist nicht notwendig. ALOHA (Begrüßung) bringt man dadurch zum Ausdruck, dass man eine LEI (Blumengirlande) um den Hals der Malihini legt. Das Luau wird an langen Tischen serviert, die auf einer LANAI (offener Veranda) oder unter einem Palmenbaldachin im Hof stehen. Das Essen wird in einem IMU (unterirdischer Ofen) gekocht, für den man ein LUA (Loch) in die Erde gräbt und es mit POHAKU (Steinen) und KUNI (Zündmaterial) füllt. Man macht ein AHI (Feuer), um die Pohaku zu erhitzen. Das PUA (Schwein), das im Imu gegart wird, heißt PUA KALUA. Wenn das Luau ein AHAAINA (großes Fest) ist, dauert es Stunden, bis es PAU (beendet) ist und alle HIAMOE (schlafen) gehen. Der Schlaf kommt schnell, denn der OPU (Bauch) fühlt sich angenehm an von so viel KAU KAU (Essen)."

Imu-Löcher wurden in den Gärten ausgehoben, als sei der Goldrausch zurückgekehrt, doch allein der Wunsch, zum Wilden zu werden, war nicht genug. Die entsprechende Dekoration musste her. Die notwendigen Utensilien, um diese Happenings auszustatten, konnte man in Baumschulen und Spezialgeschäften wie „Sea and Jungle" im Valley, bei „Oceanic Arts" in Whittier oder bei „Johnson Products" in Chicago finden. Tiki-Fackeln, Grasmatten, Palmwedel, Bambusstöcke, Fischernetze, Speere und Trommeln und alles, was es in Tiki-Form gab, war hier zu bekommen. So baute man Tiki-Hütten in Hinterhöfen und Gärten und stellte Götzenbilder an Swimmingpools und auf Veranden auf, und die Tikis wurden zu den neuen Gartenzwergen der Vereinigten Staaten.

Für den Hobbybastler gab es komplette Bausätze mit Anleitung, wie man sich seine eigene Tiki-Bar bauen konnte. In vielen Vorstadthäusern wurden die Kellerräume in Partykeller umgewandelt, in denen sich Erwachsene zu Cocktailparties und „Erwachsenengesprächen" trafen. Wenn Rattan- und Bambusmöbel nicht genug Eindruck machten, dann schafften es sicherlich die mit geschnitzten Tikis verzierten Bars und Stühle aus dem Haus Witco (Seite 43 und 253). Elvis Presley, immer ein sicherer Maßstab in Sachen Volksgeschmack,

stattete seinen „Jungle Room" in Graceland mit Witco-Möbeln aus. Elvis schwamm mit auf dem Höhepunkt der polynesischen Welle mit seinen Filmen „Blaues Hawaii", „Südseeparadies" und „Clambake", in dem die großartigste Luau-Szene am Strand von Florida zu sehen ist, die es je in einem Film gab.

SURFIN' TIKI

Kalifornien, Mitte der 60er Jahre: An den Stränden und in ihren Gärten feierte eine Generation von Mittelstandsamerikanern Rituale, die sie „Luaus" nannten, bei denen sie sich an polynesischen Getränken berauschten und Tiki als Gott der Freizeit huldigten. Von ihnen unbemerkt, gerieten ihre Kinder derweilen unter den fremdartigen Einfluss eines Phänomens, das bald „die britische Invasion" genannt werden sollte. Ausländische Popbands mit seltsamen Namen wie „The Beatles" beeinflussten eine Jugendkultur, die, wie wir alle wissen, mit langen Haaren begann und mit psychedelischen Drogen und der sexuellen Revolution endete.

Die Versuche der Eltern, den Zivilisationsstress in einem Plastikpolynesien zu entkommen, wurden schnell als lahm, kitschig und veraltet abgetan. Tikis Zauber sollte bald gebrochen werden. Doch bevor dies geschah, nahm eine einheimische Version jenes ausländischen Jugendkults Tiki für sich in Anspruch: Für Kaliforniens Surfer wurde Tiki der modische Glücksfetisch, der sie auf ihrer Suche nach der perfekten Welle begleitete. Tiki-Amulette gehörten nun zur Strandkultur und galten als cooles Teil, das sowohl städtische Beachcomber als auch Surfer trugen. Die Inspirationsquelle war Hawaii. Es war nicht nur wegen seiner idealen Surfbedingungen ein Traumziel, sondern es war die Insel, auf der der weiße Mann zum ersten Mal diesen Sport beobachtete. Der große Forscher Captain Cook entdeckte viele Dinge in Polynesien, und eines davon war das Surfen. Als er in Kealakekua Bay vor Anker ging, wo er sehr viel später durch die Eingeborenen zu Tode kommen sollte, notierte er in sein Logbuch: „Die Kühnheit und Geschicklichkeit, mit der wir sie diese schwierigen und gefährlichen Manöver ausführen sahen, war ungemein erstaunlich, und man kann es kaum glauben."

Im alten Hawaii war das Surfen eine Tätigkeit, mit der sich vor allem die Mitglieder des Königshauses vergnügten. Das Schnitzen eines Surfbrettes war, wie die Schaffung eines Tiki, von heiligen Ritualen begleitet. In der hawaiischen Mythologie sind viele Geschichten über surfende Ahnengötter überliefert, zum Beispiel diese über „Mamala, die Wellenreiterin": „Mamala war eine Kupua-Fürstin. Das bedeutete, dass sie eine Mo-o, eine Rieseneidechse oder ein Krokodil, war und ebenso eine schöne Frau, und sie konnte die Gestalt annehmen, die sie wollte. Mamala war eine wunderbare Wellenreiterin. Mit größter Geschicklichkeit tanzte sie auf den höchsten Wellen. Die Leute am Strand, die ihr zuschauten, erfüllten die Luft mit dröhnendem Applaus, wenn sie vor Begeisterung über ihre außergewöhnlichen athletischen Fähigkeiten in die Hände klatschten."

Da Surfen die Religion der kalifornischen Surfer war, ist es nicht verwunderlich, dass Tiki ihr Gott wurde. Als Talisman, auf T-Shirts und bei Strandfesten wurde Tiki zu einer Ikone, die als cool galt.

DIE KÜNSTLER

Die Schöpfer der bisher nicht anerkannten Kunstform des modernen Tiki-Stils, amerikanische Tiki-Bildhauer, sind niemals als Künstler akzeptiert worden. Ihre Produkte wurden als „authentisch" bezeichnet, ein verschwommener Begriff, der Echtheit bedeuten kann, aber nicht zwingend beschreibt, dass es sich um Originale handelt. Keiner wollte die Aufmerksamkeit darauf lenken, dass etwa die dunkle Haut des Holzschnitzers Vince Buono daher rührte, dass er einer New Yorker Immigrantenfamilie italienischen Ursprungs entstammte und nicht von einer Südseeinsel. Tiki-Stil hatte nichts mit mutwilligem Betrug zu tun, er bediente nur das Bedürfnis des Publikums nach Selbstbetrug, und daher hüllte er sich und seine Schöpfer in Geheimnisse. Die Motorsäge, die Leroy Schmaltz schwingt (Seite 242) war tabu bei öffentlichen Auftritten, wo die Schnitzarbeit mit Hammer und Meisel vorgeführt wurde. In diesem Kapitel soll einigen Künstlern, stellvertretend für alle, die unerwähnt bleiben, die gebührende Anerkennung zuteil werden.

SEITE 244–245
Leroy Schmaltz und Bob van Oosting gründeten ihre Dekorationsfirma „Oceanic Arts" in Whittier, einem Vorort von Los Angeles, in den späten 50er Jahren, auf dem Höhepunkt der Tiki-Begeisterung. Sie hatten ganz klein mit Tiki-Amuletten und Palmwedelmasken begonnen. Doch schnell entwickelte sich „Oceanic Arts" zum größten landesweiten Hersteller und Vertreiber von Tiki-Kunst und Einrichtungsmaterial. Alle großen Restaurantketten von *Don the Beachcomber* bis *Kon-Tiki* arbeiteten mit ihnen zusammen, und bei der Masse an Aufträgen war praktisch jeder Holzschnitzer der Branche irgendwann einmal bei ihnen beschäftigt. Manchmal wurden die Tikis von den Architekten oder Innenausstattern entworfen, meistens aber folgten die Holzschnitzer ihren eigenen Ideen und bisweilen übernahmen sie sogar die komplette Innenausstattung der Lokale.
Die Liste der Auftragsarbeiten im „Oceanic Arts" ist lang, denn sie hatten mit den meisten Tiki-Tempeln zu tun, die in diesem Buch dargestellt sind. Vom *Kahiki* in Ohio (S. 144) über das *Mai Kai* in Florida (S. 136) bis zum *The Tikis* in Monterey Park (Kapitel 11) kann man „Oceanic Arts"-Produkte in ganz Amerika entdecken. Selbst das anerkannte Bishop Museum in Honolulu beherbergt einige ihrer Schnitzwerke, wenn auch nicht in den Ausstellungsvitrinen, so doch an den Wänden der Cafeteria. Für das kulturübergreifende Phänomen des Tiki-Stils schloss sich der Kreis, als Götzenbilder aus der Werkstatt von „Oceanic Arts" für Hotels und Restaurants auf Hawaii, Samoa und Tahiti exportiert wurden. Heute ist „Oceanic Arts" der einzige Hersteller von polynesischen Schmuckartikeln, der den Niedergang der Tiki-Kultur erfolgreich überlebt hat und eine neue Forschergeneration aus aller Welt an die Gestade von Whittier, Kalifornien, lockt.

SEITE 246
Nördlich von San Francisco, im malerischen Jachthafen von Sausalito, hat der Ex-Offizier der Handelsmarine, Barney West, sein Lager mit seinem „Tiki Junction" aufgeschlagen. Er fand zu seiner Berufung als er im Zweiten Weltkrieg auf den Marianen strandete. Zu seinem „Tiki Junction"-Logo inspirierte ihn ein Buch, das anlässlich der ersten Ausstellung von Südseekunst in Amerika im Jahre 1946 veröffentlicht wurde; das Trader Vic-Logo soll auch hierauf zurückzuführen sein. Trader Vic, der sein Geschäft auf der anderen Seite der Bucht in Emeryville nahe Oakland hatte, wurde der Hauptkunde für Barneys Tikis. Noch heute finden sich einige dieser Götzenbilder, die seinen unverwechselbaren Stil aufweisen, in vielen *Trader Vics*-Filialen rund um die Welt. Barney entsprach ganz der Rolle des trinkfesten, frauenverschleißenden Bohemien, und er ist schon lange in den Tiki-Himmel eingegangen.

SEITE 248–249
Milan Guanko lernte das Schnitzen schon als Kind von seinem Vater auf den Philippinen. Nachdem er 1928 in die Vereinigten Staaten ausgewandert war und im Lebensmittelhandel gearbeitet hatte, fand er seine Nische in der aufkeimenden Polynesienbegeisterung. Schließlich wurde er einer der produktivsten und einflussreichsten Tiki-Schnitzer in Amerika, sein Stil wurde kopiert und für den wachsenden Bedarf der Tiki-Anhänger vermarktet. Zu seinen Kunden gehören *The Islands* (Seite 155) in Phoenix, Arizona, das *Kapu Kai* (Seite 199) in Rancho Cucamonga und Ren Clarks *Polynesian Village* (Seite 44) in Fort Worth, Texas, für das Guanko und zwei mexikanische Schnitzer, Juan Razo und Fidel Rodriguez (die das *Mauna Loa* in Mexico City ausgestattet hatten), mehr als zweihundert Tikis geschnitzt haben, manche in Form von Barhockern, andere als

dreieinhalb Meter hohe Riesen. 1960 war es ein polynesisches Vorzeigeparadies, heute ist von diesem künstlichen Tiki-Wald nichts übrig geblieben und der Verbleib seiner vielen Bewohner ist unbekannt. Auch das Schicksal eines riesigen Anaheim-Apartment-Tikis, der seinen eigenen Aussagen zufolge auf einem rotierenden Sockel stand, bleibt ein Geheimnis. Milan eröffnete sein Geschäft in Anaheim, wo er von der Rodung für das immer größer werdende Disneyland profitierte; er wurde ständig mit Palmen versorgt. Er gab offen zu, von „kiddie cartoons" beeinflusst worden zu sein, und sich kaum an einen „authentischen" Inselstil zu halten. Heute kann man seine Arbeiten im *Royal Hawaiian* in Laguna Beach bewundern, eine der ältesten noch geöffneten Tiki-Bars.

SEITE 250–251
Bob Lutz, der hier mit seinen wunderbaren Götzenbildern posiert, ist ein einmaliges, aber wenig bekanntes Tiki-Talent. Er war wohl zu gut für diese Welt, und es heißt, er habe sich umgebracht, nachdem er seine Freundin im Bett eines anderen überrascht habe. Das einzige ihm zuzuordnende Schnitzwerk, befindet sich vor der „Tiki Spa" in Palm Springs. Ein weiterer Schöpfer hochstilisierter Tikis war Andres Bumatay, der wie Milan Guanko von den Philippinen stammte. Seine absurden, mit Glupschaugen versehenen Tikis konnte man in dem „Sea and Jungle"-Geschäft (Seite 234) kaufen. Sie bildeten die Vorlage für einen Tiki-Krug und wahrscheinlich auch für den Tiki auf dem Logo des *Tahitian* (Seite 152).

SEITE 251
Charles Rosencrans arbeitete als Polier bei einer Baufirma und war Autodidakt. Seine seltsamen Statuen zierten *The Reef* in Long Beach und das *Royal Tahitian*, einen Tiki-Tempel im modernen, abgeschrägten A-Form-Stil am Ontario-Golfplatz in Los Angeles, eine Anlage, die über das „größte polynesische Freizeitgelände im ganzen Land" verfügte – zumindest wenn man den Golfplatz einfach dazurechnete. Das A-förmige Gebäude ist erhalten geblieben, doch alle Spuren von Rosencrans' seltsamer Kunst sind verschwunden. Doch gleich daneben befindet sich ein namenloses Apartementgebäude, das vier Tikis von Milan Guanko sein eigen nennt.

SEITE 253
In William Westenhavers Witco-Welt war nur ein geschnitztes Stück Holz ein gutes Stück Holz. Ob er seine „Plüschteppich-Brenn-Reliefs" oder komplette Schlafzimmereinrichtungen im primitiven Stil kreierte – keine glatte Fläche entging der Kettensäge dieses Verrückten. Wo immer er ein Tiki-Gesicht anbringen konnte, flogen die Holzspäne. Dann wurde das Holz mit einem Schweißbrenner angeflammt, um die Maserung in dicken schwarzen Adern sichtbar zu machen. Aber es war nicht nur polynesische Pop-Kunst, auch moderner und Konquistadoren-Raumdekor wurde in der Witco-Fabrik in Seattle am Fließband produziert. Eine Zeit lang hatte Witco Ausstellungsräume in Chicago, Dallas, Denver und Seattle und Westenhavers Kunst findet sich noch immer in Motels in Florida und in Trödelläden überall in den Vereinigten Staaten. Zu seinen Kunden gehörten Elvis Presley (Seite 235) und Hugh Hefner (Seite 43). Sogar einige „Häuser von schlechtem Ruf" sollen bei ihm Kunden gewesen sein. Zu seinen gelungensten Arbeiten gehören etliche Tiki-Bars (Seite 6) und Tiki-Springbrunnen (Seite 179).
Der Autor dieses Buches arbeitet derzeit an einer Monografie über das umfangreiche Schaffen dieses originellen Kunsthandwerkers. Zu guter Letzt möchte er seine Hoffnung zum Ausdruck bringen, dass das vorliegende Buch dazu beitragen mag, der Tiki-Kultur die ihr gebührende Anerkennung zu verschaffen.

FRENCH

LE LIVRE DE TIKI. LE CULTE DU POP POLYNÉSIEN DANS L'AMÉRIQUE DES ANNÉES 50

LE GUIDE DE L'ARCHÉOLOGUE URBAIN. DÉCOUVRIR UNE CIVILISATION PERDUE DEVANT SA PORTE

« La putréfaction se répand parmi les idoles – le fruit sur leurs autels devient insultant – les temples ont besoin d'une renaissance… »

(Herman Melville: Taïpi, 1846)

Ces remarques sur le destin de l'ancienne civilisation polynésienne, tirées de l'un des classiques de la littérature inspirée par les mers du Sud, semblent étonnamment appropriées pour rendre compte du sort qui a frappé le style tiki américain des années 1950 et 1960. Ses symboles, les tiki, sont en décrépitude, la cuisine polynésienne de cette époque est devenue l'antithèse de l'alimentation saine, et la plupart des exemples de l'architecture tiki qui ont survécu semblent délabrés. Mais, de même que Paul Gauguin était fasciné par l'atmosphère mélancolique du déclin de Papeete, la capitale de Tahiti, repérant « la surface trouble d'une énigme insondable » dans ce paradis déjà corrompu, l'archéologue urbain d'aujourd'hui reconnaît les vestiges de ce « Paradis perdu » de la dolce vita américaine que nous appelons le style tiki.

Les temples tiki, que l'on rencontrait jadis dans toute ville américaine d'importance, ont disparu, ou bien ont été rénovés, les « grossières images à l'aspect jovial » chassées avec un zèle missionnaire pour faire place aux nouveaux dieux (ou styles). Les cascades ont cessé de couler comme le mana qui avait permis leur installation, les torches tiki ont disparu et les poutres saillantes ont été sectionnées. Mais l'archéologue des villes a développé une sensibilité exacerbée pour les cultures disparues et leurs formes oubliées. Ignorant la peur, il explore leurs sites dans des lieux aussi exotiques que Colombus, l'Ohio ou Pomona, dans la mer urbaine de Los Angeles. Pour lui, s'immerger dans quelque secrète voie expresse jusqu'à une super périphérie non répertoriée, un jour de pollution, est aussi excitant que de naviguer à bord du Kon-Tiki au sein du Pacifique déchaîné. Tel un batteur de grève urbain, il passe au crible les débris de la culture de consommation dans les dépôts-vente, les débarras d'arrière-cours et les bouquinistes. Tout cela pour compléter le puzzle de modes de vie disparus qui ont engendré des concepts tels que celui du Paradis Polynésien Urbain. Avec un émerveillement intact, l'archéologue urbain découvre qu'il ne faut pas chercher bien loin pour explorer les mystères de traditions disparues, et que d'étranges trésors peuvent se trouver à notre porte, enfouis sous les couches du progrès et du développement. Nous voulons, à travers ce livre, entretenir chez vous cette faculté à reconnaître le merveilleux dans l'apparente banalité, offrir un guide de la culture tiki en Amérique.

AU COMMENCEMENT …

Depuis qu'il en a été chassé, l'homme a toujours aspiré à retrouver le chemin du paradis. Les premiers récits sur les îles des mers du Sud apparus dans l'Ancien Monde semblaient décrire ce havre perdu. La Polynésie devint la métaphore de l'Eden sur terre. Mais comme ses rivages lointains étaient inaccessibles au commun des mortels, les explorateurs se mirent en quête d'autres terres mythiques.

L'une d'elle était la Californie, une île mystérieuse (on croyait alors qu'il s'agissait d'un continent) que l'on croyait peuplée d'amazones. Même lorsque cette terra incognita fut colonisée et que ces débordements d'imagination se révélèrent terriblement excessifs, la Californie conserva son statut de pays de rêve. Des générations et des générations s'y établirent, cherchant à réaliser leur propre version du paradis. L'une de ces interprétations édéniques était le jardin tropical des îles des mers du Sud.

Le premier palmier fut planté et la flore tropicale se propagea. Et comme la biosphère tout autant que la psychosphère étaient parfaitement adaptées, une Polynésie américaine vit très vite le jour. On érigea des temples tiki et les gens crurent un temps à ces idoles. Ils célébraient le culte du primitivisme moderne, pratiquant avec ferveur des rites aujourd'hui tabous tels que l'alcoolisme, le racisme, la phallocratie et la consommation de viande de porc. Et de même que les Californiens imitaient la Polynésie, le reste de la nation trouvait en Californie le modèle d'un style de vie. Bientôt, chaque ville importante des Etats-Unis abrita au moins un palais polynésien.

TIKI – QUI ETAIT-IL?

Au commencement était le Verbe, et le Verbe était: « tik » ! C'est du moins ce que prétendait l'expert en ethnolinguistique, Merrit Ruhlen de Palo Alto, Californie. Il faisait remonter l'origine de tout langage humain à ce mot magique de trois lettres, qui survit aujourd'hui dans l'américain « digit » (et bien entendu dans l'argot français « trique »). Doté d'un tel pouvoir archaïque, il n'est guère surprenant que « tiki » soit devenu le cri de ralliement de toute une génération.

Mais « tiki » n'était pas seulement proche du premier mot proféré par l'humanité, il est également synonyme du premier homme dans la mythologie polynésienne. D'après le « Concise Maori Dictionary » d'A.W. Reed, cela s'explique ainsi:

1. TIKI: Le premier homme, ou la personnification de l'homme. A travers le culte ancestral, cet Adam maori devint un demi-dieu, et finalement le terme « tiki » fut utilisé dans toutes les descriptions de l'homme, comme nous le voyons dans sa signification suivante:

2. TIKI: La sculpture grotesque de l'homme dans une maison. Une description concise du type de tiki que nous trouvons dans ce livre. Mais, poursuivant la lecture, le mot révèle une signification encore plus profonde.

3. TIKI: Un symbole phallique. En effet, dans la culture maori, tiki désigne la puissance procréatrice et l'organe sexuel du dieu Tane, créateur de la première femme. Dans les îles Australes, au sud de Tahiti, « tiki-roa » (la longue figure ancestrale) était le surnom du pénis, et « tiki-poto » (la courte figure ancestrale) désignait affectueusement le clitoris.

Ce mot ayant de tels pouvoirs créatifs, nous ne sommes pas surpris de lui trouver déjà une autre signification dans les îles Marquises:

4. TIKI: Le dieu des artistes. Montrer que Tiki inspira en effet de nombreux artistes, connus et inconnus, est l'une des ambitions de ce livre, qu'il puisse aussi s'établir comme le protecteur très attendu des artistes.

L'ART PRIMITIF DANS LES LIEUX CIVILISES

« Quiconque les a vus, se trouve ensuite hanté comme par un rêve fiévreux. » (Karl Woermann, à propos des tiki, dans son « Geschichte der Kunst aller Zeiten und Völker, 1900–1911).

L'esthétique apparemment naïve et sauvage de l'art dit « primitif » pour adoucir les lignes du design moderne a été une source d'inspiration pour les fondateurs de l'art moderne. Lorsque, au début du XXe siècle, de plus en plus de « curiosités artificielles » (objets d'art d'Afrique et d'Océanie) arrivèrent des colonies dans les villes de l'Europe occidentale, une nouvelle génération d'artistes tels que Picasso, Miro, Klee et Ernst, s'en inspirèrent pour défier les canons artistiques en vigueur à l'époque. Comme le note Gauguin, l'étude des arts classiques établis « me dégoûtait et me décourageait, me donnant un vague sentiment de mort sans renaissance ». Pablo Picasso eut une révélation (« … soudain, j'ai compris pourquoi j'étais un peintre ! ») en découvrant la collection d'art primitif du Musée d'Ethnographie du Trocadéro. En fait, dès 1919, il était célébré comme un « vieil adepte du tiki », et ce probablement parce qu'il était depuis

1910 le fier propriétaire d'un tiki des Marquises qui l'accompagna tout au long de son inégalable carrière.

Alors que l'art primitif fut essentiellement apprécié par l'avant-garde durant les années 1920 et 1930, il séduisit la classe moyenne après la Seconde Guerre mondiale. On l'associait désormais à un style de vie artistique, bohème et à une conception de l'existence originale et ludique. A la fin des années 1950, on se devait de posséder une œuvre d'art tribale surprenante pour rompre un tant soit peu la monotonie du décor de son salon contemporain. L'heure du tiki avait sonné.

LE PRE-TIKI ET LA NAISSANCE DU POP POLYNESIEN

« Oh, être né sur l'une des îles des mers du Sud tel un soi-disant sauvage, pour, une fois seulement, jouir de l'existence humaine dans toute sa pureté et sans arrière-pensée. »   (Conversations de Goethe avec Eckermann, 12.3.1828) Le désir d'échanger les bienfaits de la civilisation contre un mode de vie plus simple et plus naturel est aussi ancien que la « civilisation » elle-même. Les rêveurs comme les philosophes sérieux considéraient que les premiers récits de voyages de Cook et Bougainville racontant leurs expéditions dans les mers du Sud, décrivaient l'alternative parfaite aux conditions de vie prévalant dans la société artificielle de la vieille Europe. Melville a célébré dans « Taïpi » le naturel des femmes indigènes : « J'aurais aimé voir, à l'Abbaye de Westminster, nos beautés de la cour face à ces filles des îles. Leur raideur, leur air formel et affecté, auraient produit un saisissant contraste avec la vivacité et la grâce naturelle de ces femmes sauvages. »

Le doux climat, la beauté sans artifices, des indigènes ardents, et les nourritures exotiques en abondance, semblaient promettre une existence libérée des contraintes et des tensions créées par les communautés cultivées du monde occidental. Les récits d'aventures en Polynésie, en quête de l'« évasion », devinrent si populaires qu'en 1921, la maison d'édition G. P. Putnam's Sons publia une parodie de ces expéditions dans les mers du Sud, intitulée « The Cruise of the Kawa » (1921). Bien qu'ouvertement satirique, ne serait-ce que par les photographies sélectionnées, le livre fut considéré comme authentique et son auteur invité à s'exprimer devant la National Geographic Society. Preuve fut ainsi donnée que la fiction était préférable à la réalité lorsqu'il s'agissait de traduire le paradis sur terre. Et c'est ainsi que naquit ce goût pour le fantasque qui allait imprégner le pop polynésien. Mais à l'origine, les récits rapportés de Polynésie touchaient un instinct bien plus archaïque. « Sur l'île de Otaheite (Tahiti), où l'amour est la principale occupation, le luxe favori, ou, plus exactement, l'unique luxe des habitants, les corps et les âmes des femmes sont poussés à la perfection. » (Joseph Banks, 1743–1820, naturaliste embarqué à bord de l'*Endeavour* du Capitaine Cook).

Ce genre de remarques proférées par les premiers explorateurs firent de la jeune fille indigène nue, la vahiné, l'Eve du jardin d'Eden polynésien. Incarnant les promesses d'un amour sans limites, elle devint la première et principale icône du pop polynésien. Bientôt, le palmier, la hutte, la pirogue et toutes sortes de fleurs et d'animaux exotiques la rejoignirent dans la galerie des symboles populaires de la culture océanienne. Tant et si bien que le tiki ne fut plus qu'une figure parmi d'autres de la légendaire Polynesia Americana.

L'ukulele, fit son apparition lorsque se déchaîna l'engouement pour la musique hawaïenne dans les années 1920. Les musiciens hawaïens étaient invités après leurs prestations dans les boîtes de nuit, et les clubs eux-mêmes commencèrent à puiser dans le thème tropical. Les sols et les plafonds en bambou ou en rotin, les luxuriantes plantes tropicales et les peintures murales des îles servirent de décor aux citadins en quête d'évasion, leur donnant l'illusion de se trouver dans les mers du Sud.

Et bientôt l'imagination populaire se concentra sur une autre image. Même si les premiers zoos européens avaient commencé à montrer des « sauvages »

vivants et si les journalistes se moquaient des dames de la bonne société qui se pâmaient en les voyant, la répulsion et l'attrait ressentis à la fois pour le « sauvage », son allure étrangement exotique, s'étaient inscrits dans les consciences civilisées des occidentaux. Dans le pop polynésien, cette fascination prit la forme de l'idole païenne Tiki.

TIKI : LOISIRS ET STYLE DE VIE D'UNE GENERATION

« Le système d'idolâtrie, qui prévalait chez un peuple séparé de la majorité de ses semblables par des océans infranchissables et possédant à un degré inhabituel des moyens non seulement de subsistance mais aussi de confort, est une démonstration navrante d'imbécillité, d'absurdité et de déchéance. »

(Révérend William Ellis : Polynesian Researches, 1831)

Dans les années 1950, les Américains étaient prêts à récolter les bénéfices du dur labeur qui leur avait donné l'indépendance économique et l'abondance. Ils étaient sortis de la Seconde Guerre mondiale en héros et volaient sur un nuage de succès international et de reconnaissance. Mais la même éthique puritaine du travail qui les avaient conduits jusque-là, transportait avec elle tout un lot d'interdits sociaux et moraux qui restreignaient la libre jouissance de la prospérité.

Les soirées polynésiennes offrirent un exutoire à l'homme en complet de flanelle grise, elles lui permirent de régresser jusqu'à une naïveté primitive qui faisait fi des lois : s'exhiber en chemises aloha bariolées (pas besoin de les rentrer dans son pantalon), s'enivrer de doux breuvages exotiques aux noms évocateurs d'un idiome infantile (Lapu Lapu, Mauna Loa Puki), manger le cochon luau avec ses doigts, et se lancer dans des concours de houla et de limbo, permettait de lâcher la bride et de s'amuser au sein d'une société on ne peut plus conservatrice.

Une autre liberté offerte au « sauvage de banlieue » était de pouvoir contempler des photos de femmes indigènes aux seins nus, aussi longtemps que l'on restait dans le cadre de l'intérêt anthropologique, et de pratiquer ainsi une sorte d'érotisme de type National Geographic. Mais tandis que l'on allait quérir à nouveau la vahiné et toutes les autres icônes-clichés propres aux contrées mythiques des mers du Sud, une nouvelle figure de proue du pop polynésien fit son apparition : l'idole sculptée communément appelée tiki. Nonobstant le fait que le terme n'existe pas en langage hawaïen ou tahitien, et que les statues de pierre de l'île de Pâques étaient des moai et le sont restées, toutes les sculptures océaniques devinrent pour le pop polynésien les membres d'une même famille heureuse : les tiki. Ces effigies primitives étaient un antidote au monde moderne du plastique et du chrome, des monuments élevés aux instincts primaires des hommes.

Bien qu'empruntant leur forme à leurs prédécesseurs polynésiens, les tiki américains étaient le plus souvent des interprétations libres de plusieurs styles insulaires assaisonnés d'une bonne dose de fantaisie de BD et d'un doigt d'art moderne. Même ceux que l'on aurait pu qualifier d'« authentiques » ne reproduisaient en fait que quelques originaux ayant survécu à la « fureur iconoclaste » des missionnaires. Cette attitude libérale envers la contrefaçon avait commencé dans les îles hawaïennes lors des premiers contacts avec l'Occident, comme on peut le constater dans ce rapport de 1825 : « Les officiers du navire royal *Blonde*, lorsqu'ils résidaient dans les îles, étaient particulièrement soucieux de se procurer quelques-unes des anciennes idoles pour les rapporter chez eux comme curiosités. La demande épuisa bientôt le stock disponible. Afin de vaincre la pénurie, les Hawaïens fabriquèrent des idoles et les noircirent à la fumée afin de leur conférer une apparence antique, et finalement réussirent leur supercherie. » (W. S. W. Ruschenberger : Extracts from the Journal of an American Naval Officer, 1841). Et plus d'un siècle après, le collectionneur d'art primitif Pablo Picasso, qui était un client avisé du marché aux puces, déclarait : « On n'a pas besoin du chef-d'œuvre pour saisir l'idée. Le concept ou la caractéristique d'un style est entièrement accessible dans des exemples de second ordre et même dans des faux. » Par conséquent, les artistes américains, imprégnés de l'esprit du tiki, n'hésitèrent pas à recréer les têtes des dieux au gré de leur fantaisie.

Un parfait exemple de ce style est le tiki qu'Alec Yuill-Thornton dessina pour le bar *Tiki Bob* à San Francisco. Mi-George Jetson, mi-primitif moderne, cette sculpture avait peu de choses en commun avec les objets océaniens. Mais avec la signature tiki du *Luau* de Stephen Crane elle marque en réalité le commencement du style tiki. Pour la première fois, un tiki fut utilisé comme logo, fit office de gardien à l'entrée des établissements, fut dessiné sur le menu et sur les pochettes d'allumettes, et apparut sous forme de chopes, salières et poivrières.

Bob Bryant, surnommé «Sneaky» (le sournois), avait travaillé comme gérant du bar de Trader Vic, mais lorsque les deux hommes se brouillèrent en 1955, Bob quitta le *Trader* de Cosmo Place et ouvrit son propre bar. Sa tentative de vendre son concept au *Capitol Inn* de Sacramento fit long feu. Bob ouvrit également le *Tiki Bob's Mainland* sur la Bush Street où il offrait des défilés de lingerie pour attirer les hommes d'affaires à l'heure du déjeuner.

Tiki devint ainsi la star du théâtre pop polynésien, son nom étant adopté par une multitude d'établissements à travers l'Amérique, de l'Alabama à l'Alaska, et ses différentes formes ornant les bars d'une civilisation fatiguée. L'image du tiki atteignit le sommet de sa popularité lorsqu'elle devint le logo de la série télé (produite par Warner Brothers) «Hawaïan Eye» qui fut diffusée dans les foyers américains entre 1959 et 1963, sa forme archétypale marquant durablement les esprits des banlieusards hypnotisés.

Le grand conflit des générations des années 1960 mit un terme à la fièvre tiki alors que celle-ci était à son paroxysme. Les enfants des noceurs tiki décidèrent de créer leur Nirvana personnel, où l'amour libre et le bonheur loin du monde quotidien étaient une réalité immédiate. L'alcool cessa d'être la drogue de prédilection lorsque la marijuana et les psychotropes devinrent des substances récréatives, et que la révolution sexuelle parut mettre un terme au principe puritain de la monogamie. De même que la fausse cuisine pseudo-chinoise, trop grasse et trop sucrée, les cocktails tropicaux heurtaient la récente prise de conscience de l'alimentation saine.

L'«invasion anglaise» attira l'attention des jeunes vers un autre culte étranger bizarre, les Beatles. Les Kinks se lamentaient sur cette Polynésie en plastique: «… et même les pagnes étaient en PVC!» Et de même que, deux siècles auparavant, les Polynésiens découvrirent que les explorateurs blancs n'étaient pas des dieux lorsque, à Kealakekua Bay, ils firent couler le sang du Capitaine Cook et le tuèrent, les Américains furent traumatisés lorsque leur divinité, le Président Kennedy, fut assassiné en 1963. Ce fut le commencement de la fin, la perte de leur innocence infantile, à leurs propres yeux et aux yeux du monde.

La guerre du Viêt-nam se transformant dans les consciences en une monstrueuse erreur, avec ses huttes et ses palmiers brûlant sur les écrans de télé, l'exotisme et le style tiki se voyaient dénoncés comme des rituels imposés par l'establishment impérialiste. Et tandis que de jeunes manifestants marchaient sur le Capitole de Washington, Richard Nixon sirotait des Mai-Tai dans son repère favori, le *Trader Vic's* de Washington.

Dans les années 1970, le style polynésien ainsi discrédité fut noyé par l'apparition d'un thème tropical générique indéfini, sans identité claire, sans caractère insulaire. Qu'il s'agisse des Caraïbes, du Mexique ou de la Polynésie, partout on retrouvait «Margarita-ville». Le show télévisé populaire «Fantasy Island» illustrait cette délimitation politiquement correcte de complicité culturelle, créant un monde au décor colonial en osier blanc mélangé à des plantes exotiques. Le bar habillé de fougères remplaça le bar tiki.

Les années 1980 furent la décennie de la destruction, de l'abolition du tiki et de sa culture. Rasés ou rénovés de manière à les rendre méconnaissables, les

palaces polynésiens disparurent sans avoir été reconnus comme une facette unique de la culture pop américaine. Considérés comme l'expression d'une lubie populaire, ils avaient toujours été condamnés ou ignorés par les critiques de la culture et constituaient désormais une faute de goût embarrassante. Une tradition entière disparut sans qu'on le remarquât ni qu'on le déplorât.

ERIGER UN TEMPLE TIKI

La construction d'un «Hale Tik» (maison du tiki) était une entreprise complexe, non seulement à cause des différents matériaux exotiques employés, mais en raison des concepts inhabituels utilisés pour étonner et enchanter les fidèles adorateurs du tiki tandis qu'ils ingurgitaient leurs breuvages tropicaux.

Ce chapitre donne un aperçu des motifs qui définissent, à l'intérieur comme à l'extérieur, l'architecture du style tiki, présentant ainsi un aspect de la culture pop américaine peu reconnu jusqu'ici. Bien qu'il existe une tradition distincte, instaurée par Don the Beachcomber et comportant des éléments sans cesse utilisés et améliorés, ce qui caractérise le style tiki c'est la façon dont chacun, saisi par la fièvre Tiki l'a recréé à sa façon. Des jungles artificielles aux rituels de présentation des cocktails, l'imagination s'emballait lorsque les promoteurs américains suivirent l'appel du tiki, donnant corps à leurs versions personnelles d'un sanctuaire des mers du Sud.

Le concept architectural favori était celui du pignon en A. Est-ce le fruit d'une coïncidence si, vers la fin des années 1950, le style néo-primitif tiki entra en concurrence avec son antithèse, le style futuriste de l'époque supersonique, ou bien l'un des deux était-il une réaction nécessaire à l'autre? Quoi qu'il en soit, les deux styles se rejoignaient glorieusement dans le pignon en A. Avec le terminal de la TWA de Eero Saarinen et la Première Eglise Unitarienne de Frank Lloyd Wright, les pignons s'élançant dans le ciel devinrent le jeu favori des architectes modernes, reflétant l'optimisme de l'âge de l'espace que l'on retrouvait aussi dans les ailerons des cadillacs.

Il se trouve que la majorité des habitations traditionnelles océaniennes étaient des huttes de palmier, et avaient nécessairement une forme en A. Mais comme les constructions polynésiennes, à l'exception des habitations sacrées maoris chargées de sculptures, étaient plutôt simples, d'autres groupes ethniques similaires furent mis à contribution. La maison cérémonielle de Nouvelle-Guinée, ou «haus tambaran», avec son pignon allongé et son fronton orné de masques, et la maison cérémonielle des hommes de Palau, Micronésie, ornée de peintures narratives colorées, furent la source d'inspiration de nombreux temples tiki américains. Les enfants de l'âge du jet rencontraient ceux du silex lorsque les primitifs modernes garaient leurs voitures devant ces vaisseaux spatiaux de la planète tiki, franchissant sciemment le seuil d'un autre monde où ils pouvaient pour un moment devenir membres de la tribu tiki.

Les charpentes en A étaient faciles à construire, et des bâtiments traditionnels tels que les cabanes du Wisconsin ou des maisons de commerce furent transformés en palais païens par l'adjonction d'une entrée de forme pointue. Les restaurants chinois «actualisèrent» leur style, se donnant des allures de huttes pour bénéficier de la folie polynésienne. Mais que se passait-il derrière le grand A? Afin de symboliser le seuil d'une autre réalité, il fallait souvent édifier un pont au-dessus d'un ruisseau alimenté par une cascade s'écoulant sur une paroi en pierre ponce. Le feu et l'eau entraient en scène avec des torches à gaz tiki, parfois fixées comme signaux lumineux au sommet des pignons, et des cascades intérieures et extérieures dont le doux murmure fournissait un fond sonore. Des tiki imposants flanquaient l'entrée, surgissant d'une jungle feuillue, et assuraient le rôle de colonnes de soutien.

L'intérieur était un environnement complexe qui interpellait tous les sens. Les différentes salles, avec des noms aussi évocateurs que «Le Trou noir de Calcutta» ou «Le Bar des Sept Plaisirs», étaient recouvertes, du sol au plafond, de bois exotiques, de bambou, de rotin, mais aussi de tissu pour pagne, et d'autres matières organiques. Des armes primitives et des masques accrochés aux murs, les lampes-balises et divers objets suspendus au plafond formaient une partie du décor. Des peintures murales représentant des scènes de la vie dans les îles et des dioramas en trois dimensions renforçaient l'illusion de se trouver dans un pays lointain.

La peau humaine était une autre texture essentielle. De nombreux établissements étaient fiers de leurs serveuses exotiques à peine vêtues, contrepartie vivante aux peintures sur velours noir qui étaient aussi un élément de décor commun à la plupart des bars tiki. Pour les guerriers en col blanc des années 1950, cela avait un charme particulier, qu'entretenaient les spectacles polynésiens devenus un divertissement standard dans beaucoup des clubs-restaurants des mers du Sud. Le fait que les danseurs de feu polynésiens et que les danseuses de houlah tahitiennes fussent souvent d'origine sud-américaine ou asiatique était sans importance. Les costumes et la musique, les textures exotiques, le décor tropical et les puissants breuvages, tout contribuait à faire oublier les questions d'authenticité, ce qui permettait au noceur tiki de s'abandonner au charme irréel du paradis polynésien urbain.

Les diverses lampes, très originales, suspendues en rangs serrés à la plupart des plafonds des temples tiki, faisaient partie des objets artisanaux les plus curieux. Des pièges de pêcheur jetant une faible lumière, des boîtes en bois flotté, des cages à oiseaux, des tétrodons, des coquillages et des filets de pêche et leurs bouchons de liège formaient le ciel de la *Polynesia Americana*. Mais son habitant le plus imposant était toujours le tiki, saint patron du sauvage des banlieues.

DON THE BEACHCOMBER – LE PERE FONDATEUR DU POP POLYNESIEN

Hollywood, 1934 : la «noble expérimentation» américaine de la prohibition venait de s'achever. La demande en alcool de bonne qualité était importante, et un restaurateur émigré de la Nouvelle-Orléans, Ernest Beaumont-Gatt, décida de tenter sa chance avec le rhum. Peut-être inspiré par les histoires de pirates de sa ville natale, ou par le fait que son père, qui possédait un hôtel à la Nouvelle-Orléans, l'avait emmené à plusieurs reprises en Jamaïque, Ernest ouvrit un petit bar à McCadden Place, à Hollywood, le décora avec quelques faux palmiers et le baptisa *Don the Beachcomber* (Don, le batteur de grève). Là, il mélangeait l'or liquide tel un alchimiste à la recherche de la pierre philosophale, créant de puissants breuvages qui permettaient à ses clients de s'échapper temporairement vers les rivages lointains, tandis que dehors la vie de la grande ville suivait son cours effréné. Ernest s'identifia tellement à la figure du Beachcomber qu'il troqua légalement son nom contre celui de Don Beach. Bientôt sa science des mélanges attira la foule du cinéma assoiffée d'alcool et d'ambiance, et en 1937, il transforma son bouge en un repaire des mers du Sud qui allait devenir un modèle pour ceux qui suivirent ses traces. Telle une île dans l'océan urbain, Don fit de son paradis polynésien un refuge contre la métropole qui l'entourait.

L'aménagement intérieur était composé de matériaux exotiques tels que le bambou, des nattes en lahaula et des bois d'importation. Des plantes tropicales, des fleurs, des régimes de bananes et des noix de coco entretenaient l'atmosphère exotique, tandis que des armes indigènes et d'autres objets océaniens parlaient de civilisations sauvages. Des fragments d'épaves et d'objets venus des quatre coins du monde étaient suspendus au plafond, accentuant l'illusion d'être arrivé à un havre du plaisir. Une averse tombant sur le toit à intervalles réguliers et actionnée à la main donnait l'impression d'avoir échappé à un orage tropical, tandis qu'un flot de musique douce entraînait les habitués dans des rêveries exotiques. Le dépaysement était renforcé par l'effet des puissants cocktails imaginés par Don, parfois servis dans des ananas entiers ou lourdement décorés d'étranges garnitures. Mais si Don Beach possédait le sens du spectacle et une imagination fertile, il était peu doué pour les affaires. Cette partie était du

ressort de sa femme, Cora Irene «Sunny» Sund. Elle avait proposé un partenariat d'affaires qui avait abouti à un mariage en 1937, avant de se terminer par un divorce trois ans plus tard. Ce qui ne l'empêcha pas de conserver une emprise ferme sur la boutique, si ferme que lorsque Don revint de la guerre, à laquelle il avait pris part comme colonel de l'armée de l'air, il se vit dépossédé de son propre bar. Sunny, qui avait dirigé l'ouverture du premier franchisé à Chicago, en 1940, était désormais en charge de l'opération et n'avait plus besoin de Don, juste de son nom.

Beaucoup plus créateur qu'homme d'affaires, Don parvint à conserver une position de conseiller au *Don the Beachcomber* du continent, tout en consacrant toute son énergie à son projet chéri: ouvrir son propre local à Hawaii.

Mais Don avait également créé un prototype, le «beachcomber» urbain du XXe siècle, un individu qui tenait à la fois du grand voyageur, du beatnik de plage et du noceur. Dans l'histoire du pop polynésien, d'autres «beachniks» firent leur apparition dont le plus notable fut Ely Hedley, également connu comme «le beachcomber original».

Epicier malchanceux de l'Oklahoma, il avait suivi l'appel du Pacifique et entraîné sa famille à Whites Point, une plage située près de San Pedro à Los Angeles. Là-bas, lui, sa femme et leurs quatre filles se construisirent une maison en bois flotté et entamèrent un commerce fructueux en fabriquant des lampes et des meubles avec les épaves échouées à leur porte. Ely devint si célèbre pour son style «beachcomber moderne» qu'on lui confia la décoration de temples tiki tels que le *Trader Dick's* et le *Harvey* dans le Nevada. Lorsque la fièvre tiki se répandit, il commença à sculpter des tiki et à ouvrir des boutiques de produits des îles; d'abord à Huntington Beach, puis dans l'«Adventureland» de Disneyland. Après avoir définitivement apposé sa marque sur le style tiki, Edy Hedley se retira dans la résidence «Islander» de Santa Ana, décorée par ses soins.

Entre-temps, *Don the Beachcomber* était devenu un logo commercial, l'entreprise changeant deux fois de mains pour finalement appartenir à la société Getty. La figure avait été modernisée, troquant les traits de Don contre ceux d'un noceur anonyme. Les franchisés étaient maintenant au nombre de seize, certains comme les établissements de Dallas ou de Marina Del Rey ressemblant à des OVNIS. D'autres fans de la Polynésie s'inspirèrent, à travers les Etats-Unis, du concept Beachcomber, mais aucun n'avait le flair de Don. Lui-même s'était construit un nouveau royaume dans son Centre de Marché International à Waikiki. Là-bas, il continua à innover et à créer de «nouvelles façons de produire des choses» pour la Polynesia Americana. Lorsque Don disparut en 1987, les derniers établissements de la chaîne qui portait son nom, depuis longtemps abandonnés par son mana, mirent rapidement la clé sous la porte. Mais l'influence décisive de Don sur le phénomène du pop polynésien n'a pas été oubliée.

TRADER VIC – L'AMBASSADEUR DU BON GOUT

L'américanisation de tiki, en tant que dieu des loisirs, se fit progressivement. L'un de ses plus grands émissaires fut Victor Bergeron, plus connu sous le nom de Trader Vic, qui employa même ses propres figures mythologiques, les «Menehune» ou «petit peuple» des légendes polynésiennes. Ce n'était pas tant qu'il glorifiât ouvertement la divinité mais, apparu dans les années 50, le tiki était toujours avec lui, et Trader était devenu une figure plus grande que nature, un original, appartenant à une race en voie d'extinction, disparue aujourd'hui. A la fois patriarche, gentleman et phallocrate, son succès comme restaurateur et épicurien encouragea une génération de «sauvages cultivés», à tourner le dos à la civilisation et à créer leur Polynésie à eux dans les bars, les restaurants, les jardins, les arrière-cours et les bowlings. Il éleva «la bouffe et la bibine» des mers du Sud, comme il les appelait, au rang d'art. Plus encore que Don the Beachcomber, qui aurait dit-on trouvé le nom de son apéritif le «Rumaki» en laissant tomber son doigt sur une page d'un dictionnaire des îles Cook, Trader Vic fut un innovateur culinaire. Après le succès de sa cuisine «Nouveau Polynesian», il fut l'un des premiers à proposer des plats mexicains aux consommateurs américains (par le biais de ses restaurants Seor Pico). Tout commença dans un bouge baptisé *Hinky Dinks*, à Oakland, de l'autre côté de la baie de San Francisco. Ce fut le premier établissement que Vic bâtit pour lui en 1934, une cabane de bois édifiée avec ses derniers 500 dollars. Dans l'histoire du pop polynésien, il y eut certains «centres de pouvoir», tels que le *Beachcomber* à Hollywood, le *Luau* à Beverly Hills, le *Lanai* à San Mateo ou le *Bali Hai* à San Diego, qui diffusaient le mana de Tiki. *Hinky Dinks*, qui allait bientôt devenir *Trader Vic's*, était l'un d'eux. Mais Victor Bergeron était un homme ambitieux, éminemment doué pour les cocktails étranges, et c'était exactement ce que les gens désiraient boire après l'abrogation de la prohibition. Il avait effectué un voyage d'études à Cuba et en Louisiane et étudié sur place avec les meilleurs barmen. Mais ce fut son séjour à Los Angeles qui s'avéra décisif. Dans sa biographie, il révèle: «Nous sommes allés dans un établissement appelé *South Seas* qui n'existe plus, et nous avons même visité *Don the Beachcomber* à Hollywood. En fait, j'ai même fait des emplettes chez *Don the Beachcomber*. Lorsque je suis retourné à Oakland et que j'ai raconté à ma femme ce que j'avais vu, nous sommes tombés d'accord pour changer le nom et la décoration de notre restaurant. Nous avons décidé que *Hinky Dinks* était un nom à foutre en l'air et que l'endroit devait être baptisé du nom d'un personnage dont on pourrait raconter les histoires. Ma femme a suggéré *Trader Vic's* (Vic le marchand) parce que je faisais toujours du commerce avec quelqu'un. Parfait, je devins Trader Vic.» En conséquence de quoi, la jambe de bois qu'il avait gardée d'une lutte contre la tuberculose dans son enfance (et avec laquelle il divertissait ses clients en y plantant parfois abruptement un pic d'acier) devint le fruit d'une rencontre avec un requin – l'un des nombreux contes correspondant à la nouvelle identité de Vic. Cet aveu candide concernant la naissance de *Trader Vic* venait d'un homme qui avait non seulement égalé, mais dépassé son pair et prédécesseur. Vic n'eut jamais à dissimuler ses sources, parce qu'il ne perdit jamais le contrôle de son affaire comme Don, et lorsque la vogue polynésienne prit son essor dans les années 1950, il était en position d'en tirer le meilleur profit. Il ouvrit son premier poste avancé, qu'il appela *The Outrigger* à Seattle en 1949. Une flopée de clubs-restaurants satellites prit la suite au fil des décennies: à San Francisco proprement dit en 1951, à Denver en 1954, Beverly Hills 1955, Chicago 1957, New York et La Havane 1958, et Portland 1959. Ils furent suivis par d'autres à Boston, Houston, Dallas, Detroit, Atlanta, Kansas City, Saint Louis, Saint Petersbourg, Washington, Vancouver, Scottsdale, Londres, Munich et par une multitude d'établissements à l'étranger.

Vic élargit encore son influence avec une série de livres de recettes de cuisine et de cocktails, dans lesquels il utilisait de préférence des produits venant de sa nouvelle société Trader Vic's Food Products. Dans ces publications, il exposait ses vues sur les réunions et les habitudes alimentaires de la classe moyenne, et ce dans son argot caractéristique, bien différent de la prose fleurie qu'il utilisait dans ses menus:

«J'ai eu un tas d'emmerdes pour avoir déballé ce qui se passe quand on va chez quelqu'un pour boulotter de la nourriture et se rincer le gosier, et je maintiens que la maîtresse de maison américaine moyenne a besoin d'une petite raclée dans son derrière culinaire, alors entrons dans le vif du sujet. C'est simple, les petits machins qu'on sert généralement dans les cocktails me tuent. Après avoir regardé pendant des années des centaines de plateaux en argent et leur contenu, j'en suis arrivé à la conclusion que quelqu'un aurait dû créer un prix Pulitzer pour le hors-d'œuvre le plus mortel.» Le Trader était un sacré fils de pute, et les gens l'aimaient pour ça.

Lorsque Hawaii devint la villégiature de rêve de l'Amérique, Vic fut contacté pour devenir le consultant culinaire d'United Airlines et des hôtels de la compagnie maritime Matson, les deux principales agences de voyages entre les îles et

l'Amérique. Auparavant, autour de 1940, il avait monté un partenariat pour ouvrir un établissement à Honolulu, mais suite à un désaccord il y renonça, laissant à son partenaire le droit d'utiliser le nom dans les îles. Le fait étrange qu'un *Trader Vic's* ait été ouvert à Hawaii, comme *Don the Beachcomber's*, le *Kon-Tiki* de Stephen Crane et la *Christian Hut* avant lui, renforce la thèse selon laquelle le pop polynésien est véritablement une facette de la culture pop américaine, exportée à Hawaii pour répondre à l'attente des touristes.

Cette expansion de l'empire du Trader fut rendue possible grâce au soutien financier de grandes chaînes hôtelières, telles que Western (aujourd'hui Westin) et Conny Hilton, qui pouvaient s'offrir les constructions élaborées requises par un bar tiki de grande classe. Et de la classe, le *Trader Vic's* en avait à revendre. Si d'autres bars des mers du Sud, dont beaucoup avaient copié son nom, servaient les troufions, *Vic's* était le club des officiers. Non que Vic fût snob, mais il voulait gagner rapidement de l'argent, et il y parvint en attirant les riches. Mais ce fut en définitive l'une des raisons de l'effondrement de la chaîne, car à mesure que disparaissaient les membres de la haute société fréquentant ces hauts lieux du plaisir, les nouvelles générations recherchaient des environnements plus abordables et moins chichiteux.

Les postes avancés de Seattle, Washington, Vancouver, Portland et même San Francisco ont malheureusement fermé leurs portes dans les années 1990. Mais *Trader Vic's* continue de bien se porter outre-mer et demeure la seule chaîne de bars tiki en Amérique. Ainsi, en dépit des malencontreux efforts de rénovation des années 1980, qui virent disparaître les lampes-cages à oiseaux caractéristiques, et d'autres éléments du décor considérés comme des nids à poussière, des havres hôteliers tels que le *Trader Vic's* de Chicago et celui de Munich restent les rares exemples du style tiki.

STEPHEN CRANE – L'HOMME QUI AIMAIT LES FEMMES

Dans la tradition polynésienne de Mangareva et des Marquises, tiki, le premier homme, est dépeint comme un filou et un charmeur. Après tout, c'est lui qui a créé la première femme avec de la boue, s'activant aussitôt après à faire avec elle tous les enfants de ce monde. Il paraît donc normal que celui qui reprit le flambeau tiki fût un homme de commerce agréable et un grand séducteur. Acteur raté de films de série B («Le Cri du loup-garou»), le seul titre de gloire de Crane était d'avoir été marié à Lana Turner. Bien que cette union n'ait duré que cinq mois, une fille, Cheryl, en naquit. Bien plus tard, alors qu'elle était adolescente, celle-ci connut la célébrité en assassinant l'amant mafioso de Lana, Johnny Stompanato (apparemment parce qu'elle avait déjà été victime d'agressions sexuelles par un autre des soupirants de sa mère, le Tarzan de cinéma Lex Barker). Mais Stephen resta l'ami de Lana tout en séduisant d'autres stars. Le propriétaire du *Ciro*, le principal bar de Hollywood dans les années quarante, remarquait après avoir vu Steve trois soirs de suite avec successivement Ava Gardner, Rita Hayworth et Lana Turner: «Les trois plus grandes reines de cette ville! Je n'ai jamais vu quelqu'un d'autre faire ça.»

Heureusement, l'énergie de Stephen Crane se concentra bientôt sur les mondanités et le divertissement. En 1953, il ouvrit son restaurant *The Luau* au 421 Rodeo Drive à Beverly Hills. L'endroit avait abrité auparavant le bar *The Tropics*, et Stephen broda sur le thème exotique dans l'intention de conserver la clientèle des gens du cinéma. Il le fit à sa façon, comme s'en souvient sa fille Cheryl dans sa biographie «Detour- A Hollywood Story»: «Il considérait que puisque les hommes aiment traîner dans des endroits qui attirent les femmes, il fallait rendre le lieu aussi appétissant qu'un pot de miel. Au centre du pot de papa, il y avait une stratégie peu connue, et jamais ébruitée: autoriser quelques prostituées triées sur le volet et très chères, à se mêler au reste de la clientèle du bar. Il s'agissait souvent d'ex-starlettes, elles étaient raffinées et magnifiquement vêtues, leur présence attirant les hommes sans choquer les autres femmes qui les reconnaissaient rarement pour ce qu'elles étaient.»

Et afin de tirer un profit maximum du principe de «La Belle et la Bête», Crane peupla son paradis de tiki qu'il présentait ainsi dans son menu: «Les tiki, ces grandes sculptures délicieusement laides qui vous entourent doivent attirer votre attention. Un tiki est un dieu païen, une idole. Alors qu'aujourd'hui la plupart de nos voisins des mers du Sud sont chrétiens, ils ne cessent de respecter et de vénérer les dieux de leurs ancêtres, et nous avons ici au *Luau* des tiki tels que le dieu de la pluie, le dieu du soleil, le dieu de la guerre et d'autres encore. Le tiki à la bouche exceptionnellement large est le dieu de la boisson, La Grande Gueule. Le tiki avec le plus gros bedon est notre préféré, peut-être parce qu'il est le dieu du bien manger». Cette attitude pleine d'humour et naïve envers la religion éteinte d'un autre peuple caractériserait désormais le style tiki. Pour la première fois, un tiki inspiré des deux sculptures de l'entrée, était utilisé comme emblème sur le menu, les pochettes d'allumettes, les cartes postales, mais aussi comme pied de lampe en céramique ou comme salière et moulin à poivre.

Pour le reste du décor, Stephen s'était largement inspiré des traditions du *Beachcomber* et du *Trader*. Si largement, que le directeur artistique Florian Gabriel se souvient que pour un emploi de designer chez Stephane Crane and Associates, il lui fut impérativement demandé de se rendre au *Trader Vic's* du Beverly Hilton (qui jadis se vantait d'avoir à l'extérieur cinq tiki de 4,5 mètres de haut) et de faire un croquis d'un coin du restaurant. Il y parvint avec succès et à partir de ce moment, il forma une équipe de décorateurs avec George Nakashima, qui avait auparavant travaillé pour Welton Becket, architecte du *Beverly Hilton*. Ils participèrent ensuite à la construction des îles satellites SCA qui commencèrent à s'implanter dans les autres villes américaines à la fin des années 1950.

La Sheraton Corporation, désireuse de rivaliser avec le *Hilton*, avait invité Crane à recréer d'abord son *Luau* dans leur hôtel de Montréal, où il ouvrit sous le nom de *Kon-Tiki* en 1958, en présentant au public abasourdi «des panneaux de bois gravés par les Maoris avec des motifs particuliers pour se préserver des esprits malins, des lances de Nouvelle-Guinée avec des pointes en aile de chauve-souris trempées dans le poison par les chasseurs de têtes, et un autel pour les sacrifices». Portland (avec trois cascades), Chicago, Dallas, Cleveland et Honolulu suivirent. Le *Kon-Tiki Ports* de Chicago et le *Ports of Call* de Dallas furent conçus selon le principe du touriste voyageant dans son fauteuil et donnèrent à chaque salle à manger un thème différent: Papeete, Singapour, Macao et Saïgon. Leurs histoires étaient de la pure poésie pop polynésienne: «PAPEETE – Un des quatre points d'ancrage exotiques à Ports o' Call Restaurant dans le penthouse du Southland Center, Dallas, Texas. La nature a été domptée pour ce refuge tropical. Une cascade murmure pour votre plaisir et les animaux sauvages ne bougent pas, pour que vous vous sentiez à l'aise. Mais les lances et les peaux de bêtes rappellent au convive que la vie simple a ses côtés excitants.»

Quoi qu'il en soit, le fossé que la réalité allait bientôt creuser entre la génération tiki et ses enfants manifestant contre la guerre du Viêt-nam n'est nulle part mieux illustré que dans la description du salon SAIGON: «La splendeur orientale et l'opulence marquent ce Port du Plaisir. Ces heureux habitants sont entourés de feuilles d'or fin, de soies rares, de cristal et de sculptures de temples autrefois interdits.» Ce qui était une licence poétique en 1960 était douloureusement cynique vers 1968. A la fin des années 1970, un consortium iranien offrit à Stephen Crane 4,1 millions de dollars pour le *Luau*. En 1979, l'établissement fut totalement rasé: la fin de l'ère tiki s'annonçait.

DANNY BALSZ – LE FILS PRODIGUE

La figure de Danny Balsz ne s'inscrit pas naturellement dans la lignée des ancêtres du pop polynésien. Il ne lança pas de chaîne de restaurants et n'imposa pas non plus d'innovations culinaires ou de nouveaux breuvages alcoolisés. Il n'était pas tant concerné par la qualité que par la quantité. Pour Danny Balsz, plus c'était gros et mieux c'était. Par conséquent, il construisit le plus

gros volcan sur le terrain du plus grand luau polynésien de ce pays. Là-bas, chaque nuit, une jeune fille tiki était jetée en sacrifice dans cette fosse ardente, tandis que des danseurs tahitiens, dans des costumes qui devaient plus au Las Vegas de l'époque qu'à la réalité insulaire, se trémoussaient aux rythmes de divers orchestres. Lorsqu'il découvrit que les Hawaïens étaient censés croire que plus on avait de tiki dans sa demeure et plus on avait de chance, il s'entoura de poteaux figuratifs en bois de toutes formes et dimensions, et baptisa l'endroit *The Tikis*. Plus de dieux, plus de danseurs, plus de nourriture et de boisson pour plus de 3 000 clients chaque nuit. C'était un tiki pour les masses, et Danny était Mr.Tiki !

The Tikis incarne l'apogée de l'ère tiki. Il s'éleva avec une grandeur et une décadence sans précédent avant de disparaître dans l'oubli. En butant contre les ruines de ce Disneyland des dieux oubliés, je sus que son histoire serait un jour racontée. Devant moi s'étendait la planète perdue des tiki, le cimetière des éléphants d'une espèce disparue. Qu'est-ce qui avait conduit cette civilisation autrefois grandiose au déclin? Fils d'un propriétaire de night-clubs de la ville frontière de Mexicali, Danny Balsz émigra à l'est de Los Angeles, avec en tête le souvenir de plaisirs incertains. Il travailla dix ans comme boucher d'abattoir, jusqu'au jour où il opta pour l'aménagement paysager et se spécialisa dans les cascades. Un jour de 1958, Danny fit des emplettes chez un pépiniériste japonais à Monterey Park, un faubourg rural de Los Angeles coincé entre quatre autoroutes. En s'arrêtant à un ranch voisin pour y acheter des œufs, il fit la connaissance de sa propriétaire, Doris Samson. Quatre mois plus tard, ils étaient mariés. Tout en aidant Doris avec ses poulets, Danny peaufinait ses talents de paysagiste, transformant lentement le dixième d'hectare de la propriété en un jardin tropical. En 1960, deux étudiants demandèrent à Danny s'ils pouvaient organiser une soirée luau sur ce terrain. A cette époque, les terrains de luau, qu'on louait pour des soirées, surgissaient partout dans le sud du pays. Danny et Doris décidèrent de tuer tous leurs poulets et de se lancer dans le commerce des soirées polynésiennes. Le moment était bien choisi, l'endroit prospéra, et année après année, Danny versait et sculptait de plus en plus de ciment pour créer des tunnels de lave, des grottes et des chutes d'eau, édifiant de ses mains son propre Xanadu.

A la fin des années 1960, sa clientèle, essentiellement composée de travailleurs des sociétés d'aéronautique et de transport routier, débarquait par bus entiers. Les fournitures nécessaires, comme 50 000 guirlandes de l'usine de fleurs en plastique de Hughestown, Pennsylvanie et des tonnes d'ananas, étaient payés cash, et lorsqu'il restait de l'argent, Danny rapportait de nouveaux tiki. «J'avais tout, mec: l'argent, les voitures, les bagues!», se souvenait Danny. Mais il voulait davantage. La chance de Danny tourna quand il commit le Péché de chair et il fut chassé du paradis pour être tombé amoureux de Leilani, une Hawaïenne mormon qui dansait dans l'établissement *The Tikis*. Les dieux ne virent pas d'un bon œil l'union du haolé et de la vahiné. Encore moins sa femme et ses enfants, qui constituaient l'épine dorsale de son opération familiale. Et sous la pression de voisins excédés, le conseil municipal lui retira sa licence. C'en était fini du cirque polynésien, semble-t-il. Mais Danny Balsz était monté sur des ressorts. Il remballa ses tiki et leur construisit un nouveau logis à Lake Elsinore, plus loin au sud de Los Angeles. Là, il trima pendant des années, reconstruisant un nouveau pays de lave. Ses tiki montaient patiemment la garde à l'entrée, attendant la grande réouverture. Mais les temps avaient changé et le grand jour ne vint jamais.

«La lumière qui brûle deux fois avec le même éclat, brûle deux fois moins longtemps, et tu as brûlé avec tant et tant d'éclat. Tu es le fils prodigue ! – Mais j'ai accompli des choses discutables … Et aussi des choses extraordinaires, tu as pleinement joui de ton temps…» (Extrait du dialogue du film «Bladerunner» de Ridley Scott)

KON-TIKI, AKU AKU ET THOR

«Les mystères non résolus des mers du Sud m'avaient fasciné. Il doit bien y avoir une solution rationnelle, me disais-je, et je m'étais promis d'identifier Tiki, le héros légendaire.»

Ainsi s'exprimait en 1937 un jeune zoologiste norvégien nommé Thor Heyerdahl, alors qu'il luttait pour survivre à Fatu Hiva, une des îles Marquises. Hippies avant l'heure, Thor et Liv avaient décidé de renoncer à la civilisation et de «retourner à la nature», vivant comme des primitifs en menant des recherches sur la faune locale pour le compte de l'Université d'Oslo. Mais lorsque Thor entendit Tei Tetua, le dernier natif à avoir goûté la chair du «Grand cochon» (l'homme), réciter un vieux conte le soir au coin du feu, tout bascula. «Tiki était à la fois un dieu et un chef. Ce fut Tiki qui amena mes ancêtres sur ces îles où nous vivons. Avant cela, nous vivions sur une grande terre, très loin, de l'autre côté de la mer.»

Dès lors, Thor cessa d'observer les escargots et les mille-pattes géants vénéneux, pour s'intéresser aux origines de la race polynésienne. Il avait été frappé par les similitudes entre les tiki de pierre, les pétroglyphes des Marquises, et les idoles incas du Pérou; et pendant dix ans, il travailla sur la théorie selon laquelle le grand prêtre pré-Inca, et fils du soleil, Kon-Tici Viracocha, qu'un chef de guerre avait contraint à fuir le Pérou, ne faisait qu'un avec Tiki, le dieu ancestral polynésien. Ne rencontrant que résistance et mépris de la part des archéologues, des ethnologues, des linguistes et des sociologues, Thor résolut de prouver sa théorie par la pratique. Il construisit un radeau précolombien avec cabine en balsa, sans utiliser la moindre pointe, clou ou fil de fer, et se laissa dériver avec cinq hommes d'équipage scandinaves dans le détroit de Humboldt du Pérou à la Polynésie.

Après seulement trois mois de traversée, le Kon-Tiki parvint à rallier les côtes polynésiennes. Le livre inspiré par ce voyage, intitulé «L'Expédition du Kon-Tiki» fut publié pour la première fois en Norvège en 1948, et la critique l'accueillit fraîchement, comparant la tentative à «une descente des chutes du Niagara dans un tonneau». Mais cela ne parvint pas à détourner l'intérêt du public pour cette entreprise intrépide.

Peu après la publication du livre en Angleterre et aux Etats-Unis, en 1950, il apparut évident que les éditeurs tenaient là un best-seller. «Kon-Tiki» fut finalement traduit en soixante langues, le premier livre après la Bible à connaître pareille diffusion. Le film réalisé au cours du voyage connut un destin similaire, après avoir été refusé par les distributeurs américains en raison de ses défauts techniques. Il reçut l'Academy Award du meilleur documentaire en 1951, et des millions de spectateurs allèrent le voir. Le monde sortait du traumatisme de la Deuxième Guerre mondiale et des aventures pacifiques étaient les bienvenues. L'engouement international sans précédent pour le Kon-Tiki alimenta la fascination de l'Amérique pour la culture polynésienne. Bien que le terme «style tiki» n'ait pas été courant dans les années 1950 et 1960, il devint alors une expression populaire pour désigner l'architecture polynésienne. Thor et Tiki, le dieu nordique de la foudre et le dieu polynésien du soleil, s'étaient unis pour devenir des héros populaires.

Le livre de Heyerdahl «Aku Aku» (1955), consacré à son expédition sur l'île de Pâques, eut également une grande influence sur le pop polynésien. La couverture du livre devint une icône si populaire que les gigantesques statues de pierres, les moaï, devinrent célèbres sous le nom de têtes Aku Aku, voire même de Aku-Tiki, et un thème largement répandu dans le royaume tiki américain.

JAMES MICHENER ET BALI HAI

«Bali Hai peut t'appeler, et la nuit, et le jour.
Dans ton cœur tu l'entendras, viens ici, viens ici.
Bali Hai murmurera, dans le vent, dans la mer,
Me voici, ton île à toi, viens vers moi, viens vers moi.
Tous tes espoirs, tous tes rêves,

fleurissent sur la colline, et brillent dans le courant.
Si tu essaies, tu me trouveras, là où le ciel rencontre la mer,
me voici, je suis à toi, viens vers moi, viens vers moi.»

(d'après «South Pacific» de Rodgers et Hammerstein)

Thor ne fut pas le seul auteur à succès à marquer le pop polynésien de son empreinte. Au cours de la Deuxième Guerre mondiale, toute une génération de conscrits américains avait découvert la culture des îles du Pacifique. James Michener était l'un d'eux, et son récit romancé de leur expérience, «Contes du Pacifique Sud», lui valut le Prix Pulitzer en 1948 et un extraordinaire succès populaire. Une comédie musicale de Broadway et un film en CinémaScope réussirent si bien à conférer un tour romantique aux épreuves de la guerre qu'ils donnèrent naissance à un nouveau terme pour désigner le «paradis exotique»:«Bali Ha'i», l'île des femmes. Il devint le nouveau Shangri-La, l'île de rêve de chaque homme.

C'est là-bas que le héros du roman, le Lieutenant Cable, fit l'expérience de ce vieux fantasme masculin d'un amour sans entraves avec une jeune beauté exotique. Le protagoniste de l'histoire se voit accorder le privilège de visiter l'île, «un joyau sur le vaste océan», sur lequel «les Français, avec une prévoyance et une connaissance toute gauloise de ces choses, avaient rassemblé toutes les femmes des îles. Chaque femme, qu'importe sa couleur ou son physique, qui aurait sinon été violée par les Américains, fut cachée à Bali Ha'i.» (Michener) Lorsque le bateau du Lieutenant Cable jette l'ancre, les lecteurs masculins de 1950 ne peuvent que l'envier: «Pour la première fois de sa vie, il avait vu tant de femmes, en vérité toutes les femmes, aller et venir sans le moindre vêtement … comme la jungle, comme les fruits de la jungle, les adolescentes semblaient se trouver là en une invraisemblable profusion.» (Michener)

Cable est sauvé de cet essaim de jeunes femmes par la matrone Bloody Mary qui le précipite immédiatement dans les bras de sa ravissante fille vierge Liat. Dans le film, le héros pénètre dans une romantique hutte en feuilles de palmier, où l'attend Liat, une fille ravissante et prête à l'amour. Aucune parole n'est échangée, des regards brûlants, des lèvres tremblantes, l'amour est immédiat et profond. Les archétypes des mers du Sud doivent être vrais après tout.

Les Américains de toutes extractions firent soudain la connaissance d'une culture totalement étrangère grâce à un témoin direct, et cela laissa une marque indélébile sur l'Amérique elle-même: «Qu'est-ce que je fais là? Comment moi, Joe Cable de Philadelphie, en suis-je arrivé là? Voici Bali Ha'i, et il y a un an je n'en avais jamais entendu parler. Qu'est-ce que je fais là?» (Michener). L'attitude était celle d'un émerveillement juvénile, et parce que les soldats avaient reçu un accueil chaleureux des populations libérées de l'envahisseur nippon, les souvenirs des années de service dans le Pacifique Sud étaient généralement excitants ou agréables. Par conséquent, de petites Bali Hai surgirent partout aux Etats-Unis, accueillant ceux qui y étaient allés aussi bien que ceux qui étaient restés. James Michener connut un nouveau succès avec «Retour au paradis» en 1951. Par la suite, il publia «Canailles au Paradis» (1957, avec un récit de la vie d'Edgar Leeteg) et «Hawaii» (1959) qui firent définitivement de lui l'auteur sur la Polynésie le plus lu dans les années 1950.

Michener avait visité la véritable Bali Ha'i, sur l'îlot de Mono, près de Guadalcanal. Il s'en souvenait comme d'un «village sale et désagréable», mais il se servit de son nom à cause de «sa qualité musicale». Cela n'empêcha pas le mythe pop polynésien de Bali Hai d'être finalement réimporté en Polynésie française. En 1961, gravement atteints par la fièvre tiki, un avocat, un agent de changes et un vendeur d'articles de sport décidèrent de renoncer à leur existence civilisée à Newport Beach, dans la banlieue de Los Angeles, pour s'établir à Tahiti. Là-bas, ils ouvrirent un hôtel qu'ils baptisèrent naturellement «Bali Hai». La fiction était devenue réalité, comme si souvent dans le pop polynésien.

D'AUTRES TEMPLES TIKI CELEBRES

Comme nous l'avons déjà mentionné, le style tiki avait, comme n'importe quel culte, ses «hauts lieux», des endroits magiques où le pur mana tiki se répandait librement et non dilué. Nous ne pouvons malheureusement tous les décrire, ni même les mentionner, dans ce livre qui est loin d'être le répertoire complet du style tiki. Ce chapitre évoque certains lieux qui existent toujours, et tout particulièrement le *Mai Kai* et le *Kahiki*, qui sont probablement les deux plus beaux exemples que l'Amérique conserve de cette culture disparue. Le *Kahiki* a récemment été inscrit au Registre National des Sites Historiques, ce qui est particulièrement rare s'agissant d'un bâtiment de 1961 et indique qu'une réévaluation du style tiki est en cours. Ce chapitre s'ouvre avec une «fille mystérieuse» (page de gauche) nous accueillant à la fontaine tiki de l'entrée du *Kahiki* à Columbus, Ohio. La tradition du breuvage mystérieux vient probablement du *Mai Kai* où l'attirait exotique des serveuses s'avéra attirer la clientèle.

Le premier lieu inspiré que nous visitons est une île consacrée aux temples tiki. Elle fut créée par la Navy avec le sable extrait de la baie de San Diego pour faciliter le passage de ses navires de guerre. Quel meilleur endroit pour une Polynésie artificielle qu'une île artificielle?

LE *BALI HAI*, SHELTER ISLAND, SAN DIEGO, CALIFORNIE

Le premier temple tiki érigé sur Shelter Island fut le *Bali Hai*, appelé à l'origine *The Hut* et une annexe de la *Christian's Hut* à Newport Beach. Deux ans seulement après son ouverture, le directeur de *The Hut*, Tom Hamm, reprit en mains cet établissement sinistré et le transforma en l'endroit le plus chaud de la ville. Le *Bali Hai* possédait une vue imprenable sur le port de San Diego, disposait de son propre ponton, et son spectacle polynésien était célèbre. Il était populaire non seulement auprès des Californiens du Sud, mais également auprès de Polynésiens expatriés qui, contrairement aux universitaires se moquant du tiki, étaient simplement heureux d'avoir un endroit où se souvenir de leur héritage. Le logo tiki du Mr.Bali Hai accueillait les clients à l'entrée et on le trouvait également sous forme de chope, ce qui reste un témoignage unique en son genre de manie de la part d'un chasseur de têtes. Dans une vitrine, dessinée suivant la tradition des cartes tiki de Covarrubias et remplie d'objets contemporains qui représentaient les styles tiki des différentes îles polynésiennes, la chope Bali Hai indique parfaitement son lieu d'origine.

Mais d'où vient cette curieuse tête au sommet du *Bali Hai*? Exemple significatif d'archéologie urbaine, la source de cette étrange sculpture a pu être établie à partir d'une recherche menée sur des pochettes d'allumettes:

Christian's Hut tire son nom de Fletcher Christian, fameux mutin du navire de Sa Majesté, Le Bounty. En 1935, l'histoire fit l'objet d'un film de la MGM dans lequel Clark Gable tenait le rôle du courageux officier. On choisit pour le tournage l'île de Catalina, en face de la côte californienne, et on la transforma en Tahiti. On édifia un véritable village tahitien, et près de 600 personnes (acteurs et membres de l'équipe technique) y cohabitèrent. Le bar situé sous les appartements de Clark Gable devint le *Christian's Hut*. Lorsque le tournage fut achevé, le «Hut» fut transporté à Newport Beach, où il accueillait entre autres des personnalités telles que John Wayne et Howard Hughes. Il y eut d'autres concessions, mais aucune n'atteignit la renommée de l'original, qui brûla en 1963. La signification initiale de la tête, aujourd'hui connue comme «the Goof» (Le Gogo), reste un mystère. Le mana de *Bali Hai* déversa d'autres temples tiki sur l'île. La structure en A la plus étrange s'élevait entre le *Bali Hai* et le *Half Moon Inn*, un projet dans lequel Stephen Crane se trouvait à l'origine impliqué. Son restaurant devait s'appeler le *Tahiti*, mais devint finalement *L'Escale*. Le *Shelter Isle Inn*, le *Kona Kai Club* et le *Kona Inn* respectaient tous le style polynésien. Aujourd'hui, le motif tiki a disparu, la plupart du temps sous les rénovations, ou bien, comme c'est le cas pour le *Kona Kai*, totalement étouffé par le style méditerranéen.

LE *MAI KAI*, FORT LAUDERDALE, FLORIDE

Au début des années 1950, deux frères de Chicago, Bob et Jack Thornton, décidèrent de fuir les hivers glacés de cette ville pour la Floride tropicale. Là-bas, inspirés par le *Don the Beachcomber* de leur ville natale, ils créèrent leur propre havre polynésien, le *Mai Kai*. Depuis son ouverture en 1956, le *Mai Kai*, à l'origine une hutte de quatre pièces, s'est agrandi pour devenir un village comprenant huit salles à manger, un jardin tropical luxuriant, des cascades et des tiki en abondance. Bob Thornton choisissait toujours des artistes pop polynésiens professionnels pour étendre son royaume, recrutant George Nakashima et Florian Gabriel de Stephen Crane and Associates comme architectes d'intérieur et employant un décor d'Oceanic Arts à Whittier pour donner au *Mai Kai* sa touche authentique tant prisée.

Le *Mai Kai* n'eut jamais de logo tiki spécifique, mais utilisa de manière intensive des sculptures cannibales tahitiennes apparues pour la première fois sur le menu de *Don the Beachcomber*. Un autre fétiche favori était un dieu de la pêche des îles Cook converti en bouteille de rhum. L'objet le plus remarquable est probablement la coupe mystérieuse du *Mai Kai*. Les trois dieux de la guerre hawaïens qui la soutiennent ouvrent la bouche pour y laisser entrer les pailles. Mais en dehors de sa très importante collection de sculptures, le *Mai Kai* était fier de vénérer la beauté féminine, offrant au client une troupe de beautés peu vêtues des îles Bikini pour le servir. Les photos de ces filles ornaient la publication du *Mai Kai* intitulée «Happy Talk» (d'après une chanson de «»South Pacific«), où elles étaient présentées comme starlettes et modèles, elles apparaissaient sur les calendriers et dans des films montrant le rituel du Breuvage Mystérieux.

Le *Mai Kai* est aujourd'hui dirigé avec succès par l'une de ces filles exotiques, Mireille Thornton, la veuve de Bob Thornton, venue de Tahiti pour être danseuse dans cet établissement. C'est elle qui conçoit la chorégraphie de la revue polynésienne du *Mai Kai*, le plus ancien spectacle de ce type. Le mana du *Mai Kai* est certainement la cause principale de l'importance prise par le culte tiki en Floride, où jusqu'à ce jour l'archéologue du tiki peut trouver des bars et des motels reproduisant son image.

LE *KONA KAI*, PHILADELPHIE, PENSYLVANIE

La chaîne *Kona Kai* fut la réponse du groupe Marriot au *Trader Vics* de Hilton et aux *Kon-Tiki* de Sheraton. La plage de Kona était le nouveau Waikiki des années 1960, et de nombreux établissements tiki continentaux (restaurants, motels ou résidences) adoptèrent le nom de cette Terre promise hawaïenne.

Le *Kona Kai* de Philadelphie, dessiné par Armet and Davis, était le navire amiral de la chaîne, avec d'autres succursales qui s'ouvrirent à Chicago et à Kansas City. C'était un vrai temple tiki avec des cascades intérieures, des ponts et des dioramas peints sur verre. L'origine du logo tiki classique du *Kona Kai* remonte à un ancien croquis du designer Irving Weisenberg, de chez Armet and Davis, qui figure sur la page d'ouverture du chapitre 7 (page 54). A ce stade primitif, encore appelé *Hale Tiki*, il n'a qu'une vague ressemblance avec le résultat final en bas, mais le dessin du tiki de l'entrée a certainement donné naissance à l'emblème du *Kona Kai*.

LE *KAHIKI*, COLUMBUS, OHIO

Le concept de l'île urbaine tiki n'opéra pas seulement dans les Etats connus pour leurs loisirs tels que la Floride et la Californie, où le climat facilitait la croissance des palmiers et de la végétation tropicale, mais aussi dans des zones plus froides. Entrer dans un environnement tropical faisait d'autant plus d'effet que les conditions climatiques à l'extérieur étaient rudes. Le *Kahiki*, comme on peu le voir sur son plan au sol de la page 61, est un exemple parfaitement préservé d'un tel sanctuaire tiki. La «rue principale» entre les huttes restaurants du «Paisible Village» est bordée de faux palmiers d'une douzaine de mètres de hauteur, et certaines de ces huttes donnent sur une jungle peuplée d'oiseaux vivants. Un orage tropical s'y déclenche à intervalles réguliers, tandis que de petits glaçons se forment sur les poutres extérieures. Un moai de l'île de Pâques domine la scène.

Dessiné et construit (en suivant très fidèlement le dessin) par Coburn Morgan pour Lee Henry et Bill Sapp en 1961, le *Kahiki* est une véritable trésor de l'art tiki. « ... au dessus de la porte, des copies fidèles de peintures murales primitives accueillent le visiteur. Avec ces dessins, aucun esprit maléfique ne peut entrer. » Les peintures sur velours noir sont signées « La Visse », apparemment l'un des nombreux « étudiants » d'Edgar Leeteg. Les carrelages tiki autour des portes d'entrée en style néo-maya portent l'inscription « Tectum Pan-L-Art ». Malheureusement, ce bijou est aujourd'hui convoité par une grande chaîne de drogueries, alors découvrons-le vite, le temps presse.

MENUS – L'ART TIKI

Les couvertures des menus sont les peintures à l'huile des ancêtres du style tiki, des portraits de tiki et de leurs temples depuis longtemps disparus, comme le *Dorian's* à Whittier, Californie. Ce lieu aux nombreuses poteaux figuratifs avait un bar baptisé *Happy Talk* d'après une chanson de la comédie musicale « South Pacific ». « Happy Talk » était l'idiome indigène qu'utilisait Liat, la jeune fille de l'île du Lieutenant Cable et signifiait « flirter ». Apparemment, le dessin du menu représente deux tiki conversant « joyeusement » avec un tiki féminin. Il n'existe malheureusement aucune photo de cet ensemble.

Les menus perpétuaient également la mythologie du pop polynésien, en rendant hommage à ses précurseurs tels que Don the Beachcomber, racontant les aventures des propriétaires, ou les légendes de tiki, le dieu des oisifs. Trader Vic instaura la tradition sur le dos de son menu de 1947 en déclarant : « Je salue Don the Beachcomber de Hollywood, à l'origine de cocktails aussi fantastiques que le Zombie et le Missionary's Downfall. » *The Tahitian*, dont la carte proposait 68 cocktails tropicaux, poursuit humblement cet hommage : « *The Tahitian* adresse un coup de chapeau à Don the Beachcomber, le premier des experts ès rhum dans le monde. Don a créé bon nombre de nos meilleurs cocktails au rhum, le plus célèbre étant le Zombie. Il mérite d'être applaudi par toutes les fines gueules pour sa contribution à la création d'un type de restaurants tout nouveau. *The Tahitian* salue également Trader Vic, lequel a inventé des cocktails et des plats de style polynésien délicieux. Sans prétendre à l'excellence de ces maîtres anciens, nous croyons sincèrement être l'un des meilleurs restaurants de ce type dans le monde. »

Ce type d'éloges exubérants suggéra à Dick Graves, propriétaire du *Trader Dick's*, d'arrêter la poésie et d'écrire sur sa carte : « Les gars, les mers du Sud, je ne les connais pas ... aucune de ces recettes n'est de moi ... aucune d'elles n'a fait la célébrité de l'endroit. Comment l'auraient-elles pu ? *Trader Dick's* est flambant neuf. J'ai fricoté, magouillé, emprunté et mendié pour toutes les idées et recettes que nous avons ici ... Ce sont les meilleures que j'aie pu voler dans tous les meilleurs restaurants cantonais et polynésiens, de Honolulu à New York. Et il fallait que je sache ... J'ai fourré mon nez partout ... J'ai fauché des menus, soudoyé et bavardé avec les barmen et les cuisiniers et copié toutes les bonnes choses que j'ai pu trouver. » Avec une rare honnêteté, Dick Graves ne faisait que décrire l'esprit de compétition qui prévalait dans le pop polynésien. Le *Kona Kai* de Philadelphie proposait par exemple dans son menu la légende suivante qui faisait croire au client qu'il avait atteint le but de sa quête : LE MYS-TERE DE KONA KAI. Tiki, le dieu de l'abondance et du bien-être des mers du Sud, chercha un jour l'emplacement parfait pour un paradis intemporel plein de rires et de joie. Il dépensa beaucoup d'efforts et de temps pour aiguiser ses sens, afin de savoir avec certitude lorsqu'il aurait découvert son « jardin d'Eden ». Il voyagea à travers son pays ... Enfin son périple le conduisit sur la

mer ... jusqu'à un lagon parfait nommé « Kona kai ». Il trouva là la perfection qu'il recherchait. Cette incroyable baie était bercée par des brises légères, baignée d'une douce lumière, à l'abri des orages et de la chaleur de midi. Des fleurs magnifiques poussaient à profusion et les paisibles cascades murmuraient une musique réconfortante. – Tiki est toujours à Kona Kai ... lézardant dans sa profonde perfection et bénissant tous ceux qui l'ont suivi avec joie et bonheur. » L'évangile tiki était formulé de façon beaucoup plus simple sur le menu du *Luau 400*, un sanctuaire tiki de New York : « Tiki est le dieu traditionnel de tout ce qui est bon ... Bonne santé, bonne fortune, bons moments et, bien sûr, bonne chère, font tous partie des bienfaits accordés par Tiki, le dieu polynésien. »

LES EXPERTS EN MELANGES ET LEURS BREUVAGES par Jeff Berry

Quel restaurant oserait baptiser des fruits au sirop déposés sur un tas de fromage blanc « Les Ports du Désir » ? Le *Luau* le pouvait – essentiellement parce qu'on y servait les meilleurs cocktails exotiques au rhum de Beverly Hills. De tels breuvages étaient le carburant qui faisait tourner les roues du commerce des restaurateurs polynésiens. Plus que de simples cocktails, ils furent dès le début présentés comme des fantaisies en technicolor qui s'adressaient autant à l'œil qu'au palais, servis avec des garnitures originales dans des récipients qui l'étaient plus encore. Même la glace qui les accompagnait était sculptée dans des formes inusitées, moulée en cylindre autour de votre paille, ou en forme d'igloo afin que votre boisson vous arrive « endormie dans une grotte de glace ». Un drink pouvait aussi bien arriver fumant, flambant, ou garni d'un gardénia flottant dans lequel une perle dissimulée attendait d'être découverte.

Le cocktail était le principal sujet de conversation. En quittant un restaurant polynésien, on ne parlait pas de la nourriture – on parlait de la « Mystérieuse boisson », du « Penang Afrididi », ou du « Bouquet de feu Pelé ». Et les serveurs commençaient généralement par présenter la carte dans laquelle des descriptions poétiques accompagnaient des illustrations en couleur, quasiment hyper-réalistes, des cocktails. Comme disait *The Islander* à propos de son Mont Kilauea : « Une éruption des rhums les plus subtils enflammés par les nectars sacrés des dieux tiki. »

Comme on pouvait s'y attendre, ces mélanges n'étaient pas toujours aussi bons qu'ils étaient beaux. Mais les meilleurs cocktails tropicaux pouvaient être complexes et à plusieurs niveaux ; d'abord subtils et voluptueux, avec un équilibre délicat entre douceur et amertume, puis forts et légers, fruités et secs. Et on trouvait les meilleurs cocktails tropicaux chez *Don the Beachcomber's*.

Lorsque Don ouvrit son premier bar en 1934, le rhum n'avait pas bonne réputation. D'ailleurs les alcooliques étaient appelés des « rummies ». Seuls les marins et les durs à cuire buvaient du tafia ; les gens élégants buvaient du whisky et du gin. Et si Don n'a pas inventé de cocktails à base de whisky et de gin, c'est pour la simple raison que le rhum était moins cher. Lorsque la prohibition s'acheva, on pouvait en acheter des caisses pour à peine 70 cents le litre. Dans le cas de Don, le sens de l'économie fut le moteur de l'invention.

Mais Don ne créa pas ses « Rum Rhapsodies » à partir de rien. Nash Aranas, autrefois superviseur et « garant d'authenticité » de la chaîne de restaurants du Beachcomber, raconta en 1989 que Don avait « séjourné aux Antilles où lui était venue l'idée du rhum ». Don avait probablement découvert le Planter's Punch jamaïcain et le Daïquiri cubain ; ces deux boissons sont un simple mélange de citron vert, de sucre et de rhum – trois ingrédients qui devinrent la base de la plupart des créations de Don. Au citron vert, il ajouta l'ananas, la papaye et le fruit de la passion ; au sucre, il ajouta l'anis, la vanille et l'extrait d'amande ; au rhum, il ajouta des liqueurs, des brandies parfumés ... et puis du rhum et encore du rhum. Don avait en effet découvert que mélanger des rhums bruns avec des rhums blancs créait des saveurs de base inédites, plus complexes, pour relever ses jus et ses sirops. « Don pouvait rester assis toute la journée avec ses copains à mélanger des ingrédients », se souvient Aranas. « Il testait, testait, testait, testait, comme un savant fou. » Les combinaisons étaient sans fin et variaient à l'infini, aboutissant à des inventions aussi populaires que le Vicious Virgin, le Shark's Tooth, le Cobra's Fang, le Dr.Funk et le Missionary's Downfall :

MISSIONARY'S DOWNFALL (La Chute du Missionnaire)
4 feuilles de menthe
½ tranche d'ananas
3 cl de jus de citron vert
1 cl de brandy à la pêche
½ cl de sirop de sucre *
2 cl de rhum blanc portoricain

Otez les tiges des feuilles de menthe. Faites les tremper dans les autres ingrédients et 30 cl de glace pilée. Mélangez jusqu'à obtenir un liquide homogène.
(* Pour obtenir un sirop de sucre, faites bouillir 1 kg de sucre dans deux tasses d'eau, puis laissez refroidir et mettez en bouteille).

La légende veut que le plus célèbre cocktail de Don, le Zombie, ait été improvisé afin de permettre à un client ayant la gueule de bois de participer à un rendez-vous d'affaires. Quand on lui demanda comment le remède avait agi, le client répondit : « Je me suis senti comme un mort-vivant – ça m'a transformé en zombie. » Mais la copie d'un menu du *Beachcomber* de 1941 propose une autre origine à ce cocktail : « Le Zombie n'est pas venu comme ça. C'est le résultat d'un long et coûteux processus. Au cours des expérimentations qui ont conduit au Zombie, les contenus de trois caisses et demie de différents rhums ont été utilisés et ont fini dans l'évier pour que vous puissiez aujourd'hui apprécier ce puissant ‹raccommodeur de rêves brisés›. »
Peu de temps avant sa mort, le barman et vétéran, Ray Buhen, l'un des employés du *Beachcomber* en 1934, donna une autre version de l'histoire. « Don était un chic type », se souvenait Buhen, qui avait ouvert son propre bar, le *Tiki Ti*, vingt-sept ans après. « Mais il s'écoutait parler. Il prétendait avoir inventé le Zombie, mais c'est faux. Et il n'a inventé pratiquement aucun de ses cocktails. » Buhen soutenait que le plus gros de ce travail fut accompli par les « Quatre gars », un quatuor d'assistants philippins de Don qui travaillaient derrière le bar. Une affirmation hérétique, c'est certain, mais la crédibilité de Ray ne peut être mise en cause. Durant soixante-deux années, il fut expert en mélanges dans les plus célèbres palaces polynésiens, du *Seven Seas* et du *Luau* au *China Trader* et à son propre bar, servant à boire à des gens tels que Clark Gable, Charlie Chaplin, Buster Keaton, les Marx Brothers et Marlon Brando.
Quelles que soient leurs origines, les cocktails de Don devinrent si rapidement populaires que les « Quatre gars » furent bientôt débordés. Don dut finalement recruter sept barmen à plein temps, chacun d'eux étant spécialisé dans différents cocktails. Derrière eux, il y avait encore plus d'assistants philippins découpant les ananas avec des fils d'acier, taillant de gros blocs de glace jusqu'à en avoir mal aux bras et pressant des citrons verts jusqu'à ce que l'acide leur rongeât les ongles. Pour ajouter l'humiliation à la souffrance, la sécurité fut renforcée afin qu'aucun de ces assistants ne pût mémoriser les recettes secrètes de Don. Au lieu d'étiquettes, les bouteilles étaient identifiées par des chiffres et des lettres. Selon un article paru en 1948 dans le *Saturday Evening Post*, : « Les recettes sont codées et les barmen suivent une liste de symboles qui indiquent les ingrédients pré-mélangés, plutôt que les véritables noms des concentrés de fruits et des différents rhums. De cette façon, même si un restaurateur rival parvenait à débaucher un membre de l'équipe du *Beachcomber*… le renégat ne pourrait pas emporter avec lui les recettes de Don. »
Néanmoins, cette recette du Zombie fut publiée dès 1941 :

LE ZOMBIE
2 cl de rhum brun jamaïcain
4 cl de rhum gold de la Barbade
2 cl de rhum blanc portoricain
1 cl de brandy à l'abricot
1½ cl de jus d'ananas naturel
1½ cl de nectar de papaye
Le jus d'un gros citron vert
Une cuillère à café de sucre fin

Faites fondre le sucre dans le jus de citron vert, mélangez ensuite tous les ingrédients avec des glaçons, et ajoutez de la glace pilée. Ajoutez 2 cl d'eau minérale et assez de glace pour remplir le verre, puis versez une goutte de rhum 151 proof Demerara. Décorez avec une feuille de menthe, un cube d'ananas piqué entre une cerise de cocktail rouge et une cerise de cocktail verte, et saupoudrez le tout de sucre glace.

Si Don était le Grand Patriarche Blanc du cocktail tropical, il eut de nombreux fils prodigues. Les imitations apparurent pratiquement aussitôt après l'ouverture de son établissement. Au night-club *Tropics* de Harry Sugerman, à Beverly Hills, le Zombie devint le Zoulou : « Un verre et vous êtes important ! Deux verres et vous êtes impatient ! Trois verres et vous êtes impuissant ! » Mais tandis que les autres se contentaient d'imiter Don, Trader Vic avait plus d'ambition. « Je ne connaissais rien à ce type de boissons », écrivit-il dans son autobiographie, « et j'ai pensé que j'aimerais apprendre. » Il voyagea un peu partout, observant des experts en mélanges de renommée internationale comme Constantine Ribailagua à La Havane (qui créa le Papa Dobles Grapefuit-Daiquiri pour Hemingway) et Albert Martin de la Nouvelle-Orléans (connu pour son Ramos Fizz). Lorsqu'il revint à son saloon d'Oakland, Trader Vic avait cessé d'être un imitateur. Il était devenu un innovateur.
Lorsque Vic créa le Scorpion, le Samoan Fog Cutter et le Maì Tai, il devint soudain celui que tout le monde imitait. « Ceci aggrave sérieusement mon ulcère », pestait-il, lorsque les bars de Tahiti à Tulsa commençaient à s'approprier l'invention du Maì Tai. « Quiconque prétend que je n'ai pas créé ce cocktail », déclarait Vic, « est un fichu salaud. » Il raconta l'invention avec sa modestie habituelle : « J'étais derrière mon bar un jour de 1944, bavardant avec mon barman, et je lui dis que j'allais faire le meilleur cocktail au rhum du monde. C'est alors qu'entrèrent Ham et Carrie Guild, de vieux amis de Tahiti. Carrie y goûta, leva son verre, et prononça ces mots : ‹Maì Tai – Roa Ae› ce qui en tahitien signifie ‹D'un autre monde – le meilleur !› C'est le nom du cocktail, ai-je dit, et nous l'avons baptisé Maì Tai. » Voici la recette de Vic :

MAI TAI
2 cl de rhum vieux jamaïcain
2 cl de rhum St.James de La Martinique
1 cl de Curaçao
Le jus d'un citron vert
½ cl de sirop d'orgeat
½ cl de sirop de sucre

Secouez avec de la glace pilée. Ajoutez un zeste de citron vert dans le cocktail et garnissez d'une feuille de menthe.

La controverse sur le véritable inventeur du Maì Tai ne prit fin qu'en 1970, lorsque Trader Vic porta l'affaire devant les tribunaux et traîna en justice la Sun-Vac Corporation. A cette époque, celle-ci exploitait la licence d'une gamme de cocktails pré-préparés sous le nom de Don The Beachcomber. Ironie du sort,

Sun-Vac prétendait que c'était Don lui-même – l'homme que Vic admettait avoir pillé trente ans auparavant – qui avait inventé le Mai Taï. Le tribunal donna finalement raison à Vic.

Lorsque les cocktails exotiques au rhum devinrent une grosse industrie et que les palaces polynésiens prospérèrent en les servant à leurs clients, la compétition se fit encore plus féroce. Contrairement à Don et Vic, les nouveaux venus ne pouvaient se réclamer d'aucune renommée, ils cherchèrent donc à se donner une légitimité en créant leurs propres barmen célèbres – souvent en faisant participer des membres du personnel à des concours de cocktails financés par des marques de rhum. Le restaurant pouvait ensuite faire sa publicité sur son propre cocktail créé par son propre barman légendaire, et la marque de rhum annoncer que la recette gagnante était réalisée avec leur rhum. En 1953, un serveur inconnu du *Luau*, du nom de Popo Galcini, fut engagé dans une compétition de ce type sponsorisée par Ron Rico. Il fut déclaré vainqueur et acquit ainsi une gloire instantanée, en dépit des rumeurs selon lesquelles, cette compétition, comme la plupart de ce genre, était truquée. Quoi qu'il en soit, Galcini fut vite débauché du *Luau* par le célèbre *Kelbo's*, dans l'ouest de Los Angeles, où il entama la première d'une série lucrative d'emplois de barman, qui atteignit son apogée à l'*Outrigger* à Laguna Beach. La carte des boissons du *Outrigger* annonçait fièrement «Cocktails Primés par POPO». L'un de ceux-ci était le Pikake qui obtint le premier prix lors d'un concours en 1958.

Les cocktails «primés» n'étaient pas la seule façon de se distinguer pour les bars tiki. Si on ne pouvait en revendiquer l'invention, il restait toujours l'expertise. N'étant plus méprisé, le rhum était largement répandu au milieu des années 1950, et ce en particulier grâce au prosélytisme de Vic et de Don, qui commencèrent à fabriquer leurs propres mélanges et à vendre leurs propres marques. La bonne société renonça à son whisky et à son gin pour le rhum démoniaque, désormais teinté de romantisme comme le breuvage des «aventuriers des mers» et «la boisson la plus fabuleuse et la plus discutée de tous les temps» (du moins, selon le *Hawaiian Room* à Omaha, Nebraska). Les épicuriens gravitaient autour des palais polynésiens possédant le plus grand assortiment de rhums rares, vieux, ou tout autre signe distinctif. Les restaurateurs annonçaient leurs «caves à rhum» ou exhibaient leurs vastes assortiments derrière le bar. Au sommet de sa splendeur, *Don the Beachcomber's* proposait 120 différentes sortes de rhum. Certains établissements n'annonçaient pas seulement un très large assortiment de rhums, mais aussi de cocktails à base de rhum. «Vous trouverez un choix de 36 cocktails tropicaux», rapportait une chronique gastronomique du China Trader à Burbank, «et un professeur de Cal Tech a établi un record en réussissant à en ingurgiter seize avant de sombrer dans la béatitude.» Espérons du moins que ce professeur ne s'est jamais rendu au *Luau* qui n'affichait pas moins de 74 cocktails exotiques – y compris le Martiki, la «réponse polynésienne au Martini dry».

Dans les années 1960, même les plus brillants intellectuels se rassemblaient dans les bars tiki. Les cinéastes Bob Fosse et Stanley Kubrick étaient tous deux des habitués du *Trader Vic's* de New York. C'est là qu'en 1964, Kubrick annonça pour la première fois l'idée qui, quatre ans plus tard, deviendrait *2001: L'Odyssée de l'espace*. On ignore ce qu'il buvait ce soir-là mais il pouvait sans doute en remontrer au professeur de Cal-Tech. Dans son autobiographie, Gore Vidal se souvient d'avoir emmené au *Luau* l'éminent historien Arthur Schlesinger et le Prix Nobel d'Economie John Kenneth Galbraith et, tous trois «imbibés de rhum», d'avoir brisé avec eux plusieurs barreaux du gouvernail géant de l'entrée, en hurlant: «C'est le navire de l'Etat!». Frank Sinatra était un grand amateur du Navy Grog que l'on servait au *Don the Beachcomber's* de Palm Springs. Il laissait de généreux pourboires, se souvient le barman Tony Ramos, «mais il criait et vociférait s'il n'était pas servi assez rapidement.»

A l'aube des années 1970, les goûts commencèrent à changer. Le Missionary's Downfall céda la place au Screaming Orgasm, et les maîtres mélangeurs de l'Age d'or se dispersèrent aux quatre vents … emportant avec eux leur savoir, leur expérience et leurs «ingrédients secrets». Demandez aux barmen d'aujourd'hui de vous confectionner un cocktail tropical, et le résultat écœurant donnera tristement raison à Tony Ramos qui affirme que le mélange des cocktails exotiques est un «art disparu».

Néanmoins, comme en témoigne ce livre, il existe encore une poignée d'endroits qui offrent de vrais cocktails exotiques. Le *Mai Kai* à Fort Lauderdale, Floride, et le *Kahiki* à Columbus, Ohio, continuent de servir des Breuvages Mystérieux dans des coupes fumantes, présentées par de jeunes indigènes peu vêtues, au son des gongs rituels. Et le *Tiki Ti* du défunt Ray Buhen, aujourd'hui dirigé par son fils Mike, continue de servir 72 cocktails exotiques aux habitants de Los Angeles.

Quelle meilleure façon de conclure ce chapitre sur l'histoire des boissons américaines que de citer les paroles de Ray: «C'est de l'évasion. C'est irréel. C'est du bidon», déclarait-il au sujet des faux cocktails polynésiens. Et il ajoutait: «Ah, c'était le bon temps.»

SCORPION BOWL
1½ l de jus d'oranges
0,8 l de jus de citron frais pressé
3 cl de sirop d'orgeat
1,2 l de léger rhum portoricain
1 cl de brandy

Mélanger avec deux tasses de glace pilée et verser le tout dans une chope tiki. Ajouter des glaçons. Décorer à l'aide d'un gardénia et servir avec une paille.

CHASSEURS ET COLLECTIONNEURS

«D'abord illustration d'une simple histoire, les objets dévoilent progressivement une signification plus large, jusqu'à ce qu'ils finissent par nous toucher au cœur.»   (Henry Mercer, collectionneur, 1898)

Comme un tesson de poterie ancienne renferme à lui seul la totalité d'un culture, la chope tiki est l'incarnation du style tiki. Plus d'un archéologue urbain fut pris d'exaltation en découvrant des récipients aussi étranges, représentant souvent le premier indice d'un temple tiki oublié. Les inscriptions cryptées de ces céramiques ont inspiré d'audacieuses expéditions vers des sites lointains, conduisant parfois à la découverte d'autres objets. Ainsi de splendides paradis polynésiens ont à nouveau pris forme dans la mémoire du spectateur et leurs histoires ont été arrachées à l'oubli.

La variété infinie et le style fantaisiste des chopes tiki nous renseigne sur l'esprit créatif des adeptes du tiki. Son usage dans le rituel des célèbres breuvages polynésiens amenant un état de conscience amoindri, souligne le lien du tiki avec la Culture du Cocktail.

Une multitude de bars tiki créèrent pour leurs clients, fidélisés par le rhum, des chopes portant leur logo – souvenirs de brèves vacances sur ces îles urbaines. Mais une fois à la maison, à mesure que le temps passait, de nombreuses chopes tiki furent considérées comme des fautes de goût passagères, des intermèdes esthétiques d'un soir que l'on regrette au matin, une fois l'ivresse passée, et finirent au grenier. Bien que l'origine de la première authentique chope tiki (qui remonte à peu près à la fin des années 1950, quelque part en Californie) reste entourée de mystère, le fait d'employer une effigie humaine comme réceptacle est assez ancienne et relie les collectionneurs de chopes modernes à une tradition plus obscure. Andreas Lommel, directeur du Musée d'Anthropologie de Munich, raconte dans «Prehistoric and Primitive Man» comment la croyance selon laquelle la tête humaine contenait la plus grande quantité de «mana» (ou puissance vitale) conduisit à l'adoration de la tête et finalement à la chasse aux têtes pour obtenir le plus de mana possible. D'après Lommel, «dans différentes zones du Pacifique, on employait des récipients en forme de tête humaine comme substitut de trophées de chasse ». On peut ainsi comparer les collectionneurs de chopes tiki contemporaines à des chasseurs de têtes du XXe siècle, rassemblant leurs trophées comme des reliques tribales sur le porte-crânes dans la « haus tamabaran » cérémonielle. La collection de têtes comme souvenirs n'est pas non plus sans précédent. Bien que la collection de chopes tiki soit devenue depuis peu pour certains une véritable obsession, elle atteindra difficilement les extrêmes décrits en 1896 par le major-général Robley en Nouvelle-Zélande, dans son livre « Traffic in Heads » : « Avant que les Européens ne commencent à visiter la Nouvelle-Zélande et à s'y établir, les ‹mokomai› maoris (têtes séchées et tatouées) n'avaient qu'un intérêt sentimental (le point de vue de Robley sur un culte ancestral?) et aucune valeur commerciale. Mais le désir de les exposer comme curiosités qu'éprouvaient les directeurs de musées et les collectionneurs fit considérablement grimper la demande. De son côté, le Maori était impatient d'obtenir des armes à feu, des munitions et des outils en acier. Il sut vaincre sa réticence à se séparer des têtes, et le trafic prit une telle ampleur que la demande finit par dépasser l'offre. Cela réduisit considérablement la population de Nouvelle-Zélande, mais ouvrit en revanche les musées d'Europe au culte du visage barbare, et en temps qu'entreprise commerciale, le trafic n'était pas sans profit. Des têtes de qualité inférieure puisque coupées de fraîche date prirent la place des anciennes, et l'on découvrit qu'une tête nouvellement tatouée présentait, après sa conservation, le même aspect qu'une tête ancienne. »

Les chopes tiki modernes étaient essentiellement fabriquées au Japon, le pays le moins cher pour les cadeaux promotionnels. Le principal producteur était O.M.C., ou Otagiri Merchandising. Les restaurants adressaient leurs dessins à O.M.C. qui les transformait en récipients de céramique. Cela conduisit parfois à des malentendus, comme avec la chope « Pub Tiki ». Ses motifs abstraits et son inexplicable « »1 1/2« sont un mystère jusqu'à ce que l'on consulte la pochette d'allumettes qui annonce 1 heure 1/2 de parking gratuit, apparemment un véritable privilège à Philadelphie. Mais la fièvre tiki engendra une surprenante variété d'objets, autres que des chopes, dessinés à l'image de l'idole des mers du Sud. Bols tiki, bouteilles, cendriers, briquets, bougies, tout ce qui pouvait être utilisé dans les soirées ou comme décor de bar à la maison emprunta les traits du fétiche phallique. Les influences de style allaient des différentes îles polynésiennes à la Micronésie, la Mélanésie, l'art moderne, Dalí et Disney. L'authenticité et l'exactitude culturelles étaient secondaires aussi longtemps que les objets renfermaient l'esprit de tiki, un mélange de sauvagerie, d'art naïf et de bizarrerie. Si les masques, par exemple, étaient extrêmement rares en Polynésie, la figure grimaçante aux yeux rougeoyants éclairés par des ampoules électriques était un classique du style tiki américain.

Lorsque le tiki urbain cessa de plaire, ces effigies furent dispersées ou cachées, partageant le sort de leurs équivalents polynésiens lorsque les missionnaires mirent fin à l'idolâtrie et au culte des ancêtres. Aujourd'hui, les archéologues urbains dénichent ces reliques chez les brocanteurs, aux Puces et dans les liquidations. Malheureusement, l'internet a fait perdre à la chasse au tiki son caractère aventureux en permettant à des explorateurs en chambre disposant d'assez de temps et d'argent de récolter des raretés en quelques clics de souris – il aurait normalement fallu déployer d'audacieux efforts tels que des expéditions dans des banlieues lointaines pour les obtenir. Résultat: des guerres de prix délirantes sur des sites de ventes en ligne tels que e-bay, qui font grimper le prix d'une chope du *Mainlander* de St. Louis à une somme absurde de 103 dollars. Ce type de chasse au trophée n'est guère sportif. D'un autre côté, nous devons fortement décourager la « collectionnite » de masse qui entraîne le pillage des rares sites tiki encore existants, dont le mana déjà affaibli sera anéanti par un tel saccage.

… ET LES DIEUX FURENT DIVERTIS

Hawaii, 1820, c'est la fête. Observant les indigènes en train d'offrir des leis (guirlandes de fleurs) à une idole au cours d'un marathon de houla, le missionnaire Hiram Bingham s'efforce de comprendre. « Quelle est la fonction de votre dieu, à quoi est-il bon ? » Leur réponse simple l'intrigue: « A jouer ! » Ce qui était alors inconcevable pour le puritain, les Américains seraient aptes à le comprendre un peu plus d'un siècle plus tard. Leur droiture et leur modestie leur avaient permis de surmonter la dépression et les avaient aidés à gagner la Seconde Guerre mondiale. La sécurité économique paraissait accordée à chacun et le temps était venu de jouer. Mais il n'était pas facile de mettre au panier la morale inébranlable des aïeux qui réfrénait ces désirs. Il fallut créer un autre monde où l'on pourrait assumer une personnalité moins restreinte. La culture apparemment insouciante de la Polynésie devint un univers parallèle pour ceux qui étaient en mal d'évasion. Là où l'on pouvait s'amuser, tiki régnait.

Vu la multitude d'idées mises en pratique pour distraire les clients, les bars tiki étaient déjà devenus de véritables petits parcs d'attractions. Y intégrer des temples tiki ou créer des parcs tiki était donc dans l'ordre des choses. La Californie et la Floride, lieux de villégiature par excellence, offraient une parfaite combinaison de personnes en quête de loisirs et de climat doux, et l'on vit surgir des univers tiki tels que *Tiki Gardens* et *The Tikis*. Naturellement, le Grand Kahuna des parcs d'attractions, Walt Disney en personne, ne fut pas en reste. Client assidu des clubs-restaurants polynésiens, il décida de créer un restaurant tiki qui surpasserait tous les autres. Walt était un animateur, et pour lui l'étape suivante fut logiquement de donner vie au décor habituel: fleurs, oiseaux et tiki. Ce fut l'esprit du tiki qui inspira à Disney l'idée des « Audio-Animatroniques » qui deviendraient le cœur de nombre d'attractions de Disneyland. Mais alors que le projet allait être conduit à terme, il s'avéra que la technologie futuriste des 225 robots, dirigés par une bande magnétique à quatorze canaux alimentant cent haut-parleurs et contrôlant 438 actions différentes, avait débordé largement l'espace du restaurant. Plutôt que de compromettre la complexité du spectacle, Walt résolut de supprimer le restaurant et d'en faire une attraction. Lorsque « Le Salon Tiki enchanté » ouvrit ses portes en 1963, le *New York Times* écrivit: « LA BANDE POLARIS AIDE L'ANIMATION DE DISNEY – De nouveaux procédés de synchronisation permettent aux totems de parler … Dans le Salon Tiki enchanté, une profusion d'oiseaux artificiels colorés parlent, chantent ou sifflent. Des effigies de dieux païens jouent du tam-tam et chantent dans d'étranges langages. Des orages éclatent et les fontaines se mettent en marche. Des perroquets artificiels discourent en différents dialectes. »

Un compte-rendu exalté mais plutôt intellectuel, écrit par Don D. Jackson, M.D., professeur à Stanford et directeur du Palo Alto Mental Research Institute, comparait le Salon Tiki à d'autres lieux enchantés créés par l'homme : « JEU, PARADOXE ET FOULE: CRAINTE A DISNEYLAND … C'est parce que je prétends avoir éprouvé en étant assis dans le Salon Tiki artificiel de Disneyland un aussi grand sentiment de crainte, d'émerveillement et de respect que dans quelques-unes des grandes cathédrales – Chartres, Reims et Notre-Dame … Dans une fausse hutte, de faux perroquets chantaient des chansons intéressantes, mais leurs plumages étaient une explosion de couleurs et les perroquets ouvraient et refermaient leurs becs avec précision – d'abord ce groupe, puis cet autre, cela sans la moindre hésitation et de façon toujours surprenante. Puis dans différents coins du salon hexagonal, les grands totems (tiki) se transformèrent en visages mobiles et chantant, et bientôt les chants des fleurs s'unirent à ceux des hommes et des oiseaux. C'était comme un moment d'un rêve compliqué dont on garde un vague souvenir. » Et Jackson poursuit en célébrant le créateur: « Disney fut un entrepreneur exceptionnel, capable de rassembler des quantités d'individus talentueux pour réaliser les détails de sa vision enfantine. Innocent, Disney n'a pas accepté les limites ordinaires imposées par la connaissance.

Toutes ses productions créatives réalisent les visions de l'enfance – elles vont au-delà des étoiles. »

Parmi les individus talentueux que Walt impliqua dans le projet du Salon Tiki figurait l'artiste Rolly Crump, qui dessina l'arbre tiki et les statues du Jardin Tiki (la zone d'attente devant la hutte), et l'animateur Marc Davis, l'un des « nine old men » de l'équipe de Disney. Davis avait commencé comme assistant-animateur sur *Blanche Neige et les sept nains*, collaboré à *Bambi* et dessiné le personnage de Cruella De Ville dans *Les 101 Dalmatiens*. Son intérêt pour l'art papou de Nouvelle-Guinée se reflétait dans ses dessins pour l'intérieur du Salon Tiki.

On créa des parcs à thèmes tiki dans toutes les dimensions possibles, des golfs miniatures aux promenades de bord de mer. Le *Pacific Ocean Park*, situé jadis au bout de la jetée de Santa Monica, offrait une promenade autour d'un lagon et d'un volcan artificiels, tous deux construits sur une plate-forme séparée de la pointe de la jetée, et reliés à celle-ci par un téléphérique.

Les bowlings furent également de la partie. Les bars adjacents, mais parfois aussi les établissements entiers, étaient généralement dédiés au dieu des loisirs. Le bowling était né dans les monastères allemands, où les moines demandaient aux fidèles de renverser un objet en forme de bouteille baptisé « Kegel » pour prouver leur dévotion. Le kegel de bois représentait le diable, et le renverser lavait le fidèle de ses péchés. On ignore si des quilles en forme de tiki ont jamais existé, mais dans de nombreux endroits, les chemises aloha et les chemises de bowling se mêlaient allègrement, tandis que les boissons tropicales calmaient les lancers des noceurs tiki. L'un de ces endroits était le très sélect *Kapu Kai* (Mer interdite) à Rancho Cucamonga, une banlieue de Los Angeles (voir également page 55). Quatre arches en A accueillaient les fervents disciples. Les tiki dressés entre les pistes et autour du bâtiment avaient été sculptés par Milan Guanko. Les reliefs tiki de la porte d'entrée accueillaient avec un sourire les noceurs, mais ceux de l'intérieur adressaient une grimace à ceux qui s'en allaient. Des tapis tiki couvraient les sols et le Salon du Feu tahitien présentait d'impressionnantes peintures murales. Et pourtant, malgré son design remarquable, le *Kapu Kai* ne survécut pas à la fin du 20e siècle.

HÔTEL, MOTEL

Le tourisme et les tiki marchaient main dans la main dans l'Amérique des années 1960, et comme les enseignes des motels étaient les totems de la culture routière américaine, de nombreux établissements utilisèrent le tiki pour attirer l'attention. Phares dans la mer urbaine, leurs torches tiki en néon ou alimentées au gaz clignotaient pour les voyageurs épuisés et les négociants. La Polynésie était désormais accessible par la route. Le motel, une mutation américaine de l'hôtel, fut créée pour la vache sacrée à quatre roues, symbole du progrès et de la prospérité qu'est la voiture américaine des années 1950. A cette époque, il n'y avait d'autre limite que le ciel pour les constructeurs d'automobiles, les dimensions et les formes de leurs produits soutenant la comparaison avec les vaisseaux spatiaux. Ces aéroglisseurs avaient besoin de ports facilement accessibles où leurs pilotes puissent se reposer avant le prochain voyage. Afin de signaler ces ports de l'espace dans le vaste univers urbain, de gigantesques emblèmes rougeoyants furent érigés au bord des grandes artères de circulation.

L'emblème du motel est un symbole classique de la culture américaine. Le fait que la ville d'Anaheim, patrie de Disneyland et qui attire les touristes du monde entier à la recherche de la culture pop américaine, ait détruit en 1998 la plupart des emblèmes tels celui du « Pitcairn », est donc un véritable « signe » d'ignorance. On a remarqué qu'une icône culturelle est particulièrement menacée de destruction juste avant que sa valeur soit redécouverte. Par conséquent, il faut s'attendre à ce que de mauvaises répliques de ces emblèmes soient érigés dans quelques années à Disneyland. L'emblème du *Hanalei* à San Diego est un parfait exemple « Avant » et « Après » d'ignorance commerciale où, au nom de la modernisation, une fade standardisation se substitue à l'expression individuel-

le. Tout comme l'emblème « Stardust » à Las Vegas (page 114/115), il a été remplacé par un banal caractère standard sans rapport avec le thème. Etant donné que le style polynésien a été considéré comme « dépassé », même si l'intérieur du restaurant *Islands* de l'hôtel *Hanalei* est demeuré pratiquement intact, la nouvelle entrée ne suggère plus en rien la présence des trésors tiki dissimulés dans le bâtiment. Beaucoup d'objets dans le restaurant et dans l'atrium proviennent d'un autre important site tiki, l'ancien *Luau* de Beverly Hills (page 100). La fermeture de ce lieu polynésien a coïncidé avec l'ouverture de la nouvelle extension de l'hôtel *San Diego*. Le premier propriétaire était un « polynésiaque » avéré et avait soi-disant obtenu pour le nouveau bâtiment la bénédiction d'un Kahuna hawaïen original. La Floride était naturellement prédestinée à la culture du tourisme tiki et, aujourd'hui encore, l'archéologue urbain consciencieux peut y trouver, sur la côte Atlantique comme dans le Golfe, des motels qui invoquent la divinité.

De même que pour d'autres temples tiki, les motels tiki ne fleurirent pas seulement dans les régions au climat doux, mais également dans d'autres Etats américains. Le bâtiment principal du *Tiki Motor Inn* à Lake George, dans l'Etat de New York, était entouré de palmiers artificiels qui restaient verts sous la neige. Toutefois la seule authentique chaîne de motels tiki est apparue dans les villes du désert californien : Ken Kimes dirigea jadis quarante motels dont cinq étaient ornés de tiki produits par les artisans de Oceanic Arts : il s'agissait du *Tropics* implanté à Indio, Blythe, Rosemead, Modesto et Palm Springs. Quatre d'entre eux présentent toujours des tiki qui ont bien survécu grâce au climat sec. Le *Tropics* de Palm Springs est le plus élaboré, bien que le bar « Reef » ait été rénové dans le style mexicain. Espérons que la redécouverte de Palm Springs comme centre du modernisme des années 1950 aidera à conserver ce précieux temple tiki.

SANS EGAL DANS LA VIE DU CELIBATAIRE

« Traversez la passerelle sculptée au-dessus du puits ardent de la déesse Pelé ; là où la lave est sur le point d'entrer en ébullition et la terre de trembler. Vous vous trouvez alors dans le meilleur des mondes, loin du stress, des ennuis et des soucis, mais à quelques minutes seulement des transports en commun, des églises et à quelques secondes de la terre ferme … Dans ce décor fantastique, Pelé sait tout. Elle a été et demeurera dans le panthéon hawaïen. Vous vous détendrez et vous prélasserez au soleil au bord du bassin bordé de palmiers, dont l'eau, issue de la fontaine de corail, se déverse dans le splendide lagon. Sur la passerelle intérieure, vous vous retrouverez au milieu des ruines de son royaume, là où les vestiges de Hopoé et de Lohiau se sont transformés en deux grands rochers au sein des eaux tumultueuses qui s'écoulent sur la pente couverte de lave d'un volcan en éruption. Ici, réconforté par les dieux, vous pouvez trouver le repos du guerrier et vivre au milieu du magnifique décor de palmiers sans égal dans la vie du célibataire … Prenez votre clé et devenez l'un des habitants de ce petit village exotique au centre d'une ville animée. »

Cet exemple évocateur de poésie pop polynésienne extrait de la brochure de la résidence *Pele* donne une idée du mal que se donnèrent les promoteurs pour créer ces établissements « polynésiens ». Les concepts architecturaux s'appuyaient sur les bars et les restaurants tiki, et dans le cas unique de la résidence *Pele*, on copia les caractères et les notes de pochette d'un célèbre album de musique exotique. Le « Pele » d'Arthur Lyman inspira le nom d'un prototype de voiture, fabriqué par le producteur d'aluminium qui avait construit le dôme du bâtiment où Lyman avait enregistré son disque … Henry J. Kaiser, magnat de l'industrie et propriétaire de l'entreprise Kaiser Aluminium, était un « polynésiaque » qui avait voulu prendre sa retraite à Hawaii mais, une fois arrivé là-bas, il avait construit le *Hawaïan Village Hotel* et le dôme Kaiser Aluminium pour accueillir sa musique préférée. En 1960, le « primitif » moderne n'avait qu'une idée : habiter la résidence *Pele*, conduire la voiture « Pele » et écouter le jazz « jungle » de l'album « Pele » d'Arthur Lyman.

Le même promoteur conçut un autre complexe d'appartements attrayant, *Shelter Isle*, mais la brochure publicitaire annonçait, vingt ans à l'avance, la décadence à venir: «Lorsque l'on quitte l'espace récréatif et que l'on flâne le long des chemins sinueux, on se trouve soudain au milieu des ruines d'un village indigène abandonné, au bord d'un petit lac arrosé par des cascades descendant des parois couvertes de lave d'un volcan bouillonnant.»

Lorsque l'archéologue urbain découvrit cette installation au milieu des années 1990, il ne subsistait de ces «vestiges» que des rochers de lave noyés dans un bassin. Généralement, les villages tiki (ensembles résidentiels polynésiens) fournissent à l'archéologue un environnement plus gratifiant, car ils ont bien mieux survécu à l'abolition de l'idolâtrie que les temples tiki (restaurants et bars) qui leur ont donné jour. Moins soumis aux changements de goût que l'industrie de la restauration, ils représentent parfois des sanctuaires virtuels de ces espèces menacées que sont les tiki.

Même si certains propriétaires et gérants ont tenté de les mettre au goût du jour avec un zèle de missionnaire, et que de nombreux tiki se sont dégradés ou été volés par des pilleurs de sépultures, parcourir la mer urbaine de Los Angeles en quête de palmiers géants et de pignons en A peut toujours générer des découvertes spectaculaires. Au «Tahitian Village», dans la San Fernando Valley, les archétypes du feu et de l'eau sont représentés par deux sculptures indigènes à la Gauguin qui flanquent la passerelle de l'entrée. La figure masculine crachait autrefois de l'eau dans ses mains, qui à leur tour la déversaient dans le fossé, tandis qu'une flamme de gaz jaillissait de la main de la figure féminine. Un masque en ciment de 2,20 m de hauteur, des poteaux tiki et des lances croisées sur des boucliers en acier répartis tout autour sont quelques-unes des caractéristiques de ce complexe d'habitation.

Les torches tiki du «Polynesian Village» de Playa del Rey se sont éteintes, ainsi que les feux volcaniques qui avaient coutume de jaillir de la cascade principale. Mais les poutres extérieures sculptées, les jardins et l'architecture en lave/ciment d'Armet & Davis, demeurent de parfaits exemples d'un style qui s'est développé à une époque où l'on souhaitait en même temps «retourner à l'état sauvage» et vivre à proximité d'un aéroport. C'était une époque où les voyages en avion étaient chic et n'évoquaient pas le bruit, la pollution et le stress: «Les luxueux et élégants équipements aérodynamiques, reflets de l'âge du moteur à réaction, sont habilement mariés avec les couleurs, le romantisme et le charme des îles des mers du Sud afin de créer un nouveau et délicieux mode de vie, à la résidence polynésienne de Playa del Rey … Les figures sculptées de dieux tiki veillent sur ces paysages splendides et luxuriants tout en promettant santé, bonheur et sérénité.»

Tout comme les temples, les villages étaient répandus dans toute la Californie mais, également comme eux, leur présence ne se limitait pas aux endroits les plus chauds. Tout le long de la West Coast, autour de Seattle, à Tacoma et Bremerton, ville de construction navale, on construisit de nombreux lotissements tiki. Partout en l'Amérique, des communautés plus ou moins organisées acclamaient l'effigie du dieu des loisirs. Les noms de ces îles de banlieue étaient aussi évocatrices que leurs styles. Du style «Beachcomber», «Asiatique», «Primitif», «Bambou» au style «Gros Samoa», ils représentaient tous des éléments de l'esthétique tiki. Certaines ailes ou parties de ces résidences avaient leurs propres désignations telles que «Port abrité» ou «Mauna Loa», empruntées à des sites hawaïens ou à des hôtels.

La Résidence *Exotic Isle* à Alhambra, dans la banlieue de Los Angeles, aujourd'hui essentiellement peuplée d'immigrés asiatiques, fut jusqu'à une date très récente une autre manifestation impressionnante de la foi tiki. Une salle de détente située au-dessus de la cascade centrale en constitue le centre et peut être considérée comme l'équivalent tiki de «Falling Water» de Frank Lloyd Wright.

Le *Kona Pali*, le seul ensemble a avoir une résidence jumelle en un autre point

de la ville, le *Kona Kai*, a même survécu aux dommages causés par le récent tremblement de terre de Northridge. C'est un trésor de raffinement tiki. A l'entrée, nous sommes accueillis par un «Aloha» en ciment incrusté de coquillages et, en inspectant le porche en A, nous découvrons une autre caractéristique plaisante: dans le coin droit, quatre petits tiki se détachent du plâtre moucheté d'or. Mais seul un œil exercé pourra remarquer les dernières traces d'un autre trait remarquable du pignon: si on les regarde sous un bon éclairage, les panneaux ovales et rectangulaires inclinés révèlent de faibles reflets de masques tiki peints au pochoir. Ce bâtiment a vraiment dû valoir le coup d'œil! Partiellement dissimulée derrière les bananiers et les torches tiki, la façade est scandée par une suite de poutres tiki sculptées et profilées selon le style tiki moderniste aérodynamique. Les blocs de la climatisation sont dissimulés derrière des masques tiki «comédie/tragédie». Une autre caractéristique remarquable de cet établissement tiki est le portail derrière la porte de verre: en traversant la passerelle de l'entrée au-dessus d'un fossé jadis bordé de plantes tropicales, nous trouvons sur notre droite une carte des îles Hawaii en carreaux de mosaïque. Le côté gauche est recouvert de panneaux de bois et défendu par des tiki grotesques sculptés dans différents styles classiques, menaçant de damnation le briseur de tabou ou répandant fortune et bonheur sur l'initié.

Pico Rivera, dans la banlieue de Los Angeles, vaut le déplacement. On y trouve en effet trois résidences tiki alignées l'une derrière l'autre dans le bloc 5400 de Rosemead Boulevard. Les habitants nous jettent un regard soupçonneux tandis que nous explorons le *Aloha Arms*, avec ses curieux bâtiments en A incliné de trois étages (voir page 61). La résidence «Samoa» est juste à côté et là, derrière un mystérieux terrain non construit, surgit le *Kapu Tiki*, dont le pignon est surmonté d'un tiki peint à la main qui tient une torche à gaz depuis longtemps éteinte. Les lampes en forme de boules étaient probablement suspendues à des filets pour rappeler les flotteurs des filets de pêche japonais ramassés sur la côte hawaïenne. A l'extrémité droite de la façade est fixé un masque tiki solitaire dont les yeux étaient autrefois dotés d'ampoules électriques, et dont la bouche crache une cascade d'eau dans un coquillage géant.

En d'autres points de l'Amérique, il existe des sites à inspecter, comme le *Sands West* à Phoenix, Arizona, dont la brochure publicitaire promettait: «A Hawaii, les Maoris cessaient traditionnellement le combat au coucher du soleil, se retirant dans leur halé pour savourer à la lueur d'un feu l'awa, le poi et ce délice local qu'est le poulpe. A *Sands West*, votre guerrier familial peut se reposer de sa bataille quotidienne dans son lanai privé, et se détendre le soir en famille. Plutôt que de se réjouir d'un poulpe grillé ou d'un breuvage au piment fermenté, votre Kau Kau pourra s'attabler devant un opulent barbecue dans votre patio couvert. Grâce au confort que procure tout l'équipement électrique, vous aurez l'impression à *Sands West* que tout le travail est accompli par les légendaires Menehune (le petit peuple). Votre habitation est également protégée des méfaits de Kumumahanahana – le dieu de la chaleur – grâce à l'air conditionné et un approvisionnement en eau chaude de qualité supérieure.»

Les dieux étaient nombreux dans les villages tiki, et bien que la plupart d'entre eux soient détruits ou renversés, ceux qui restent se dressent comme les gardiens d'une culture oubliée, nous rappelant l'esprit créatif et surprenant qui imprégnait le style tiki.

LA POLYNESIE A SA PORTE

Par plus d'un côté, le désir de l'Américain moyen de «retourner à l'état sauvage» était une régression à l'enfance. Il était facile d'oublier les responsabilités du travail et de la famille lors des garden-parties «luau», un genre de fêtes d'anniversaire pour «les grands» où l'amusement et les jeux étaient de nouveau permis. On revêtait des chemises hawaïennes fleuries et des «Muu Muus», on absorbait des aliments doux et on ingurgitait des breuvages encore plus doux qui ramenaient l'intellect à un état de conscience infantile, les adultes blancs dansaient le houla et s'essayaient aux chants en langue hawaïenne: « Tous les KANES, VAHINES et KEIKIS (hommes, femmes et enfants) veulent WIKI WIKI (se précipiter) à un LUAU (fête) hawaïen. Les MALHINIS (nouveaux venus) veulent connaître la signification des mots étranges qu'ils entendent au cours du luau. Les vahinés porteront des HOLOKUS (robes de princesses hawaïennes avec une traîne) ou des MUU MUUS (tuniques flottantes à fleurs). Les Kanés portent des chemises ALOHA (chemises de sport bariolées). Aucun PAPAPLE (chapeau) n'est requis. LES ALOHA (vœux) sont exprimés en plaçant un LEI (collier de fleurs) autour du cou du malihini. Le luau est servi sur de longues tables placées dans un LANAI (véranda ouverte) ou sous un baldaquin en feuilles de palmiers. La nourriture est cuisinée dans un IMU (four enfoui dans la terre) réalisé en creusant un LUA (trou) dans le sol, et en le remplissant de POHAKU (cailloux) et de KUNI (petit bois). Un AHI (feu) est allumé pour chauffer les pohaku. Le PUA (cochon) cuisiné dans l'imu est un PUA KALUA. Si le luau est un AHAAINA (grande fête), il faudra des heures avant qu'il soit PAU (achevé) et que tout le monde rentre pour HIAMOE (dormir). Le sommeil vient vite car l'OPU (estomac) est satisfait après tant de KAU KAU (nourriture). »

On creusait des trous imu dans les jardins et les cours comme si la ruée vers l'or avait recommencé, mais le simple désir de retourner à l'état sauvage n'était pas suffisant. Il fallait un décor approprié. On pouvait trouver les éléments nécessaires à ces happenings dans des pépinières et des magasins spécialisés tels que « Sea and Jungle » dans la Valley, « Oceanic Arts » à Whittier, ou « Johnson Products » à Chicago. On pouvait y obtenir les torches tiki, les nattes en chanvre, les feuilles de palmiers, les poteaux de bambou, les filets de pêche, les lances et les tambours, et tout objet en forme de tiki. C'est ainsi que l'on construisit des huttes tiki dans les jardins et que des idoles furent érigées au bord des piscines et dans les patios, devenant ainsi les nouveaux nains de jardin de l'Amérique.

Le bricoleur adroit se voyait proposer des kits complets avec les instructions pour construire son propre bar tiki. Dans de nombreux logements de banlieue, les caves se transformèrent en salles de chahut, où les grandes personnes se rassemblaient pour des cocktails et des conversations « entre adultes ». Lorsque le bambou et le rotin perdirent de leurs attraits, on ajouta des bars tiki sculptés et des chaises de la maison Witco (voir pages 43 et 253). Toujours à la pointe du bon goût, Elvis Presley équipa sa « Jungle Room » à Graceland avec du mobilier de chez Witco. Elvis surfait sur la crête de la vague polynésienne avec des films tels que « Blue Hawaii », « Paradise Hawaiian Style » et « Clambake », qui montre le meilleur luau jamais filmé sur une plage de Floride.

SURFIN' TIKI

CALIFORNIE, milieu des années 1960: sur les plages et dans leurs jardins, toute une génération d'Américains de la classe moyenne se livraient à des rituels appelés « luaus », au cours desquels ils s'enivraient de breuvages polynésiens et adoraient le tiki, dieu des loisirs. A leur insu, leurs enfants passèrent sous l'influence d'un phénomène étranger qu'on appellerait bientôt « l'invasion britannique ». Des groupes pop étrangers avec des noms aussi étranges que « The Beatles » inspirèrent un culte jeune qui, nous le savons tous, débuta avec les cheveux longs et s'acheva par les drogues psychédéliques et la révolution sexuelle.

Les tentatives des parents d'échapper au stress de la civilisation dans une Polynésie de plastique furent rapidement considérées comme dépassées et franchement ringardes. Le charme du tiki allait bientôt être rompu. Mais avant cela, une version locale de ce culte jeune allait revendiquer tiki. Pour les surfeurs de Californie, le tiki devint le fétiche à la mode qui les guidait dans leur recherche de la vague parfaite. En tant qu'élément de la culture balnéaire, les amulettes tiki était le truc cool que portaient aussi bien les douceureux beachcombers urbains que les surfeurs. L'inspiration était Hawaii. Ce n'était pas uniquement une destination de rêve à cause de ses vagues éblouissantes, c'était aussi là

que l'homme blanc avait découvert ce sport. Le Capitaine Cook, grand explorateur s'il en fut, découvrit bien des choses en Polynésie, et le surf était l'une d'elles. Sur le point d'entrer dans la baie de Kealakekua, où beaucoup plus tard il serait tué par les indigènes, il nota dans son carnet de bord: « L'audace et l'adresse avec lesquelles nous les avons vu accomplir ces difficiles et dangereuses manœuvres était tout à fait sidérantes et on a peine à le croire. »

Dans l'ancienne Hawaii, le surf était une activité que pratiquait surtout la famille royale. La fabrication d'une planche de surf s'accompagnait, tout comme la création d'un tiki, de rituels sacrés. Dans la mythologie hawaïenne, il s'est transmis nombre d'histoires à propos des dieux ancestraux du surf, et notamment celle concernant « Mamala qui chevauche les vagues ». « Mamala était une princesse kupua. Cela signifiait qu'elle était un mo-o, gigantesque lézard ou crocodile, aussi bien qu'une femme ravissante, et pouvait prendre la forme qu'elle désirait. Mamala était une merveilleuse surfeuse. Elle dansait avec beaucoup d'adresse sur les vagues les plus violentes. Les gens qui la regardaient de la plage emplissaient l'air d'applaudissements lorsqu'ils frappaient dans leurs mains, enthousiasmés par ses extraordinaires qualités d'athlète. » Le surf étant la religion du surfeur californien, quoi de plus naturel que Tiki devînt son dieu? En talismans, sur les tee-shirts et dans les fêtes de plage, les tiki étaient considérés comme des idoles parfaitement cool.

LES ARTISTES

Les créateurs de cette forme artistique qu'est le Moderne Tiki, les sculpteurs de tiki américains, n'ont jamais été acceptés comme des artistes. Si leurs productions étaient déclarées « authentiques », il ne fut jamais clairement affirmé qu'elles étaient originales. Personne ne voulait attirer l'attention sur le fait que le visage basané d'un sculpteur tel que Vince Buono, par exemple, provenait de ses origines italo-new-yorkaises et non des îles des mers du Sud. Le style tiki n'était pas une trahison intentionnelle, il répondait simplement au besoin du public de s'illusionner, s'entourant ainsi que ses créateurs d'un épais voile de mystère. La tronçonneuse de Leroy Schmalz, que l'on voit en pleine action (page 242), était proscrite dans les démonstrations de sculpture publiques, au cours desquelles on recourait au maillet et au ciseau. Ce chapitre voudrait donner à certains de ces artistes, choisis pour représenter tous ceux que nous ne pouvons citer, la reconnaissance qui leur est due.

PAGES 244 ET 245

Leroy Schmaltz et Boob van Oosting fondèrent leur entreprise d'objets décoratifs « Oceanic Arts » à Whittier, dans la banlieue de Los Angeles, à la fin des années 1950, au plus chaud de la folie tiki. Après un démarrage modeste avec des amulettes tiki et des masques en feuilles de palmier, « Oceanic Arts » devint vite incontournable comme fabricant et fournisseur d'art et de matériel tiki du pays. La société décrocha des contrats avec toutes les chaînes importantes, de *Don the Beachcomber* à *Kon-Tiki*, et pratiquement tous les sculpteurs de cette industrie travaillèrent avec elles à un moment donné. Si les tiki étaient parfois dessinés par les architectes ou les décorateurs, la plupart du temps c'étaient les sculpteurs qui réalisaient leur propre vision et qui parfois concevaient l'ensemble de la décoration intérieure.

La liste des réalisations d'« Oceanic Arts » est considérable, puisque cette société a eu partie liée avec la plupart des temples tiki figurant dans ce livre. Du *Kahiki* dans l'Ohio (page 144), ou le *Mai Kai* en Floride (page 136), aux *The Tikis* du Monterey Park (chapitre 11), on retrouve des objets d'« Oceanic Arts » dans toute l'Amérique. Même le très respectable Bishop Museum de Honolulu expose, sinon dans ses vitrines, du moins sur les murs de sa cafétéria, certaines de leurs sculptures. Le phénomène de croisement culturel du style tiki atteignit son apogée lorsque les idoles manufacturées d'« Oceanic Arts » furent exportées dans des hôtels et des restaurants de Hawaii, de Samoa et de Tahiti. Aujourd'hui, « Oceanic Arts » est l'unique fournisseur de décors polynésiens à avoir survécu avec succès à l'abolition du tiki, attirant une nouvelle génération d'explorateurs du monde entier sur les rivages de Whittier, Californie.

PAGE 246

C'est de l'autre côté du Golden Gate Bridge, au nord de San Francisco, dans le pittoresque port de plaisance de Sausalito, que l'ex-marin Barney West installa son « Tiki Junction ». Il avait trouvé sa vocation au cours de la Seconde Guerre mondiale, alors qu'il était retenu dans les îles Marianne. Le logo du « Tiki Junction » fut trouvé dans un livre publié à l'occasion de la première exposition d'art des mers du Sud aux Etats-Unis, en 1946, livre qui inspira également le logo de Trader Vic. *Trader Vic* étant situé de l'autre côté de la baie, à Emeryville, près d'Oakland, il devint le principal client des tiki de Barney. On trouve encore certaines de ces effigies au style inimitable dans les établissements de la chaîne *Trader Vic*, à travers le monde. Barney jouait à la perfection le rôle du bohème cavaleur et buvant sec, et il a depuis longtemps rejoint le paradis du tiki.

PAGE 248

Milan Guanko apprit la sculpture auprès de son père, au cours de son enfance aux Philippines. Après avoir émigré aux Etats-Unis en 1928 et travaillé dans l'épicerie, il trouva son créneau lorsqu'apparut la folie polynésienne. Il devint finalement l'un des sculpteurs tiki les plus prolifiques et les plus influents des Etats-Unis, son style étant copié et commercialisé pour répondre à la demande croissante des noceurs tiki. Au nombre de ses créations figurent notamment *The Islands* (page 155) à Phoenix, Arizona, le *Kapu Kai* (page 199) à Rancho Cucamonga, et le *Polynesian Village* (page 42) de Ren Clark à Fort Worth, Texas, pour lequel Guanko et deux sculpteurs mexicains, Juan Razo et Fidel Rodriguez (qui avaient équipé le *Mauna Loa* à Mexico), sculptèrent plus de deux cents tiki, les uns en tabourets de bar, d'autres en géants de 3,5 mètres de haut. Exemple du paradis de l'art polynésien en 1960, rien n'a subsisté de cette forêt virtuelle de tiki, et l'on ignore où se trouvent la plupart des ses habitants. Ce qu'il est advenu d'un tiki géant réalisé pour la résidence Anaheim, et qui d'après le témoignage de Milan était monté sur un socle tournant, est également une énigme. Milan ouvrit son magasin à Anaheim, profitant d'un approvisionnement régulier de palmiers abattus pour l'extension de Disneyland. Il revendiquait les dessins animés pour enfants comme une des influences qu'il avait subies, suivant rarement les styles « authentiques » des îles. Aujourd'hui on peut admirer ses travaux au *Royal Hawaiian* de Laguna Beach, l'un des plus anciens bars tiki encore en activité.

PAGE 250

Voici, posant devant ses surprenantes idoles, Bob Lutz, un talent tiki unique en son genre mais peu connu. Bien trop bon pour ce triste monde, on raconte qu'il se serait suicidé après avoir surpris sa petite amie faisant l'amour avec un autre. La seule de ses sculptures qui soit encore en place se trouve au *Tiki Spa* de Palm Springs. Un autre créateur talentueux de tiki superbement stylisés fut Andres Bumatay, d'origine philippine comme Milan Guanko. Ses absurdes tiki aux yeux d'insectes étaient vendus au magasin « Sea and Jungle » (page 234) et inspirèrent une chope tiki et probablement le logo du *Tahitian* (page 152).

PAGE 251

Contremaître dans une entreprise de construction, Charles Rosencrans apprit seul à sculpter dans un style naïf/primitif. Ses étranges statues ornaient *The Reef* à Long Beach, et le *Royal Tahitian*, un temple tiki moderne avec un pignon en A incliné dans le Golf d'Ontario (Los Angeles). Celui-ci prétendait offrir le plus grand territoire polynésien du pays en raison de son terrain de golf. Le pignon en A est toujours là, mais toute trace de l'art étrange de Rosencrans a disparu.

On peut cependant trouver, juste à côté, un immeuble anonyme abritant quatre tiki de Milan Guanko.

PAGE 253

Dans l'univers de Witco de William Westernhaver, un bon morceau de bois était un morceau de bois sculpté. Qu'il s'agisse de ses tableaux faits de « reliefs en bois brûlé sur tapis épais » ou de ces ensembles complets pour « chambre à coucher primitive », aucune surface lisse n'échappait à la tronçonneuse de ce fou. Partout où il pouvait tailler un visage de tiki, les copeaux s'envolaient. Le bois était ensuite brûlé au chalumeau afin de faire apparaître sa texture en d'épaisses veines noires. Il n'y avait pas que de l'art polynésien, les décors modernes et de style conquistador étaient également produits en série dans la fabrique de Witco à Seattle. On peut encore voir les travaux de Westernhaver dans des motels de Floride et dans des magasins d'articles d'occasion dans tous les Etats-Unis, Witco ayant eu à une époque des salles d'exposition à Chicago, Dallas, Denver et Seattle. Sur la liste de ses clients figuraient Elvis Presley (page 235), Hugh Hefner (page 43) et même, à ce qu'on dit, certaines « maisons de mauvaise réputation ». Parmi ses œuvres les plus remarquables, on note une grande variété de bars (page 6) et de fontaines tiki (page 179).

L'auteur de ces lignes prépare actuellement une monographie consacrée à l'œuvre prolifique de cet original. Enfin, il désirerait exprimer son espoir que le présent ouvrage pourra contribuer à ce que la culture tiki retrouve auprès du public l'attention qui lui est due.

CREDITS

The publishers wish to thank the copyright holders who greatly assisted in this publication. Every effort was made to identify and contact individual copyright holders; omissions are unintentional. The following are credits for copyrighted material; all illustrations not mentioned here are from the collection of the author, Jeff Berry, Doug Miller, Pete Moruzzi, Kevin and Jody, Bosko Hrnjack, Otto von Stroheim, John English, Chris Nichols, Dale Sizer, Kiara Geller, Martin McIntosh, Bobby and Al, Bamboo Ben, Byron Werner, Janet Austin, Chester and Cheryl, Florian Gabriel, Domenic Priore, Jim Heimann, Luis Reyes, Sylvia Stoddard, and Dewey Webb.

Carlos Alejandro, House Magazine, New York (NY): 177; Armet & Davis, Los Angeles (CA): 2, 27 top, 61 top, 65 center, 66 center, 142, 198 top left, 210, 216 and 217; Janet Austin, Los Angeles (CA): 126 bottom center, 235 top left; Automotive Hall of Fame, Dearborn (MI): 212 bottom center; Bamboo Ben Archives, Huntington Beach (CA): 74 left; Forde Photographers, Seattle (WA): 87 bottom; Jörg Hauser, Göttingen: 58 left and bottom; Herling & Robinson Commercial Photographers, San Diego (CA): 135 top right; House Industries, Wilmington (DE): 167, 169, 173 (typefaces for the recipes), 63, 133, 213 (typeface for the graphics) and typefaces for the cover; Kunstindustrimuseet, photograph © Ole Woldbye, Copenhagen: 179 center left; Ulli Maier, Düsseldorf: 253; Fred Milkie Photographers, Seattle (WA): 86 top; Pete Moruzzi, Los Angeles (CA): 13 center; Museum für Völkerkunde, Staatliche Museen zu Berlin – Stiftung Preussischer Kulturbesitz, photograph © E. Postel, Berlin; Oceanic Arts, Whittier (CA): 27 bottom, 28, 29, 66 bottom right, 67, 152 bottom, 198 top right and bottom center, 199, 214 top, 230/231, 233 bottom, 244, 246, 247 bottom left and right, 250, 251 center and bottom; Rautenstrauch-Joest-Museum für Völkerkunde, Cologne: 12/13 top, 22 center, 32/33 top left; 58 top, 59 top; Rue des Archives / Brierre, Paris: 26 top right; San Francisco Library, San Francisco (CA): 47 left, 82 bottom right; Bill Shepherd, Dayton (OH): 117 bottom left; S.S Archives / Shooting Star, Hollywood (CA): 172 top; Beau Sterling, Harrisburg (PA): 78 bottom left; Tom Vano Photography, San Francisco (CA): 6; © 1962 Walt Disney Productions: 232 top right; Delmar Watson Photography-Archives. Inc., Hollywood (CA): 100 top left; © 1999 Bunny Yeager, Miami (FL): 43 left

© 2000 TASCHEN GmbH
Hohenzollernring 53, D–50672 Köln
Design: Armando Chitolina, Milan
Cover artwork and design: Moritz R®, Munich
Endpapers: One of six murals designed by Miguel Covarrubias for the
1939 Golden Gate International Exposition on Treasure Island
German translation: Bettina Blumenberg, Munich
French translation: Patrick Javault, Strasbourg
Production: Horst Neuzner, Cologne
Editing and coordination: Michael Konze, Cologne

Printed in Italy
ISBN 3–8228–6417–X